chancer

chancer

HOW ONE GOOD BOY SAVED ANOTHER

A MEMOIR

DONNIE KANTER WINOKUR

Published by Grand Harbor Press, Grand Haven, MI

www.brilliancepublishing.com

ISBN-13: 9781503942905
ISBN-10: 1503942902

Cover design by Faceout Studio

Printed in the United States of America

To my children, Morasha and Iyal; my husband,
Harvey; my parents;
and the animals we forever love.

AUTHOR'S NOTE

A memoir is filtered through the memory of the author. To the best of my knowledge, the individuals and events described in this book have been part of my family's journey. All the names are from real people; however, a few names have been changed out of respect for their privacy.

While I have offered the most recent statistics and definitions of fetal alcohol syndrome (FAS) and fetal alcohol spectrum disorders (FASDs), these may change by the time this book is published, which may be a good thing. FASDs are a group of conditions that can occur in a person whose mother drank alcohol during pregnancy. People need to know the numbers, even though they are staggering. The prevalence of FASDs is a public health crisis: up to one in twenty U.S. school children may have FASDs. The effects of FASDs will last a lifetime but are completely preventable if a developing baby is not exposed to alcohol before birth.

I wanted to share our family's story because I believe it's bigger than just FASDs and service dogs. Awareness, education, and compassion are necessary to foster a deeper understanding and respect for all people experiencing "invisible disabilities." Fortunately, education can take place through unexpected, but nonetheless inspired, sources. Especially those that give these disabilities human faces—and furry, wagging tails—amid the many battles and victories of families like mine.

PROLOGUE

My ability to breathe vanished the same moment I realized my son, Iyal, had disappeared.

Sometimes in your life, the universe reveals a jubilant symphony, a harmonic convergence of illumination, tranquility, and hope in consonance with others, choreographing the perfect dance, the perfect plan for your future.

This wasn't one of those moments.

Then I saw him through the kitchen's open glass doors. Iyal had climbed onto the railing and was sitting with his twelve-year-old feet dangling from the edge of our three-story deck. He looked as if he might launch himself off any second, like a seasoned swimmer entering the pool, and just let gravity take its course. I froze as a million thoughts collided and stalled in my mind. Among them, a taut but frazzled thread pulled me back to when my children had arrived home from school an hour earlier. In other words, how the hell did this happen? How had this very real scenario slipped through the psychological barricades I put in place every day while awaiting the arrival of my son, the emotional stormtrooper?

Until then, the day had been good, a fairly quiet afternoon. The weather—always mild in Atlanta for this Jersey girl—held the promise of spring. The dreaded yellow pollen that finely and annoyingly dusted everything everywhere had come and gone and left the faint scent of mud and honeysuckle in the air. That morning, I had stood with a cup of coffee in hand for a long time, just staring out the sliding glass doors, enveloped by the emerald curtain of moss-covered trees providing a private reserve around the back of our house. Just standing still seemed like a vacation. With my husband, Harvey, a rabbi, off to work and the kids out the door, I actually had time to read the paper, obsess over lengthening to-do lists, and check my e-mails. With our golden retriever, Chancer, sprawled like a twenty-four-karat rug nearby, I experienced a rare moment. Life was good.

Nearing thirteen, Iyal and his sister, Morasha, were changing before my eyes, not just physically but emotionally. Adolescence had kicked in, and so I never knew who would return from school that day, the boy and girl I once recognized or the strangers taking over their bodies. That day, it was the latter. Iyal and Morasha burst through the door like a hurricane reaching shore and began peeling away backpacks, jackets, shoes, all the while shouting at each other. Chancer immediately descended on Iyal with licks and kisses, paying special attention to read his mood. Iyal seemed especially irritable and exhausted, overwhelmed by trying to translate the day's activities and academics into something meaningful. Which was virtually impossible.

They made a beeline for the kitchen, not to see me so much as to scavenge the pantry and root around in the fridge for snacks, with Chancer on their heels.

"Hey there," I said, trying to sound nonchalant, which I thought important around preteens, and as welcoming and cheerful as possible, determined to show no grief for the end of my solitude. Not that they would notice if I had turned into Spider-Woman cleaning cobwebs around the house while they, mere mortals, scrambled around the kitchen.

"How was your day, honey?"

Iyal ignored me as he began frenetically shuffling boxes and cans around in the pantry, quickly exasperated.

"Fine," mumbled Morasha. "But I really need to study for my history test if I'm going to get an A this semester, because we got our group project grades back and we only got a B! Didn't I *tell* you this would happen? I don't know why Mrs. Stevens couldn't just let us do it by ourselves."

"Mom!" Iyal demanded in his abrupt staccato delivery. "Where are the cookies? You know, the Oreos!"

Staying calm, I soothed him. "Don't you see them in the pantry?"

"No!" He roared his response. "They're not in the pantry! I already told you!"

"Mom, did you call Alicia's mother today about the sleepover this weekend?" asked Morasha. "You said you would do it yesterday, so I hope you didn't forget again."

Without responding to Morasha's insinuation of middle-age memory loss, I drew on my quickly draining reservoir of peace and serenity, forget namaste, and suggested, "Did you look on the second shelf? I saw them there—"

"Yes! They're not there, I said. I can never find them—I give up!" Iyal slammed the pantry door just to make sure we heard him in all caps.

"Yes, I called Alicia's mother," I told my daughter. "It's all set."

"Thanks, Mom," she said, rewarding me with one of her scarce smiles before diving into the details of the sleepover.

I nodded and stood from my chair at the kitchen table in my perpetual attempt to connect with Iyal. "Here, honey, let me help you," I offered, while also trying to keep eye contact with Morasha. I felt like a Ping-Pong ball being swatted back and forth as the inevitable competition between them escalated, each vying for my singular attention while simultaneously attempting to aggravate the other into submission.

"No!" he yelled and pulled away from me. "You can't help me—nobody can! This is the worst day of my life!" Then, shoving past me, he boomed, "I'm running away!" and wrenched open the glass door, thundering outside to the deck before disappearing around the corner to his left.

Meanwhile, Morasha continued talking about what she wanted to wear this weekend and when I would take her to the mall. Wait. Didn't we just have this conversation? Like, this morning? And last night? So overall, just another typically normal afternoon in the Winokur household. Oh, come *on*, you don't seriously believe this is *normal*, do you? Then go back and read between the lines.

And the lines themselves. You need to be prepared.

Chapter One

When my husband, Harvey, and I decided to adopt Iyal and Morasha, we knew that we would have a steep learning curve to parenting. But I could never have predicted just how draining this motherhood gig would actually be. Parenting isn't always a party—nor is it an agonizing nightmare. It is, however, sometimes both: an eagerly anticipated gala that begins with a string quartet and little canapés and ends up looking like a frat house the morning after. The ongoing clash between my expectations of domestic bliss and the reality of daily life as a new mother immediately began to erode my self-confidence, reshape my marriage, and exhaust a reserve I didn't even know I had, forcing me to confront parts of myself—and my husband—that I didn't particularly like.

To be clear, Harvey and I weren't your typical American parents. We were older, both divorced, in our forties (me a lot closer to forty), and keenly focused on building a family together. We only dated for two months (I know . . .), got engaged Labor Day weekend, and were married by Thanksgiving in 1997. Northerners by birth, we now lived in Atlanta, where Harvey served as the founding rabbi for a Reform congregation at a synagogue in the northern suburbs. His core congregants initially called me Rebbetzin Barbie, a fashion statement on my edgy, nonconservative wardrobe. I would have been upset with feminist indignation if they hadn't resorted to calling me Mrs. Rabbi after we married, which I thought hysterical, considering I was a two-time Hebrew-school dropout.

Trained as an actress in college, I had, over time, explored many variations on this theme, including an on-air drive-time personality for an FM country station and writing and producing original music, commercials, video, and ad campaigns, which kept my maternal instincts at bay. But by the time Harvey and I met and soon married, those maternal instincts began to gush forth, causing me to stockpile baby wipes and sippy cups in the back of my closet.

After a year when nature didn't take its course, at least not by the route we had anticipated, we began the process, like many couples, of helping the biological journey along. We met with a reproductive specialist, a scientific pathfinder, to help egg and sperm rendezvous at the desired location. However, after two disappointing artificial inseminations and one in vitro, our doctor, trying to be realistically kind and financially responsible, told us my eggs were too old to cross the finish line and qualify for the Olympic relay race known as conception.

So as the end of our infertility journey loomed closer, I was already rehearsing conversations in my head with Harvey about pursuing adoption, a choice that had always intrigued me even when I had been single. I didn't want to call it "plan B" because it assumed that "plan A" was preferred and we were settling for less. I never wanted our kids to think they were ours by default, second place, runners-up, consolation prizes. After several weeks of collecting information about adoption seminars, searching the Internet, and talking with other adoptive parents, I was ready to say the words out loud to Harvey.

"Hey, Harve, how do you feel about adoption?" I quietly asked him one night after dinner.

He studied me for a moment as crinkles framed his eyes, bookending the broadening smile below. "Oh, Donnie. I think it's a great idea! I wondered how long it would take to have this talk."

"Oh my God! That's great!" I went from a whisper to nearly a scream. I was pretty sure we were on the same page but absolutely wanted confirmation before my fantasy family became fully formed in my imagination.

"Look," he said, "I want to be a father as much as you want to be a mother. It doesn't matter how it happens." Then, with a beaming smile and raising his wineglass, "To parenthood."

"To parenthood," I repeated and exhaled.

I fell in love with Harvey all over again, my barometer of a happy marriage.

I knew what was important to me. Falling in love doesn't happen just once with someone; it should happen again and again throughout a marriage. It's like when your spouse smiles a certain way and you feel faint, and not because you forgot to take your meds, or you notice your spouse is finally ironing their own underwear without your threatening to throw the stupid underwear out altogether. We underwear-ironing people are a dying breed. Mark this down somewhere.

But truly, even climbing in and out of the relationship ditches, I knew that Harvey felt the same way.

And now we were starting a family together.

After Harvey and I started the adoption conversation, we found a direction based on my research and more consultations with adoptive parents. Adopting from a mother in the United States was a high-stakes poker game of waiting and hoping and taking chances about whether a child was available and when we would have a child, because it often depended on marketing ourselves to a birth mother. The process for adopting internationally, while still tedious and complicated, usually went faster and guaranteed results sooner. With no time to waste from our viewpoint (I hadn't yet forgiven my uncooperative, over-the-hill ovaries), we decided to go international and therefore chose an agency called European Adoption Consultants (EAC) out of Ohio.

Knowing we didn't want to jump the impossibly high hurdles of a domestic adoption, we then had to choose and prioritize which countries and cultures we preferred. Harvey had traveled to the Soviet Union in 1988 as part of a refuseniks mission. Refuseniks were Soviet Jews caught in the turmoil of oppression and deprived the freedoms of non-Jews who were able to leave the country. They were denied visas based on the sole fact that they were Jewish. For years, Jews all over the world stood in solidarity and fought for their freedom during this devastating time. I was in high school then and participated in rallies to free the Soviet Jews, one of the first times I would learn the value of advocacy and the immediate pain of connecting with those whose lives were dictated by others. Harvey felt strongly because of the many historical and cultural ties we had that the Soviet Union should be our first choice for adopting our children.

While I was contemplating several countries, I sensed Harvey also worried about the triple threat for a child (a Chinese baby girl, for example) not being Caucasian, being adopted, and being the child of a rabbi (the legendary curse of clergy offspring), which, in total, could result in being bullied. I didn't agree with his line of thinking but became slightly neurotic about what lay ahead for my children. But with further conversation, Harvey persuaded me to consider our heritage and pay homage to traditional treasures of the Soviet Union such as an inspiring palette of pierogi, schnitzel, and caviar (although I personally found the idea of eating fish eggs revolting).

After we made our decision, I skydived into a euphoric atmosphere without boundaries. With rabbinic and rabbinic-wife prayers in place, our babies would be from Russia.

With assistance from the EAC, we had a map, and it was time for some serious hiking on what I suspect is the world's most arduous paper trail. The dossier we had to complete—the Mount Everest of applications, documents, affidavits, and legal forms—more than stunned us. I thought that closing on a house involved a ton of paperwork, but I had no idea how signing my signature 347 times on page after page of redundant, unintelligible forms would expose the minutia of my life.

Oh. I forgot. I had been divorced. Right.

It hadn't been enough that my first marriage had died and I was then a divorcee, abandoned by my husband. I had also felt like a widow at the age of thirty. I didn't know how I would go on with this gaping hole by my side where a husband once stood. And yet, on I went when the magnitude of divorce papers officially sealed my fate, but not without disclosing enough skeletons that a walk-in closet was insufficient. In truth, nothing was funny about my divorce. Not then. Not now. But let's move on.

Some of the best advice we took from other adoptive parents was to hire a paperwork magistrate, someone who could walk us through the process quickly and directly, a kind of word Sherpa to guide us up the steep slope. Ours raced in and out of government offices and agencies throughout downtown Atlanta, obtaining every signature, every notarized seal of approval, and every apostille needed. What the hell's an *apostille* anyway? Turns out it's not a kind of Russian espionage device but a form of authenticating legal documents between countries that participated in the Hague Convention of 1961. Seriously—I can't make this stuff up. Needless to say, this woman was worth every penny we paid her to help translate the legalese and to expedite reaching the summit of Mount Dossier.

We knew things were moving fast, which is my preferred speed, but when we submitted our completed dossier to the EAC in May, neither Harvey nor I could have imagined holding two children in our arms before the end of the summer. But in August 1999, just three months later, we were landing in Moscow before flying on to Astrakhan, just days away from meeting the two people we would soon love as our son and daughter forever. Our cold war of parenthood melted when two Russian infants captured our hearts and launched us into a flood of love beyond what we could have ever imagined.

—

Choosing our son and daughter had indeed been providential. After the EAC had accepted our dossier, the hard part began: reviewing video clips of infants and toddlers who might become our children. I remember calling Harvey at the office when the first referral video package came. We watched a thirty-second video of a cute little boy, with fair skin and blond hair, just sitting there. The EAC said they would try and physically match us to our adopted children, so Harvey and I both inherently assumed that by adopting Russian babies, they might actually resemble us with our darker hair and complexion. Were we wrong to want our adopted children to look like us?

We played the thirty-second video a second time and a third before either of us said anything. There were no fireworks, no musical cascades in our ears. Something just didn't feel right. We didn't feel any connection to the little boy. We also were concerned that his head looked a little too large for the rest of his body—not exactly a red flag, but maybe a mauve one. And this was before we really had a clue about red flags.

Then came the guilt. How would we look if we didn't accept this little boy into our home? What kind of monsters could reject a needy orphan? Were we being spoiled American consumers "shopping" for the children of our dreams? Harvey and I didn't have to discuss our decision; the synchronicity of our silence voiced the answer. After making the call, we felt a mixture of relief, regret, remorse, and sadness.

Later we heard about adoptions taking place in Kazakhstan, where the process sounded agonizing. Adopting parents saw no photos, medical records, or videos of their prospective family. They would arrive at an orphanage, the children would be paraded in front of them, the parents would interact with the children for a certain period of time, and then they would choose. Mothers told me about children crying out to be picked, reaching desperately toward the prospective parents. The vision alone steals my breath.

I couldn't imagine being in that situation and fortunately didn't have to. We knew we had made the right decision later when we saw the referral video of the twelve-month-old baby boy who would become our son. In just ninety seconds, we both fell heart over head in love with this little guy. We sort of smiled at the way the orphanage worker tried to guide his head toward the camera, showing him off like a trainer positioning a puppy at a dog show. In the background, we heard someone calling his given Russian name, "Andrey! Andrey!" to get his attention. He kept trying to crawl to the left, and they kept redirecting him to the right, while he navigated in the opposite direction.

Although Andrey's body was clearly hypotonic, floppy from lack of physical stimulation to the muscles, all I could see was this impossibly angelic baby with thin dark hair, translucent skin, and deep, soulful brown eyes. Harvey and I both just knew. He was our son.

Being the rabbi that he is, my husband softly whispered, "I think we should say a *Shehecheyanu*." As the newly married rabbi's wife, I agreed that this special prayer for new beginnings was appropriate, but I was also caught off guard by the intensity of taking something liturgical into the context of our living room . . . you know, *real* life. At the time, I sensed the moment's sacredness, but I could never have known the infinite number of prayers that would follow our acceptance of this little baby in the referral video from Astrakhan, Russia.

Harvey and I had already decided to uphold a Jewish custom in which a child is given the name of a beloved deceased relative, or a name that begins with the same initial as the relative's. Consequently, we had chosen Iyal, (eye-ˈahl) meaning strength or deer in Hebrew, as our son's name to honor both my grandfather and Harvey's. They were both named Isador, apparently a rather popular name for a Russian Jew in the late nineteenth and early twentieth centuries.

Within two weeks of accepting Andrey, who would become our beloved Iyal, we received a videotape of an infant girl. Her tape was slightly longer, but in an instant, we knew we had discovered our daughter. Olga, whose new name would be Morasha, gazed directly at the video camera as if to say, "Hi there. Here's my crib. Let me show you around." This twelve-month-old darling, dressed only in her diaper, stood in her crib with an outreached hand that floated above her as though she were a ballet dancer. She calmly walked along her crib, carefully holding on to the railing with one hand while the other curved just so, extending gracefully toward the camera as she uttered something that seemed to make sense to her, if to no one else. I loved that my new daughter had conviction.

Morasha captivated every cell in my mind and in my body. With one look at Harvey sitting next to me, who was hypnotized by this tiny Russian dancer, I knew both of us had found her. This precious girl was ours.

Morasha was adorned with a stunning lack of hairstyle. In other words, she was bald. But she could pull it off! No one in the orphanage offered a reason, and we never asked. It didn't matter. She wore her exotic look like she might never even change it, even if she could. How could a twelve-month-old baby be so intentional in her movements and facial expressions?

I simply couldn't take my eyes off her. She was olive skinned with soft, fawn-like brown eyes that held a story we might never know. But she seemed unafraid. Something about her presence hinted that what lay ahead in her life would be safe and good. A life where *she* chose what was good for her.

After she chose *me* in those very first seconds of her video, everywhere I looked, I saw her. From then on, I seemed to superimpose her image into every scene I was in. And in a way, I still do. Lucky me.

For our precious daughter, we chose to honor my maternal grandmother by selecting the most beautifully unique name I had ever heard: Morasha, which means legacy or inheritance in Hebrew. I love explaining the meaning of their names; it feels magical every time.

Middle names were chosen with just as much careful thought. Iyal's middle name is Navon, translating to wisdom, after my uncle Nathan on my dad's side of the family. Rael, which is Morasha's middle name, denotes guardian of Israel and honors two of my aunts, Rhoda and Rosalyn.

—

After spending the night in Astrakhan, the big day had finally arrived. We loved every minute of being "there," because "there" was where our babies were born! We wanted to absorb every piece of Astrakhan and hold it precious for our children. Every possible scent, taste, and image we could savor we gratefully stored away in our emotional scrapbook.

Despite our joy and enthusiasm, however, our hotel room was a tad challenging. The room was so small, barely accommodating two mini twin beds, we could open only one suitcase at a time! Then we each had to carefully stand on a bed, balancing the suitcase between us so one of us wouldn't fall over and land in the bathroom. An alternative maneuver was when one of us stood outside in the hallway, hunched over, hanging on to the door frame with each hand so the suitcase could open on top of our backs. Of course we were laughing so hysterically the suitcase would fall and we would have to start all over! Olympic Russian gymnasts we were not.

The first morning, I chose to wear a black "good luck" dress my mom had given me, pairing it with black sandals and a leopard-print diaper bag. Okay, perhaps I was trying too hard to be a stylish new mom. Don't judge. I intended to maintain my trendsetting looks into this motherhood thing. Little did I know that spit-up would become the signature logo for my *entire* wardrobe.

First, our van driver pulled up to the orphanage where Iyal lived. We could barely contain ourselves as we practically catapulted out of the van, parcels spilling out as we tried to gain composure. Not wanting to miss a moment of this milestone he had waited so long for, Harvey dramatically videotaped our entrance. He described the entire scenario in his quiet, intense voice like a sportscaster narrating the Masters golf tournament in Georgia. The pauses were as effective as the words he spoke.

I took in the rusted steel gate, the barren and cracked cement play area, and the two-story white-brick building. Marina, our faithful EAC translator, led us in where a Russian woman in a white blouse and ankle-length print skirt greeted and directed us down the hall to a bright, sunny meeting room. Through translation, we were informed we wouldn't be allowed to tour or see any other part of the orphanage. All interactions had to take place in this meeting room. I might've worried about this were it not for the anticipatory wave of awe that began to spread over Harvey and me. We counted orphanage caregivers, one by one, proudly bringing six babies into the room to meet their new parents. I thought I would faint from lack of oxygen. Then we saw him.

A smiling attendant carried in Iyal and placed him on the floor before us and stepped back to let us begin a love story with our new son. Harvey and I couldn't help ourselves and began to murmur sounds we had never before made. Iyal wore a cotton blue, green, and white–checkered playsuit. My new son looked frighteningly pale and fragile, but oh so sweet.

The EAC had instructed us to bring baby diapers and clothes several sizes smaller than we might expect due to the malnourishment of the infants. It saddened us to see this was true.

Because he wore no shirt underneath his playsuit, we saw how translucent Iyal's skin was, with sharp shoulder blades poking through his back like rods with rounded ends. We could see the ripple of his spine as he bent over, his dark hair still wispy like in the video and his tiny feet barely able to keep on little blue-and-white socks.

Harvey and I grinned at each other and then couldn't take our eyes off our son. Immersed in joy, we held Iyal in a standing position as he took one finger from each of our hands. We formed a triangle, and he becomes the center of our universe. Without a sound, he followed our faces with an intense concentration in his eyes. It was all I could do to not scoop him up and snuggle him through me, out the other side, and then back again into my arms. But the staff at the EAC had advised us not to overwhelm the babies with too much affection and touch on our first visit.

Harvey leaned in and whispered, "What an adorable face! You are such a handsome little one, Iyal."

My smile morphed into words as well. "Oh, my love . . . we are finally here to take you home. You are more beautiful than in your photo—more beautiful than we could have ever imagined!" I felt lightheaded with glee and gratitude and overflowed with compassion, the joy of motherhood. I couldn't believe the softness in Harvey that his new little son was producing. My strong, thoughtful rabbi melted like a marshmallow in front of my eyes.

No longer a fantasy, but living, breathing flesh and blood. A dream fulfilled.

We had our son.

Each country has its own rules and regulations about adoption. Russia required us to wait two days after our initial meeting so that more paperwork could be processed and, I suppose, so that adoptive parents could reconsider (the thought itself crumbles my heart into tears) now that they had actually seen the baby who was about to be forever placed in their care. But we couldn't even imagine having second thoughts; we felt only impatience at wanting to take our babies home. Having to leave him after such a short visit was achingly painful, knowing that we wouldn't see him again for another two days. I felt like a new appendage had replaced a vacancy on my body and was then taken away again after I felt a new kind of wholeness.

My consolation was that I got to meet Morasha next. I was already crazy in love with her and couldn't fathom the miracle she would become in our lives.

At a similar but different children's home, we repeated the introduction process and were ushered into a small carpeted room with a high ceiling. Moments later, the director entered, cradling our baby girl in her arms. Morasha's hair had grown in since we had seen her extraordinarily chic un-hairstyle in the referral video more than three months earlier. Wearing a light-pink dress with ruffled short sleeves and matching pink kneesocks, she was beyond edible. Marina looked from the baby to me and exclaimed with a genuine smile, "Oh, Donnie, she looks just like you!" Staring at Morasha, I could barely speak as my heart grew inside my chest, taking over every other organ's function until I found my voice. I was completely, irreversibly enraptured with this precious breathing doll baby.

As the director handed her toward me, Morasha reached out and grabbed my finger and looked directly into my eyes.

Complete. Baby. Magic.

At that moment, every dream flew open, every maternal instinct unfurled with yearning, and I just could not stop beaming.

"Hello, sweet girl," cooed Harvey. "Aren't you a cute one?" Morasha turned with a smile toward Harvey, further dissolving him into mush.

"That's your daddy," I explained. "We are so lucky to have you at last! How did you get to be so lovely so fast?"

This whole exchange happened within a six-inch space between my face and hers. Her ability to be intimate with me clearly indicated that she had attached to someone before and was unafraid of the close physical proximity. Morasha immediately seemed capable and willing to trust me, even at fourteen months. The importance of a baby attaching to a primary caregiver or parent sets the stage for self-soothing, the development of trust, and a feeling of security without fear of abandonment.

Holding her close, I made ridiculous baby faces at Morasha, watching her dark eyes track my expressions. Harvey continued sermonizing in baby talk, holding out his finger for his daughter to hold. I gently tapped her nose, hoping to get her to smile. And she did. With each passing moment she was in my arms, I sank deeper into an all-consuming bliss.

Fast-forward more than a decade later, and those early memories seem worn and faded, as ornately sentimental as the icons I purchased at a flea market near Red Square in Moscow. So much had happened that, some days, I didn't recognize myself anymore. Although I truly never had second thoughts or any regrets about the gift of having Iyal and Morasha as our son and daughter, no one told me how the journey would change me, challenge my vulnerabilities and my sensibilities, carve and chisel away at hard places, and leave me in fragments.

So there I stood in the kitchen, momentarily kidnapped by paralysis, when a golden blur whizzed past me and out onto the deck. Chancer had sensed the danger that Iyal was now in just as I had, only Chancer's reflexes took over. In suspended animation, I watched as Chancer, not just our family pet but, foremost, my son's service dog, used his mouth to pull Iyal's shirt and draw him back down to the safety of the deck—a task for which Chancer was not officially trained. I had just witnessed the kind of miracle I had heard about service dogs! My belief in Chancer as an anchor for Iyal was cemented in a new reality, one I had fought for with my entire being.

Released from the horrifying picture of this potential catastrophe, I flew through the doors to Chancer and Iyal, grabbed my son by the waist, and held him. Attempting to de-escalate my own panic,

I breathed deeply and said, "Honey, why would you climb onto the railing of the deck?" I exhaled. "That was so dangerous! Why would you *do* that?"

Rule number one, reader. Pay close attention because this is an important theme in the story. Think twice before you ask a person who experiences the organic brain damage of fetal alcohol syndrome (FAS), "Why did you do that?" Because at certain times in life, like this one, they usually don't know why they do most things, and right then, Iyal simply answered, "I just wanted to see what would happen."

This was Iyal's truth, his reality, as we had come to realize that the concept of cause and effect would remain an elusive one throughout his life. Can you imagine not being able to make judgments based on past mistakes? Not having a sense of chronological order about which events in your life occurred before others? Being ruled by your emotions in ways that feel uncontrollable and arbitrary? This is the life of a child who was exposed to alcohol before they were born, a life that would be drastically shaped by FAS. This is the life of my son.

My story isn't the typical boy meets dog, boy loves dog, dog loves boy, and they live happily ever after. This story isn't a disease-*du-jour* book intended to educate you or persuade you to donate money to a cause. It's simply an extraordinary tale birthed from a mother's desperation, a dog's second chance, and a family's unexpected gift of hope.

We've learned that hope may not look like what you expect. In fact, I'm convinced that catalysts of real hope and positive change rarely do. They may slumber or prance, speak a different language, alert us to invisible harm or imminent danger, and carry around almost anything you can imagine in their mouths. Nothing about the process was easy—as you'll see—but now I can't imagine my life without Chancer any more than I can imagine life without Harvey and our kids. Our family found hope between a wet nose and a wagging tail and in unending love covered in fur.

Chapter Two

The first morning after returning home from Russia, Harvey and I awoke, still groggy with jetlag, looked at each other like strangers who couldn't remember the night before, and then suddenly realized, "We have two babies now!" We launched ourselves out of bed and into the kitchen, where my parents sat at the table, each holding a baby and cooing like mourning doves. This portrait had waited a long time to be painted.

My folks had offered to stay with us for those first six weeks after we arrived home, giving us the opportunity to rest and assimilate the miraculous but astounding change in our lives. And as grandchildless seniors, they had a lot of spoiling to do.

In fact, their adoration had started before Harvey and I even brought the babies home from Russia.

The minute we accepted the referrals of our two new babies, Harvey and I immediately made a VHS copy with both referral videos on it and sent it to New Jersey by carrier stork. That was early May 1999, so from then until Morasha and Iyal were cradled in their arms at the end of August, my mom and dad religiously watched all two minutes and forty-eight seconds of the combined video of their soon-to-be grandchildren *every day*.

Here was their ritual. My dad would wake up first, having set the coffeemaker the night before. He would go downstairs, prepare two cups of coffee with skim milk in both and a half packet of Sweet'N Low in his, and head back up to their bedroom. They would settle on the bed with their coffee and put in the videotape of the kids. And they would watch. And watch. Oh, maybe for ten to twenty minutes at a time. Every single day! They must have memorized every movement, every baby blink, every second of this tiny window into the lives of their new grandchildren. As Morasha and Iyal would be my parents' only grandkids, their impending arrival lit up each day with joyful anticipation.

Harvey's parents promised to come later, when his father, a real estate attorney, could take some vacation. The dream of a complete family had materialized, and our children had four healthy and infatuated grandparents to adore them. At long last, I felt like a maternal success, having given my mom and dad their ultimate *nachus* (Yiddish for pride), so richly deserved.

Our homecoming the night before had ushered in an intoxicating age of innocence, a parenting honeymoon, and a hypnotic spell that captured our consciousness and rendered us silly in love with Morasha and Iyal. I will forever relive those first few years with the babies this way, a gift to be opened again and again when the hard times descended. Sort of like trying dreadfully to remember what you first loved about your spouse years later when every ridiculous little thing they did drove you completely nuts.

—

As we glided off the escalator in the international terminal at the Atlanta airport, we felt like grand marshals leading the Rose Parade. Facing me in her carrier, Morasha looked alert and amused, finally calm after her sixteen-hour screaming marathon, as though all that crying in the plane took place in some other baby's body, leaving *her* completely refreshed. Giddy from exhaustion, I envied Harvey's Olympic burst of adrenaline (Where and from whom did he get it? Clearly, his body didn't manufacture it, and would it disqualify us from the eight-thousand-meter parenting freestyle?) as he bounced up and down with Iyal on his back, only the top of our son's little head visible in the carrier. We were both reverberating with excitement.

Immediately, we found several expansive, grinning faces—my mom and dad, hovering somewhere higher than our plane's cruising altitude, along with our dearest friends, Ellen and Eddie and their three kids, all holding colorful posters welcoming our new family members. After initial hugs and kisses, our parade float shuffled to a vacant waiting area, and no one could keep their hands off the babies.

Morasha and Iyal both seemed enthralled and a bit dazed by all the attention (or were they just exhausted—do babies get jetlag?). While one of the Ten Commandments of international adoption proclaims, "Thou shalt limit the number of people the babies meet for the first few weeks so they have time to adjust to their new surroundings," we desperately wanted to show them off, like new puppies. And plus, we had more than three hundred families back at the temple congregation waiting to be introduced, along with our many noncongregant friends.

But for that magical moment in the airport, our little party was just right.

Before we left for Russia, a good friend, someone who actually knew how to use tools without hurting himself, had installed six baby gates above and below the three sets of stairs in our home. Our kitchen cabinets were safer than Fort Knox. Brick fireplace mantles were overlaid with quilts, and coffee tables had to be covered with rubber strips, framing their life-threatening corners. Soft and contained became part of our "new look."

Morasha and Iyal had their first visit to the pediatrician the week after we arrived home. Weight, height, and head and chest circumference were all revisited. Inoculations brought on wails of distress—mostly from me. Mom and Dad were with us for moral support. Vials of blood were drawn to check for parasites and any other unwelcome foreign bodies.

After charting their height and weight against the norm of American infants at fifteen months, we realized they both were significantly physically and perhaps developmentally delayed. In the Russian orphanages, the infants were fed a kind of gruel, a ground-up- meat-with-milk mixture. Rumors in the adoption community claimed the bottles were often just propped up between the crib bars or playpens so that no caregiver actually had to take any time to hold a bottle for each baby. This image appalled me and still bends my heartstrings almost to breaking.

But I vowed that I would have no hungry babies in *my* house. We transitioned from formula to soft food within the next few weeks per doctor's orders and to finger food pretty much on schedule. I can't even begin to tell you the combinations of Cuisinart-processed meals I created, such as Brie and ground hamburger, and asparagus mixed with hollandaise sauce and chopped boiled eggs. I became determined to develop a superior gastronomic palate for them as early as possible. Their gourmet appreciation lasted until eighteen months, at which time they stubbornly refused their sophisticated meals and begged to eat Gerber's (where had I gone wrong?) and other typically bland baby food.

Our pediatrician had recommended a full evaluation from the state agency that assesses ages zero to three and recommends therapies as needed. We contacted the agency in September and were informed that the soonest a caseworker could conduct an intake interview would be in November. No problem—we weren't concerned. We were parental honeymooners!

In the meantime, we had converted our downstairs den into an award-winning playroom one might find in *House & Garden* magazine. Well, minus the garden and, to be completely honest, minus the picture-perfect house as well. In other words, all my cute cubbies and clever toy-storage bins didn't work as well as planned. All those bright-smiling families standing around admiring their clutter-free rooms on the cover of each toy package. Who were these people anyway? And why didn't they come and smile in *my* playroom?

At first, Morasha and Iyal played together nicely, interacting with each other and sharing toys. To be sure, we knew this wouldn't last, and it didn't. When I watch the videos Harvey took of those early months, I still smile when I hear my mom's endearing voice sing with liquid love, "What a good girrrrl. What a good booooy." In several scenes, my dad, who was always lying down to become one with the floor for months to be right on a level with the babies, makes absurd kissing sounds toward Iyal as he discovers a "push toy" and bravely learns to walk. Iyal toddled independently within two weeks after we arrived home. Yay! Four weeks later, Morasha began pattering about with arms stretched straight out in front of her—our diminutive darling Frankenstein.

As our period of "commandment quarantine" was now complete, we were more than ready to share our Russian treasures. The temple sisterhood had planned a winner-takes-all baby shower in our temple social hall. The kids met the sisterhood (whose membership magically increased for the shower), and the women watched the video of us first arriving home at the airport. The women were beside themselves watching Harvey carrying Iyal on his back in his BabyBjörn carrier. If anything could surpass the sacredness of carrying around the Torah, this was it.

As I now understand, a congregation needs to feel their rabbi has a complete rabbinate, his "extended immediate family." I swear the term *rabbinate* makes me think of a rabbit hutch. So much to learn as a rabbi's wife. According to what he had shared with me, Harvey's first marriage felt vacuous rather than fulfilling. His former wife seemed to want no part of synagogue life, and as many congregants openly shared with me, she was far from approachable. During our brief engagement, Harvey said with genuine enthusiasm, "Donnie, if you bring a plate of chocolate chip cookies—even the Pillsbury ones you can just throw in the oven—to the sisterhood once a year, they will adore you!" Even the Pillsbury kind? Wow.

"You're the opposite of what they've experienced, and they're going to go crazy over you!" It was a relief that I had no act to follow and Harvey trusted me to find my own path as a rabbi's wife. He didn't know how woefully challenged I was with absolutely no sense of direction, which meant *I* could also wind up wandering in the desert for forty years. But *I'd* stop and ask someone for directions. If there was someone there to stop. What? Have you never considered there might have been someone else who was lost? The desert is a big place.

So our baby shower was overwhelming, joyful, and generous. Besides all the equipment and accessories we had borrowed from congregants, we were now flooded with so many lovely gifts from this extravaganza. Swelling with thankfulness and disbelief, we hauled all the presents back home and drew up a blueprint for an annex.

Within weeks, teeth started to sprout all over the place! Both babies had two on top and two on the bottom when we left Russia, but suddenly teething became a full-time occupation with overtime on holidays. Their hair began to grow like Samson's and Rapunzel's, seemingly an inch longer overnight. The miracle of proper nourishment produced dramatic effects that blew us away. Now, Iyal was sporting his signature "bowl cut" coif that distinguished him throughout childhood, much to our dismay. Our little boy simply couldn't grow a part—and even today uses styling gel for management. Either teenaged Elvis Presley or young Edward Scissorhands emerges from his bathroom daily.

One of our caveats in the adoption process was that we absolutely, positively had to be back in Atlanta in time for the Jewish High Holidays, which were in early September that year. One week after we arrived home, Harvey was frantically fine-tuning his four biggest sermons for the year. He put enormous pressure on himself, while I promised him the congregation would understand if, under "new parent" duress, he made up his own commandments, added an extra day to the story of creation, and reorganized the order of the Torah.

At sixteen months, the babies were communicating in their own Rosetta Stone language, neither Russian nor English, but demonstrating that they knew they were ours and we were theirs.

Morasha flirted with males and with me, melting her tiny body against mine like a layer of spandex. Sometimes I would play the piano while she sat on my lap, swaying to the melody and clapping her hands. My joy during these duets felt incomparable. Everyone said, "Donnie, you're just a natural mom. Look at you. No effort . . . it just happens!" Motherhood did feel so natural and satisfying and defined me differently from the person I was before.

My parents reluctantly returned to New Jersey after their initial six-week indoctrination as grandparents. Was there a traumatic adjustment for us? Well, without them, Harvey and I practically murdered each other after the first forty-eight hours. Friends offered to come over and play or run errands or babysit. We were *so* not ready for anyone to babysit—especially if they didn't have our DNA. But Harvey had to eventually get himself back into his rabbi groove, and I had to take on this daunting responsibility on my own during the day and often the night.

Things were happening fast. Before we knew it, we were preparing the babies (and ourselves) for their conversion to the Jewish faith. The conversion required the babies to be given Hebrew names and be immersed in holy water at a *mikvah*. Baby boys had an extra-special step that I'll save as a surprise. Friday, November 5, 1999, was the first baby naming. Harvey and I crafted a service so our parents could be a part of it as well as the babies' godparents. The congregation had been waiting for this moment. Witnessing their rabbi on the pulpit with two toddlers running around as he chased after them meant hearing congregants say, "Yes, he is human! He's just like us!" "Wait. Is that what we want?" "Really. Like *us*?" "No, he can't keep up with his own kids!" "Yes, that *is* what we want!" "Mazel tov!"

I composed a song for the service that our cantor beautifully sang. Then all hell broke loose—yes, inside a synagogue! During the service, Morasha at some point pulled off her size-zero black patent-leather shoe and held it in her hand like a scepter. Our little princess knew an opportunity when she saw one. Meanwhile, Iyal purposefully climbed up and down the two steps on the bimah (the platform where the service takes place) like a pro in toddler boot camp.

On the video of the service, you can see some adult family member ducking down, trying not to be seen on camera running after one toddler, while another adult would appear holding the other in their arms, until the first appears again, this time with a terribly strained look on their face. Imagine something like a British farce. Except better.

During the naming service on the bimah, in place of traditional davening, when a Jew is rocking forward and back chanting Hebrew prayers, Harvey bounced up and down holding Iyal and defying synagogue gravity, and I swayed side to side, trying to contain Morasha from somersaulting out of my arms. As participants ascended and descended the bimah to speak their parts, Harvey and I had to stand far enough apart so that Morasha didn't clop her brother on his head with the scepter in her hand. A few moments later, Iyal began purring and gurgling while Morasha dropped her shoe and attempted to organize the papers on the pulpit. The service was extraordinarily interactive.

And just in case we hadn't celebrated enough, we held *another* naming ceremony two days later on Sunday for the Jewish community "at large." Rabbis and their families joined us on the pulpit with a modified ceremony, wishing blessings for Morasha and Iyal. This time, relatives flew in from the East and West Coasts as well as dear friends from New Jersey to become part of the covenant assembled to welcome the babies into Judaism. A gala reception followed the service in our social hall as friends and family were interviewed on videotape, sharing their well wishes. The toddlers were passed around like trophies, bestowing their own blessings on those who let them taste the desserts.

Harvey's mom and dad and his sister, Randy, and her daughter, Nadia, remained for several days after the naming and savored the opportunity to imprint themselves on the babies. Since Morasha and Iyal had started the sixteen-month-old "Mommy and me" class at the temple, they had mastered "Itsy Bitsy Spider," "Mr. Sun, Sun, Mr. Golden Sun," and "Ten Little Monkeys Jumping on the Bed," with accompanying hand gestures. The entire family performed the repertoire, with everyone clapping at the end, and often held a standing ovation, giggling, "Bravo! Good job!"

Also in November, Iyal had a circumcision performed at a hospital with a rabbi colleague and a pediatric urologist in an outpatient operating room. If it had been a traditional bris, a mohel would've been the religious expert who would cut the foreskin off the penis—while all males present murmured prayers. Prior to the act in a traditional bris, the baby would be swaddled and a small taste of red wine would be placed in the baby's mouth, with the intention of providing a slight buzz for the baby boy during the impending deed.

I've attended many a bris where the mothers can't be anywhere near the actual circumcision (sometimes waiting at a neighbor's) because they might faint, throw up, or begin to calculate the imminent psychiatric bills incurred to help the boy move past the trauma. For Iyal, the anesthesia erased the entire event, and the circumcision brought him deeper into the Jewish covenant.

Next up our entire close family brought the babies to a mikvah, for their conversion, which is the final official tradition that anchors them in Judaism. We had assumed they weren't born Jewish just based on the population of Astrakhan being primarily Russian Orthodox. The mikvah was held inside another synagogue, and three Reform rabbis had been invited to officiate, as Harvey was supposed to be a father, not a rabbi, for this symbolic ritual.

The babies were undressed in a private area and paraded out to a very small pool of holy water. Not a lot of water is needed when it's holy. Engraved on the stone above the water were the prayers in Hebrew and their transliteration (phonetic interpretation of the Hebrew). The babies would be immersed three times with three prayers spoken by us in between the "dunks."

Harvey and I in bathing suits walked down the few steps into the warm water, holding Morasha and Iyal. While Morasha naively and enthusiastically began waving like Miss America at the people assembled, Iyal splashed about as if searching for a water toy in a bathtub. The rabbis spoke Hebrew, we triple dunked the babies sandwiched with prayers, and before they knew it, we were done! Celebratory food awaited, and relief replaced the anticipatory anxiety that accompanies any event in which two toddlers are the stars.

And stars they were. Although we didn't exactly have a red carpet, we pretty much had every other item on a toddler's interior-decorator wish list. By then the playroom boasted wall-to-wall toys and miniature household appliances. A pink-and-gray galley kitchen equipped with Pottery Barn–like plasticware produced elegant invisible meals. A molded-plastic three-foot-tall refrigerator with a top freezer became an item of competition, with each baby pushing the one standing inside outside, and vice versa. The life-sized dolly bassinet also offered the opportunity to tease each other, with one of them constantly being dumped out and demanding equality before repeating the process.

In the background, besides hearing Rafi on the cassette, baby piano sounds repeated their prerecorded nursery rhymes while helicopters whirred, buses beeped, toys with animal faces emitted matching sounds, and adults imitated them all. The babies either participated or stared vacantly at the adults, waiting for something more important to happen. Iyal would sit on the floor, the toy of the moment in front of him, hunched over with rounded back, preferring to bang on it rather than move its parts.

The golden glow of new parenthood was great fun.

Until it wasn't.

I'm just being honest here. I loved being a mom and was all in. Yet after the first year or so, I sensed an impending shift in the paradigm of parenting, like the breeze had subtly gained momentum, becoming a headwind leading to a hurricane, something unexpected as well as inevitable. With no one else at the house doing everyday tasks and chores like doing laundry and picking up toys discarded on the floor when a new one came into view, showering and feeding myself seemed next to impossible. All my energy was sucked out of every pore and consumed by the toddlers.

Maybe it started that first year when we finally received our initial evaluations from Babies Can't Wait. We had read and researched and were already prepared to hear about developmental and physical delays. From the report, Morasha showed only slight delays in speech. She was already holding a pencil appropriately to draw, and her fine motor control, that ability to manipulate objects with her fingers, was above average.

Cleaning up the playroom every night was akin to straightening the deck chairs on the *Titanic* in the movie *Groundhog Day*. Why bother when the ship's going to sink again tomorrow? Mom and Dad had given two miniature wicker rocking chairs to the toddlers so Morasha and Iyal would sit and rock side by side mesmerized by *Snow White*, *The Wizard of Oz*, *Peter Pan*, and *Teletubbies*. Over and over again. And then some more. I knew children loved hearing favorite stories and lip-synching with characters repeatedly, but some kind of subliminal message had to be hypnotizing them and holding them prisoner to the TV. I became frightened when I, too, found myself speaking familiar lines word for word, out loud in the grocery store, keening in temple, murmuring at the doctor's office.

Even though my parents came down from New Jersey to visit about every couple of weeks, in between, I began to feel weathered, while dark clouds rolled in and out and I dodged the depression that threatened me on and off throughout my life. The combination of constant fatigue and self-doubt left me empty and lost. And the effort to hide my struggle just added another level of exhaustion. Harvey's work at the temple seemed to have increased in proportion to the demands of the kids. Were *all* toddlers this much work? I assumed so but had no real basis for comparison.

Even though everyone could see that Iyal was lagging behind his sister in development, the occupational assessment for Iyal indicated deficits in fine motor and oral motor function. Looking back on this initial evaluation, I realize how naive Harvey and I were.

"Well, this is just a standard evaluation and doesn't really mean much other than we need to strengthen Iyal's upper body and work on developing his fine motor control," I said to Harvey.

He listened attentively and then asked, "So, what does this 'oral motor function' mean?"

I answered, "You know how Iyal's mouth just stays open a lot?" Harvey nodded. "Those muscles that keep his mouth closed aren't working right, which affects his speech and his eating. So we have to work on this."

As time went by, I realized that the "delayed development" diagnosis from Babies Can't Wait was much more common than I knew. A developmental delay may appear as a delay in what is considered the achievement of normal developmental milestones during infancy and early childhood, like sitting, talking, or walking. The failure to meet these milestones would raise a red flag for the evaluator. These delays might be caused by psychological, organic, or environmental factors or any combination. When our kids were small, we met numerous families whose children were also given a diagnosis of delayed development, many of whom were adopted. The term seemed to be an appropriate net to catch children who might otherwise have fallen through the cracks while their peers grew at the expected pace both chronologically and developmentally.

What I learned after Iyal was diagnosed, through many conversations with doctors and hours and hours of reading about fetal alcohol spectrum disorders (FASDs), is that in most cases, the symptoms of FASDs often don't evince themselves until about ages two to four as children begin to socialize with each other on the playground or in a day care or school setting. Sometimes the symptoms of prenatal alcohol exposure may appear as subtle disturbances in a normally developing child. Although experts in FASDs were beginning to gain attention in this new territory in 2002, breaking through the known boundaries of developmental disorders, when the kids were four years old, FASDs were barely a blip on the radar screen of most occupational, speech, and physical therapists. Now we know that FASDs last a lifetime and can be diagnosed at any age.

Harvey asked me about how Morasha fit into this regimen of therapies. "The neat thing, Harvey, is that even though Morasha seems to be developing on schedule for the most part, she will also benefit from Iyal's therapies."

"How does that work?" Harvey asked.

"The people who conducted Iyal's evaluations said that the therapists come to our house, and their protocol states that any child who lives in the home will also be involved in the therapy."

"So that seems like a bonus!" Harvey said.

"I think so," I responded. "What I know is that my, uh, our, days will be filled with a lot of therapy."

I couldn't imagine at this point just how scheduled our lives would become with wall-to-wall appointments and often very little to show for it.

—

Consequently, we began weekly speech and occupational therapy and had monthly physical therapy visits. As part of Iyal's therapy, both babies were taught sign language, which I found cool. We all learned to sign "Twinkle, Twinkle, Little Star" and important words like *more* and *no*. Our dear friends Caroline Figiel and her daughter, Kelly, knew American Sign Language and brought over videos of *Little Red Riding Hood* and other fairy tales signed by one of the current human performers on *Sesame Street*. We watched these videos over and over until the tapes were silently screaming for mercy.

Naturally, tantrums were on the rise in both children, but because they were two years old, we knew we had it coming. But I discovered parenting has its own math system, and the "terrible twos" times two didn't equal four. It was four *fucking thousand*! Do you hear me? Parenting takes too much fucking energy! By the end of the day, after the kids were down for the night and Harvey would just be returning home, he would eventually locate me on the den floor in the fetal position.

Remember Thing 1 and Thing 2 from Dr. Seuss's *The Cat in the Hat*? Corralling my two little tornados that twisted and shouted in tandem was impossible. If one cried, they both cried. If one was hungry, then of course they both were! And I began to notice that Iyal was usually the follower, the one taking his cues from his sister.

—

By this point, their little personalities had begun to surface. Morasha had a talent for accessorizing at an early age. Years ahead of the trend, she was never seen without some "extension" in her hair—often a scarf or fake braids attached to a headband—with which she could maximize her femininity. Killer runway looks included when she would strategically place her bib over her head, pulling back her bangs at mealtimes (which Iyal also mastered), or when she wore her favorite flannel nightgown secured on her head and strode around the house, her "hair" swaying with a dramatic flair while she tried not to trip on it.

Morasha initially wowed us with her strong will when during her first week home, she would hold her breath if she was not in agreement with our plans. Her face turned an angry plum color, and she simply cried so hard she was not breathing! We blew puffs of air at her nose, not knowing if there was some more scientific remedy for her oxygen-related political stance. Eventually, she resumed normal breathing, knowing she had won that battle. Eardrops? Don't get me started. We needed a minyan (a minimum of ten people assembled for prayer) to hold her down.

Two days before we'd left Moscow to come home to Atlanta, we'd captured on video the physical examination performed by our EAC-designated Russian pediatrician. These exams were required in order to obtain the kids' passports. You can't imagine how ludicrous the means were with which he weighed the babies. The doctor, who came to our hotel room, literally sat on a bed, placed his hands under their armpits, and lifted each baby up in the air twice. Satisfied with his measurement, he noted on paper and to us, "This one. The little girl. She"—he paused—"she's nine pounds." After weighing according to a measurement system I was unaware of, he announced that Iyal was twenty-five pounds. Of course, the babies wailed the entire time, and I just watched, astonished, the ignorant-but-proud, brand-new mother.

When we arrived in Atlanta, Iyal had weighed a mere eighteen pounds, not twenty-five as ridiculously estimated by the Russian doctor. By twenty-two months, he had almost doubled his weight to thirty-four pounds and appeared quite active. He, too, began to reveal his personality—but only in response to Morasha's. Whatever she asked for, he asked for. Whatever food she chose, so did he. He clearly adored her, and she would learn to take full advantage of this worship over the next few years until it no longer benefitted her.

At two, both toddlers were now enrolled in our temple's pre-K school three mornings a week and also at the local Jewish community center's program. The staff at both preschools loved the kids, of course, and their time at school gave me a much-needed break. However, more than one caregiver commented that Iyal seemed to need "a lot of redirection" since his focus wandered frequently, as he seemed transported to another planet. His coordination appeared off, and one preschool teacher suggested that we test him for something called "auditory processing."

Nervous about what she might be identifying, I reconnected with Babies Can't Wait and began another set of assessments. Something inside me sensed that there was more to Iyal's lack of focus than what these trained therapists observed. But at this time, my understanding of the larger medical machine just didn't exist. I'd have to rely on my developing sixth sense that began to frame my expectations for Iyal's health. And my hopes. From this visit, we learned Iyal's vocabulary was increasing, but his "low oral motor tone" worsened, meaning his mouth gaped open more than it was closed. Occasionally, he drooled without awareness, and we needed to remind him to close his mouth. Sucking on his two fingers, which he instinctively did as he began to become increasingly overwhelmed by the subtlest demands in his environment, calmed him.

The evaluations showed that Iyal could draw vertical lines but had difficulty with horizontal lines (this is called "crossing midline") and drawing a circle with the end points meeting. He struggled to pull up his elastic pants because doing so involved the movement of both hands at the same time. For instance, he'd forget that he had a left hand, and his arm would lie motionless at his side.

Iyal's watercolor paintings in preschool revealed an inner universe that was somewhat disconcerting.

Iyal's teacher explained to me, "When I asked Iyal to paint a picture of what it felt like when he was mad, here's how he 'told me.'" I looked at the picture of figures that appeared to be creatures or something not quite human. I could feel my heart slow its beating, as though a slower heartbeat might offer a softer cushion to absorb the blow I knew was coming. His teacher continued, "Iyal said to me, 'I'm screaming. There's a big thing. It's a pillow, and I'm hitting my mommy, and I can't stop it even though I want to.'" There was the blow, the first of too many to count. By age three, Iyal's picture of our family showed four figures, each labeled appropriately with our names. Harvey, Morasha, and I are smiling, but Iyal has no face. It is completely blank.

This tiny glimpse into Iyal's psychological world was even more distressing to me than all the physical assessments combined. Even if I didn't wholly understand why, I was able to *see* the impact his delayed development had on his motor control. But we were not yet stumbling into the emotionally damaged terrain of Iyal's injured brain. I didn't even have the questions to ask, but I sensed an even greater weight would be placed on Iyal and my family.

Our parental reflex was to begin an aggressive litany of different therapies: a brushing protocol to stimulate nerve endings for sensory calming and joint compression to strengthen Iyal's ability to tolerate incoming stimuli. Yet transitioning from one activity to another became an ordeal in and of itself, especially if it was unexpected. Iyal needed a lot of extra time because he became frustrated with activities not under his control. Sand timers, special visual clocks with changing colors, and contraptions that made sounds all had trials as we searched for the right cues to help him prepare for change.

Our attempts included the Samonas therapeutic listening program to help with his ability to self-regulate. These CDs had calming music used with a specific headphone that emitted a random tone of frequency I imagine made dogs yowl in chorus all over the neighborhood. But it didn't seem to have much effect on Iyal. If he was distracted, he couldn't navigate his environment no matter what kind of auditory or visual cues prompted him to focus, which meant constantly supervising him and keeping him on track.

Over time, we understood that when Iyal was in a situation where he had to use trial-and-error reasoning or predict the consequence of an action, he disengaged and sought sensory stimulation. He zoomed into walls without registering pain or plowed into people, knocking them off balance. Like pain, Iyal's barometer of temperature was distinctly different from those whose brains were healthy. He would confuse the words describing pain and temperature when speaking. Hot and cold weather didn't have any impact on his comfort level or his choice in outerwear. It just didn't seem to matter.

Other seasoned parents reassured us that Iyal would "come out of his shell" any time now. But by age four, Iyal couldn't make any decision for himself without knowing what Morasha was doing. He literally could not make a choice without his sister as the foundation. Like any good sister, she quickly tired of his constant copycat mode and began to complain. I started to wonder if my son could actually think for himself. On the rare occasions when he wasn't with Morasha, he seemed lost and had no idea what he wanted or even needed.

Later I would learn that the process of decision making is rather more complicated than most people appreciate. The human brain learns to eliminate some options in order to make one choice, which isn't an easy process when some of the hardware is broken or missing in one's operating system.

Before the children, I had no idea how vital the relationship was between our senses and behavior. High levels of sensory input could get Iyal's attention back on track, and he could reengage in an activity he chose. He needed "deep pressure" to self-calm, which translated to receiving tight hugs, being squished between two big pillows like the jelly in a PB&J sandwich, or wearing a weighted vest—a vest literally filled with different-sized tiny weights in the lining that fit snuggly against his body. Three weeks of the vest and into the closet of failed therapeutic interventions it went, adding to our inventory of promises of change that didn't deliver.

I had no idea of the havoc that disordered sensory systems could evoke.

—

Their creative play was often hilarious as, admittedly, Iyal's persona appeared as a shadow of Morasha's. She was an early learner and developed diva syndrome, casting productions that showcased her talents, which meant she played the drama queen and Iyal was more of her sidekick.

Between the temple's and the Jewish community center's pre-K curriculum, they had been inundated with Bible stories read from both left and right—their father, formerly the rabbi, had become executive producer for their productions. As a result, playing house often seemed more Jewish history lesson than Disney fairy tale. For example, here's perhaps my favorite:

CAST:

Morasha starring as Zipporah (Moses's wife)

Iyal as Best Supporting Actor in the role of Moses

ACTION:

> Zipporah shrieks at the top of her lungs to Moses at the far end of the driveway, who is struggling to keep his tricycle upright and moving in any direction at all,
>
> "Moses! Get your camel over here. I need some groceries. Now!"
>
> Moses woefully responds, "I wuv you, 'Porah. But my camel is sleeping."

And the fun didn't end there. One sunny spring afternoon, we had a landscape company install some new plantings in the front yard. Morasha and Iyal were creating masterpieces on the driveway with chalk and blowing bubbles from the ever-present bottle of detergent-based goo that was constantly being spilled and refilled. Morasha looked up and noticed the team of men working in the yard, which included several African Americans. In her best "Zipporah voice," she bellowed to me across the yard, "Mom! Are those slaves?" I pretended to be invisible and vaporized myself to the back of the house to dissolve into a fit of laughter and die of mortification.

My parents encouraged Morasha's and Iyal's love of make-believe and theatrics. While the kids were toddlers, Mom and Dad would put in VHS tapes of *Cinderella* and *Peter Pan* among other classics. Although now people might tweet while watching a movie on TV, at the time, we didn't have a device to enhance the watching experience. But Mom and Dad designed other ways to bring the movie to life. They would ransack Iyal and Morasha's toy chest and pull out bits and pieces of costumes to create characters from these movies. I remember Dad wearing half a black eye mask that Mom carefully trimmed to become the face of Captain Hook. My parents attached a stuffed bird (not necessarily a parrot, but it didn't matter) to my dad's shoulder with strips of ribbon. Tinker Bell, formerly known as Giggy (my mom's nickname), would hop from the sofa to the chair to the floor and up to the chair again. Morasha's ballet tutu fit over some part of Mom while wings from a discarded angel costume became the means that enabled her to flit around the room. They were ready for their Tony. The kids laughed and clapped, and so did I.

As they approached four, Iyal and Morasha began another pre-K in different public school classes funded through the Georgia state lottery. Soon thereafter, Iyal's teachers gave us discouraging reports. Harvey and I were prepared to receive negative feedback but couldn't have anticipated the disastrous and painful notes that bombarded us. Here's a typical partial week's report:

Wednesday: "Iyal crawled out onto the lunch table today. He threw toys at Shirley during nap time, pinched her, and tried to hold a beanbag chair on top of her." Iyal? *Our* Iyal?

Thursday: "Iyal could not keep his hands to himself. He hit children in line. From the morning greeting circle on, he was unable to *sit* in any group at any time. Could not be quiet, made noises, and was talking all day, often to himself, except when sleeping during lunch. Launched a chair across the room." Crap.

Friday: "Had hard time listening all day. Stared into space when not bothering other students."

Well, shit.

Our world was becoming a foreign country, and we had no passports.

Harvey and I knew that with the number of children in the classroom, Iyal would be challenged to focus, especially without Morasha there to guide him. On the one hand, we were glad that Morasha wasn't with Iyal in class. At only four, we already thought she needed a break from her two-day-older brother. She couldn't know, but *we* knew that Iyal's personality was beginning to scrape away at the edges of *our* personalities. On the other hand, we realized that Morasha's real presence seemed almost tangible to Iyal, like a soothing breeze that she gently wrapped around him.

One afternoon during a phone call with Harvey, he asked, "Don, do you think we should go in to school and have another meeting with Iyal's teacher?"

"What would we say to her?" I responded. "Other than apologize and ask for different ways to keep trying to modify Iyal's behavior, I'm not sure she even knows what else to do."

I could hear Harvey's sigh on the other end of the line. "I know." Quietly, he said, "I just can't believe we could be *so* frustrated about such a *little* guy."

It was my turn to sigh. We said, "I love you" to each other and returned to our respective tasks, feeling that we were stalled in our attempts to help our son but steady in our commitment to each other.

Polite comments like "Oh, my son was like that" from caring friends became fewer as they distanced themselves, afraid Iyal's behavior might be contagious to their own children.

Around this time, Iyal had taken to "squishing" my upper arms to the point where I wore bruises as badges of courage. He developed a fetish with other people's feet and toes and couldn't stop touching them. Complete strangers in sandals were up for grabs. The "touchables" thought it was "so cute" that this little three-then-four-year-old wanted to play with their toes. But his sensory cravings were getting out of control, and we felt a growing pressure to monitor him all the time.

Rather than showing improvement, Iyal was freefalling into a black hole of progressively worse behavior. Despite our growing list of challenges and treatments, Iyal didn't yet have an individualized educational plan (IEP), a formal document recognized by most accredited education systems that requires them to accommodate and modify the curriculum of students' special needs. As his kindergarten behavior became more and more unpredictably chaotic, we requested the school evaluate Iyal in order to qualify for an IEP.

Meanwhile, as Iyal continued to struggle in the classroom, we had hoped to receive some answers from his doctors. Although we adored our pediatricians, they were at a loss for how to diagnose Iyal with something, because he didn't neatly fit into any profile. His symptoms were so all over the place. Friends who had adopted their children as babies and struggled with their frustrating behaviors reached out to us. They understood that we didn't know where else to turn. Barbara and Dick lovingly recommended a developmental pediatrician, Dr. Alan Weintraub, who specialized in diagnosing behavioral disorders and developmental disabilities.

No parent wants to believe that our unhappy and sometimes destructive children might stay that way. Yet anyone in the room with our son knowingly or not would feel on edge. Iyal was a virtual wrecking ball, and he was battering our hearts.

Something had to be done; increasing stress became the frame on which our lives were being stretched. However, after making the phone call using our referral, I was told there was a nine-month wait for an initial evaluation. Shit. I moaned. "We can put you on the waiting list, as sometimes we'll get a cancellation. Would you like us to . . ."

"Yes, please," I pleaded, on the verge of tears.

Nine more months of *this* without any answers?

How would Iyal survive?

I hated to even ask myself. How would *we* survive?

Chapter Three

Our appointment with the developmental pediatrician couldn't come soon enough.

Harvey and I started to consider that perhaps Iyal would be diagnosed with ADHD or ADD, one of the more popular default diagnoses at the time, because he was certainly hyperactive, couldn't concentrate, and seemed to space out frequently. I had read about conduct disorder, which renders an individual capable of oppositional, violent, and deviant behaviors. Those who live with conduct disorder may start fires, maliciously injure others, and hurt animals, all without remorse. I thought if I had a child who hurt animals, I could only wither and die. Considering a life where every day might mean protecting myself or my family from one of my own was just beyond my imagination. How do people *handle* this?

Our naiveté fueled our denial that something was terribly wrong with Iyal. He was requiring an enormous amount of tactile input, literally climbing on top of me to hug me. His need for immediate gratification was immense. He was totally unable to wait in line or for whatever was supposed to happen next. Anywhere. Ever. I would pull into a gas station and Iyal would rail that it would take too long to put gas in the car: "Why do we have to do this? I can't wait, it's taking too long!" When we arrived at a red light, the little four-year-old in the car seat behind me would start kicking the back of my seat, screaming, "Hurry up, stupid light! *I can't wait!*"

On cue for comic relief, Morasha would announce some little treasure like, "Mom! I'm going back to God for curly hair." Yup, the eloquent daughter of a rabbi. And thank God for her steady self-esteem, priorities, and knowing who she was! Her burgeoning sense of self only highlighted Iyal's lack of personality, which left him to be defined by his tantrums and idiosyncrasies. I knew there had to be more inside him—more creativity, more curiosity, more joy, all the things you delight in seeing in children—but I didn't know how to access it.

When noises were too loud, Iyal would cover up his ears with his hands and seem unable to modulate his voice. And yet he spoke at a consistent level of a sonic boom. If you asked him to speak more softly, he spoke louder. If Iyal was watching a movie and didn't want to see what was on the screen because it was too scary, he covered his ears—not his eyes—with his hands, clearly a disconnect between his brain and sensory receptors.

Iyal was constantly moving and touching things and became substantially exhausting to keep up with. To get his attention, I would have to physically hold his face toward me, tell him to look in my eyes, and then hold his shoulders; otherwise, he would drift away to another planet where perhaps his wiring was less entangled and he discovered some momentary peace.

Still to this day, even as a young adult, Iyal confuses temperature. For example, he believes that the purpose of the freezer is to make things warmer, not colder. Just a few years ago when I injured an eye and could have become blinded, Iyal wanted to know if I went blind, would *he* be able to see me? The filing cabinets of stored information in Iyal's brain were not only unalphabetized and randomly organized, but he was unable to access simple understanding like you and me.

We came to accept Iyal would always be challenged by abstract concepts. He needed things to be concrete.

Driving the car, I'd be frustrated by traffic and say, "Oh, for Pete's sake!" Iyal typically responded, "Who's Pete?"

Sitting at the kitchen table, eating lunch, Morasha noticed that Iyal wasn't eating, which was unusual. When she asked, "Iyal, why haven't you touched your food?" he looked at her and then began to handle all the food on his plate. We learned comments like "hit the road," "piece of cake," and "no-brainer" (already offensive enough to me) only led to confusion.

He would never be able to "do math" beyond a second-grade level without a calculator, and then only if you told him which operation he would need to use. Although he could identify a dime as ten cents and a nickel as five cents, he couldn't put the coins together to equal one dollar.

Sometimes Iyal didn't know what he didn't know. Other times he did. A peculiar kind of silence in which he and I stayed connected would follow these instances as we both processed his frustration and disappointment. Acknowledging his sadness at his understanding of living with a disability seemed so important. And then he and I would talk about what he *could* do that made him special.

By the time we finally had our appointment with the developmental pediatrician to whom we'd been referred, I was no longer sleeping, because Iyal couldn't sleep. He would be whipping up a frenzy in his room: somersaulting on his bed, literally climbing up his walls, rearranging furniture randomly, until he passed out. But within a few hours, I'd hear him charging up the stairs to our room, a baby rhinoceros roaring through the house. My internal nighttime security guard clocked in.

Iyal's night terrors created my own. Harvey and I knew it was common for young children to have night terrors before they were old enough to explain them. You would see these haunting scenes in movies and plays. However, when it was happening in your home and your toddler was at once asleep and acting out his role in the never-ending nightmare, it was hard to ever let that moment go.

As it was, I fought myself in an attempt to *not* project onto my children my own feelings and thoughts. Certain images of orphanages, real and imagined, would slip into my own dreams, waking me up to go flying down the stairs during Iyal's night terror episodes. Thank God that Morasha would remain peacefully sleeping. Standing in the doorway of the bedroom they shared, I'd watch, at first trying not to cry, while Iyal heroically fought his demons, often with screams and tears, other times in a quiet squall.

As years crept by, I'd go over to Iyal's crib, then his toddler bed, then his twin, and now his double, and I'm still unsure how I translated these moments in Iyal's life. All I could do was rub his back, speak softly, and gently reassure him that "everything will be all right, Iyal. We are here, and you are safe." It wasn't until much later that I would understand the myriad ways in which a brain—and the hearts of the person's loved ones—could be injured.

Iyal obviously had some major disorder, disease, or disability, and its manifestations were only getting worse. Instead of moving closer to the shore of order, stability, and treatment, we seemed battered and tossed even farther out to sea. My anxieties about Iyal and his future had begun to confiscate my waking hours and infiltrate my dreams. I had night sweats and panic attacks as I heard him careening into our room. When and how would this ever stop?

Harvey was at a loss just as I was. Usually exhausted by the time he made it home, he had his own issues to battle at work—budget committees, staff meetings, congregational conflicts. And even though he often tried to corral Iyal and get him under control, when Iyal didn't respond to reason or to negative consequences (time-outs were nothing more than momentary containment before the fire in Iyal blazed brighter than ever), Harvey left it to me. He either didn't have any energy left to deal with Iyal or thought it better that I try my own techniques to subdue the current raging storm. Sometimes when Harvey was feeling protective of *my* well-being, he would become so angry with Iyal and lose control, which just escalated Iyal's already-accelerating flight-or-fight tango. As Iyal's fears of abandonment surfaced, so did the tears in my eyes.

Any sense of control in our home became elusive, where it felt like every man, woman, and child for themselves. Although Harvey never said or even implied that Iyal's disruptive behavior was my fault, I somehow felt responsible, as if I'd failed Iyal as well as my husband, that somehow I should be able to keep us all together in a state of domestic tranquility. I was unsure why I felt this way, but I did. All I could do was try to hang on until our doctor's appointment as my urgency for answers circled around me like a cyclone.

Finally, the evaluation with Dr. Weintraub took place over the course of two days in October 2002. Iyal was four years and four months old. Harvey and I sat in a secluded booth (which reminded me—ironically—of the setup on the old *Newlywed Game*) with a one-way mirror and headsets so we could observe Iyal's interaction with the doctor. We watched and listened as Iyal completed test after test and performed one assessment after another.

He identified pictures, matched items (or didn't) with spoken words, and attempted to recreate designs from blocks, which I later learned assessed his visual-spatial abilities. Much of this time, Iyal would jump out of his seat, exploring the room, mumbling, or hopping about. At one point, he crawled under the testing desk, emitting animal sounds, and then couldn't figure the way back out. I watched with my mouth gaping and dry and my hands trembling and sweaty. I would have cried if I could, but my tears seemed contained behind the dam of fear clenched tight in my gut.

When we received Dr. Weintraub's initial evaluation, we could never have been prepared for all we were given to digest. Here are some highlights that leaped off the page at me from his report:

> *"As testing wore on, Iyal became more motorically hyperactive. Some anxiety was noted with some oppositional defiant tendencies. In this setting, Iyal was never blatantly oppositional, but he clearly demonstrated that he 'wanted things his way.' He became upset with the examiner when a peg dropped on the floor and he wanted to pick it up with his feet and the examiner had picked it up with his hands."*
>
> *"Iyal's distractibility, impulsivity, and hyperactivity increased with time, and his attention decreased with me. When discussing pictures presented to him, Iyal frequently raised mildly violent themes."*
>
> *"Throughout testing, it was very easy for Iyal to comment 'I can't' before he would try a task."*
>
> *"Iyal's human figure drawing was a frog. It had a fair amount of detail around the head, with arms and legs emanating off of the head, no body. This was closer to a three-and-a-half-year-old level."*

Okay, at the time, being only a year in delayed development didn't seem so critical. But here's what remains truly noteworthy: right now, at eighteen years of age, Iyal still draws like a kindergartener. At least now his humans look like human-kind-of-spiders, with their appendages coming from more appropriate parts of the body. I can show you a picture of a person Iyal drew at age five and one he drew last week, and they would look fairly identical. His ability to artistically express his inner imagination is still elementary. Yet he has been creatively writing and illustrating stories on the computer for several years now. He is proud of himself, and I am proud of him!

So where did Dr. Weintraub's evaluation, this interpretation of our son's unique behaviors, leave us after nine months of anguish and excruciating unanswered doubts? I'll cut to the chase. Of course, the report contained realistic positive observations that softened the blow even as it hurled a speeding bullet at us in slow motion.

Ignorance wasn't bliss for us, but knowledge of what we were facing didn't provide any of the immediate relief I had hoped to find. Other signs and symptoms reinforced the diagnosis that seemed plain and clear from Dr. Weintraub's expertise. This is the substance of a written report from Dr. Weintraub.

> *On physical and neurologic examination, Iyal does demonstrate several stigmata, which, as discussed with his parents, are consistent with the diagnosis of fetal alcohol effect or alcohol-related neurodevelopmental disabilities. As discussed with his parents, we can make this diagnosis clinically, but to formally confirm the diagnosis, one needs a formal history in regard to the biologic mother's ingestion of alcohol. We may never have this piece of it.*

And here is where it becomes confusing. Specific medical organizations do or don't mandate that evidence of the birth mother consuming alcohol be confirmed. When I think about all these exposed children being adopted from other countries, confirming that the pregnant mother had drunk alcohol would be difficult. In the United States alone, "children in foster care are 10–15 times more likely to be affected by prenatal alcohol exposure than other children,"[1] according to the National Organization for Fetal Alcohol Syndrome. Many individuals who are prenatally exposed to alcohol will never be diagnosed or appropriately treated.

> *Consistent with the diagnosis is relative microcephaly* (a smaller head circumference that has become one of the criteria for a medical diagnosis), *a flattened occiput* (midsection of the face), *a flat nasal bridge which causes the eyes to appear smaller, and a thin lip with a long philtrum* (the area between the upper lip and nostrils, which is smoothed out to certain degrees depending on the amount of alcohol ingested when the facial features were being developed, usually between days eighteen and twenty of gestation).
>
> *Iyal also demonstrated hypotonicity* (low muscle tone).
>
> *Cognitively, Iyal's skills are felt to be in the average-to-bright range. His skills are age appropriate per another preschool language scale.*
>
> *Significant visual motor integrative deficits are noted.*

Dr. Weintraub observed the gap between Iyal's chronological age and his developmental age (known as dysmaturity, another hallmark of FASDs):

> *Iyal was seen to be distractible, impulsive, hyperactive, and frenetic or driven. Oppositional defiant behaviors were also noted.*

Amid all this medical and psychiatric jargon, four words formed the corners of our new plane of existence: fetal alcohol spectrum disorder. I was vaguely aware of it, and it seemed fairly self-explanatory, but now it provided a label (which I thought would be beneficial, and I still subscribe to this belief) to this collective struggle in my son's life. After the doctor's assessment and six clinical diagnoses, a total of seventeen recommendations followed, including medications, books for Harvey and me to read, and a four-week follow-up. Over ten more diagnoses, including mental retardation (now called cognitive or intellectual impairment), reactive attachment disorder, psychotic disorder not otherwise specified, and post-traumatic stress disorder would be added by various physicians along the way.

At the time, though, Harvey and I went into triage mode. I read everything I could get my hands on and head around in order to parse the real meaning lurking behind every school report, conversation with a teacher, and discussion between Harvey and me. It was like learning a foreign language in another language's alphabet, so *not* easy and extremely disturbing.

I was becoming a student in my son's world, and I didn't know if I would make the grade to be the mother I'd need to be. My education began with basics that became a dictionary I would refer to over and over again. When a baby is exposed to alcohol while in the mother's womb, he or she may be born with a condition along the continuum of FASDs. As defined by the Centers for Disease Control and Prevention, FASDs "are a group of conditions that can occur in a person whose mother drank alcohol during pregnancy."

This description became a blueprint of sorts for Iyal's dysregulated world. The understanding of FASDs also legitimized this invisible cape that swirled around Iyal, shutting down the most basic of abilities he needed to survive in our world. FAS is the most involved disorder on the spectrum and currently the only disorder with a clinical diagnosis. The manifestations of FASDs can range from mild to severe in their impact on an individual's and family's life. Most people are unaware that FASDs are the leading preventable cause of intellectual disability in the Western world. Besides intellectual disability, FASDs can include social, emotional, behavioral, and physical challenges, with a predisposition to a host of developmental conditions and psychiatric illness. FASDs may be accompanied by intellectual impairment, obsessive compulsive disorder (OCD), oppositional defiant disorder (ODD), reactive attachment disorders (RAD), learning disabilities, seizures, attention-deficit/hyperactivity disorder (ADHD), and autism spectrum disorder (ASD).

So in 2002, the conclusion of Dr. Weintraub's assessment meant that Iyal had a diagnosis of fetal alcohol effect (FAE) or alcohol-related neurodevelopmental disabilities (now disorder; ARND). The term FAE, no longer used, was never meant to be a diagnostic term but was used when an outcome was known to be from prenatal alcohol exposure but didn't meet the full criteria of FAS.

I know, all these letters, this alphabet soup of diagnoses and nondiagnoses put me into a tailspin, and I didn't know how, or if, it would ever stop.

Following Dr. Weintraub's diagnosis, a good friend whose daughter was also experiencing similar symptoms mentioned to me that a clinical study at the (then) Marcus Institute in Atlanta was looking for children to participate. If the child was suspected of having symptoms of FASDs, he or she might be chosen to become part of a four-year study.

After Iyal's diagnosis of FAS, I was ready to find others who knew about FASDs and what treatments were available to help him. The study sounded like the perfect environment for Iyal. I immediately contacted the staff at the Marcus Institute to see if he would qualify. As part of the study, your child had to meet the criteria of FAS through an evaluation by a pediatric neurologist and another specialist. If Iyal qualified, he would be followed for four years in a specific program that included a variety of interventions and educational opportunities.

The program also offered parenting skills, which I knew would be an essential component to our new life, as it was sorely lacking in our "old" life.

Iyal qualified, which was a good and bad thing. I'm sure you understand my thinking here. As part of the study, a pediatric dysmorphologist confirmed Iyal's diagnosis of FAS. I assumed this second opinion meant that Iyal, indeed, was prenatally exposed to alcohol, which explained *a lot.* The expanse of this diagnosis would, in time, actually shrink our world, as our focus on Iyal precluded the activities of our former life.

Iyal was enrolled, and over the next four years, our whole family participated in the program at one time or another. Iyal was provided with play and educational therapy, several sessions per week. A neuropsychological evaluation was initially performed, which provided us with a baseline of Iyal's intellectual scores as well as "adaptive reasoning" scores. This neuropsychological exam became a marker with which we could measure his developmental, neurological, and psychological growth. Iyal would be eligible for this evaluation every three years. The evaluation tracked the broad and specific changes that occurred in Iyal.

Ninety percent of fetal-alcohol-exposed individuals who don't meet the medical criteria for FAS still experience the same kinds of organic brain damage to one degree or another. Without the physical characteristics associated with the exposure, people with the invisible injury become more and more challenged as the expectations of our culture, educational system, and justice system impose an impossibly complicated world.

Because the majority of fetal-alcohol-affected kids look just like your neighbor's child, noticing any difference in their behaviors is unclear until spending maybe fifteen minutes with them. Then the hidden challenges emerge as the kids repeat sentences over and over, disconnect from the moment, unknowingly interrupt, and bulldoze through the conversation. These behaviors that show a lack of social skills also express the impact that severe impulsivity can have on individuals who experience FASDs. As I understand it, impulsivity is the space between thought and action. Most of us are able to edit our thoughts and consider the risk of saying or doing something. Impulsivity can drive people to make poor choices and carry them out because they can't take the time to evaluate a possible outcome. And not everyone has the patience to help someone living with FASDs organize his or her thought process. Doing so is hard work.

In other words, we learned that FASDs are hidden or invisible disabilities currently impacting up to one in twenty school-age children in the United States. That statistic is just staggering and leaves me outraged! To make matters worse, this lifelong disability is greatly misdiagnosed or never recognized for what it is. Our diagnosis was just words on a page—black-and-white symbols that couldn't begin to capture the Technicolor, 3-D, all-encompassing lifetime of IMAX effects on display in my son's life.

I started poring over any piece of information I could find. In 2002, quite a bit of material on FASDs was on the Internet, in medical journals, and in books written by professionals or parents. However, I wasn't able to connect with the content or process it or feel my customary empowerment at gaining knowledge. The more I learned, the more anxious and ultimately depressed I became about Iyal's abilities to one day lead a "normal" life. The literature couldn't reach the unrelenting anguish forming in my stomach and the fact that my heart felt fractured as I began to realize the enormity of Iyal's lifelong birth defect that would eventually hold our whole family hostage.

And no ransom could ever equal the emotional let alone the financial cost of living with a person who experienced a life full of misunderstanding. Families caring for children with severe birth defects or mental illness can become bankrupt financially and emotionally.

"Morasha asked me if I was angry with Iyal's birth mother," I mentioned to Harvey one night as I lay reading FASD material in bed. "She said to me, 'Doesn't it bother you that this didn't have to happen?'" Even at seven, Morasha spoke directly, with the confidence of someone beyond her years. It startled me that she could understand her feelings internally and express them so articulately. Her pointed observations often caught me off guard, and I didn't always have a response that felt honest.

When those moments froze me, I would say to her, "Morasha, I'm so proud of you for caring about Iyal and how his FAS affects me and Dad. Right now, I don't have a good answer, but you've given me something to keep in my head, and when I'm ready, we can talk about this more." I'd nod. "Okay, sweetie?" She usually offered me a hug, or a shrug, depending on her age and mood.

Harvey looked at me, grasping for words, and said, "I can't even describe how it makes me feel. Sometimes I want to explode, and sometimes I want to cry."

"Of course I'm angry," I said quietly, wondering how long before Iyal came bounding into our room to share some catastrophe or irrational request. "But not at Iyal—and not even at his birth mother. She probably never knew the impact drinking alcohol would have on her unborn child. I don't think the young women in Russia, especially in an impoverished area, would have access to any education about these things.

"Harve, look, we don't know what she was facing, the kind of life she lived or what it was like for her. At least she made a plan for her baby. I think that shows she *did* care. And what if drinking was the only way she thought she could survive?"

"And I'm not sure as a father I can fully accept what this diminished life means to Iyal or to us." I felt a wave of compassion for Harvey at that moment. I was beginning to get an inkling of how difficult it is for fathers to cope when their children have special needs. I had already heard too many nightmares about fathers abandoning families because they couldn't take the pressure, stress, financial loss, and emotional duress that could accompany a diagnosis like Iyal's. I was keenly aware that until recently, the risk of marriages ending in divorce was as high as 80% while parents raised a child with special needs. Studies now show that the divorce rate may be significantly lower than first estimated. But when I first heard that number, it burned my heart and haunted me, especially when the stress on our relationship seemed unbearable. That disheartening statistic rumbled through me when insecurity coerced its way into the marriage. Which was happening more than I would like to admit.

"Hey," I said, reassuring myself as much as Harvey. "We'll figure this out, okay? I'm not sure how, but knowledge is power, right? I feel validated just to know that we're not the only people ever to walk this path. And, Harve, we're good partners, we've learned how to tag team so we aren't destroyed by Iyal's challenges." Tears formed at the corners of my weary eyes as I stuttered with emotion, "I—I just wish we could make Iyal's life easier, happier. He deserves to be happy as much as any other kid." Tiny pieces of my heart shattered every time I realized that Iyal's path to happiness was detoured at every turn. And I felt helpless knowing that his burden would always be greater than ours.

I couldn't explain to Harvey the connection I had been growing with Iyal as I watched his mental illness take shape and residence along with the other brain disorders he already possessed. I didn't yet have any words to describe what I saw in Iyal that felt familiar to me. And giving these ideas life before I could better understand what it all really meant was premature. I was afraid it might distance me from Harvey rather than create more intimacy, which was already becoming shredded.

Harvey shifted his position in bed, leaning back, his face tired and sad. "I wish I could make all our lives easier," he said, combing his fingers through his hair over and over again, a gesture that filled in the spaces when words couldn't. "But I can't. This is just something we have to deal with."

"Yes," I said, "we do. We all have to deal with it because it isn't going away. Not for Iyal"—I swallowed some of my sorrow and continued—"and not for us."

Certain seasons of life can seem blurrier than others around the edges. Maybe the clarity of memory escapes because it was such a hectic, chaotic time. But I'm convinced some seasons of life fade in our memories because we can't handle the blunt trauma of catastrophic events no matter how far removed in time we may be when recalling them. And the lingering impressions often manifest themselves in the same kinds of fear, anxiety, and depression ignited by those past events, a kind of PTSD that can haunt both body and soul. These uninvited bullets of psychological pain can sear through the present and reopen wounds you assumed were healing.

And you never see them coming.

The next three or four years following Iyal's diagnosis has crystalized in my memory like shards of glass broken over and over again, always underfoot with each step we tried to take. Days back then might have involved an appointment with some kind of therapist, pediatrician, neurologist, or psychiatrist. Each one was like the day before, as though it never had existed, attempting to contain Iyal, keep him entertained, or hold him tight in the waiting room before he jettisoned from my arms and threw himself against the wall or crawled under a chair. His vocabulary increased by increments, and whatever volume control he had in the first place seemed to disappear.

A few years later when Iyal was around eleven, we noticed how he literally couldn't stop talking. This is sometimes called "pressured speech." It can be symptomatic of several different disorders. His speaking came out like rapid machine-gun fire, nonstop. He spewed words constantly without taking a breath and usually repeated sentences and phrases over and over again. While feeling genuinely sympathetic, I was certain a daily root canal would be more endurable than this constant torture. I knew Harvey would agree.

Occasionally, Harvey would accompany us, but most of the time, he was tied up with work. Family friends sometimes offered to go with me, and sometimes I accepted their kindness, but usually it only compounded the chaos as Iyal pulled on their arms, examined their shoes and feet, or shouted from across the room about his latest bathroom accomplishment. Then we had to go home, eat lunch, pick up Morasha, and struggle through an evening. By the time Harvey came home, usually the kids would have already eaten, been bathed, PJ'd, and read to. I'd try to chat with Harvey like any other wife might (using my rationed reserve), all while trying to defuse whatever storm was brewing in Iyal.

"Iyaaaal!" moaned Morasha when she realized he had gone into her room without her permission. Again. "Iyal, I told you so many times to leave my stuff alone!"

Iyal looked up from his Game Boy for a few seconds before returning his eyes and fingers to his game. "I didn't *do* anything, Morasha," he muttered.

Morasha marched over and hovered above Iyal with her hands on her little hips as he sat glued to the floor. "Oh yes, you did!" Morasha yelled back. "So where is it? Where did you put my game, Iyal?"

"I dunno." His number-one response in his limited repertoire.

Morasha turned and stomped out of his room, slamming his door. "Moooom!" And then it was my turn.

My concern for her well-being had created its own little chamber of fear and worry in my heart.

Over time, we found different ways to describe to Morasha the brain damage Iyal had experienced, and she seemed to grasp what she intuitively knew already: her brother suffered from something over which he had no control. I'm not sure she treated him any differently, maybe at first, but overall he was still her pesky brother either imitating her (and thus infuriating her) or teasing her until she thundered back at him.

Did she feel invisible, unheard, trapped within the limits of the "United Nations of Iyal"? She had to dodge grenades ready to explode with her brother's behavior while finding and securing a safe place in our family. I anguished over her predicament as the sibling and felt helpless that the cast of characters in our home never seemed to be in sync.

When he was there and got caught in their crossfire, Harvey would either try to separate and calm them like any father might do with his battling children or else he would try and ignore them. Needless to say, neither strategy was particularly effective—except at making me feel like more of a failure, more alone in this war we seemed destined to lose.

And maybe it was my own arrogance or pride that made me all the more determined to find solutions for my son's struggles and their impact on my family, so with each week I survived, I tried to be a student of my son and his disability. But unraveling Iyal was like trying to take apart a matryoshka doll, so many layers to pull apart without ever getting to the solid core of who he was beneath his behaviors. Wistfully, I'd catch him in a moment of sheer joy, perhaps feeling proud of something he did at school or slightly embarrassed by Morasha's teasing. In those moments, Iyal would work his mouth into this adorable grin, lips slightly parted, lower lip moving up and down as if battling his effort to shape a full-blown smile. Those moments made my heart soar and kept me going when I felt I could only coast in anticipation of the next crashing event that would leave me feeling totaled.

I was determined to catch those smiles and weave them into my own safety net.

—

Most of the time, Harvey (and Morasha) considered me too easy on Iyal. Feeling self-conscious as I corrected Iyal, though, I was often caught between wanting to be firm and consistent so that Harvey would approve, while wanting to be encouraging and understanding so that Iyal would know just how much I loved him. As a result of this tension, I'd try to walk the high wire and keep my balance, coming on strong for my husband's benefit and then softening the edge by using "we" for my son's, as in "We need to give Iyal more time to process what we are saying to him. He is trying his best, but he cannot keep up with us." I often wished I had a PET scan of Iyal's brain, so Harvey and Morasha could see how certain parts light up when activated by shouting or his own perceived threats. Most people have difficulty seeing beyond the behavior and realizing that the brain is the culprit.

And depending on whatever was firing or not firing in his brain at the moment, Iyal might nod and sulk away like any first grader or he might turn into a Mini-Me of the Incredible Hulk. This kind of uncertainty often left both Harvey and me brimming with anxiety, usually for different reasons, sometimes the same ones. My anxiety's partner, depression, was never far away, waiting to pull me beneath the stormy clouds that defined the intermittent sorrow I was committed to hiding away in a closet growing full of a staggering grief.

I felt obligated to contain my emotional responses to our life in order to keep some stability in our script. I knew when triggered, Iyal was unable to turn the switch off until his feelings played out, which in actuality was a cascade of neurotransmitters gone haywire. Whenever his impending rage began to percolate, I could observe changes taking place in Iyal as he was slowly engulfed by something beyond his control—beyond my control or anyone's. The son I knew was nowhere to be seen.

Bedtime was often like negotiating a peace treaty in the Middle East. Either Iyal didn't want to go to bed or else he was so tired and grumpy that he found himself detonating as a result of his fatigue. I would lie in bed at night, willing my mind to shut down and my heartbeat to hit the brakes and obey the after-dark speed zone. Usually, Harvey would already be snoring next to me, which only annoyed me more—not that he snored so much as that he could seemingly go right to sleep. Feeling sleep-deprived no matter how much I actually slept, I wanted to scream at him, "Shut the fuck up! *Please.*" Harvey often offered to go sleep on the sofa if I thought it would help. But then, of course, my guilt kicked in and I played the martyr with my seasoned dramatic Jewish flair.

Momentarily, I would hear something and anticipate the "slumber shutdown." I could hear the wooden floor complain beneath Iyal's steps, bounding upstairs like he was about to jump on a horse at the rodeo. Then, like a bronco buster, he'd barrel in as if it were the middle of the day, not midnight, and ask me why his bed felt funny. And when I couldn't produce a satisfactory answer despite my most creative attempts, I could smell the fire burning closer to his fuse. Then his neurons would explode, and soon the entire house—and maybe the neighborhood, for all I know—would be awake as collateral damage of my son's emotional rocket launch.

No wonder I couldn't sleep. If I wasn't dealing with the aftermath, I was anticipating the next encounter. Anxiety lodged itself inside me like a bullet, blood bubbling up through my veins as I listened for the opening shots of the next battle.

—

I used to think of people who are emotionally constipated or numb to their experiences and feel the urge to ask, "Don't you want to be fully alive before you die? Don't you want to engage with your *own* life?" These people would seem to hold their connection to their core feelings at arm's length, hoping to slide beneath the barbed wire that makes people keenly aware that life is sharp if they step the wrong way, mini bayonets waiting like sharks' teeth to shred your dreams apart.

But then I realized that perhaps they became frozen involuntarily, as if their emotional and physical receptors have blown a circuit, frozen, and can no longer register feelings. The pain became too intense, like subzero cold burning their skin, as they found themselves stretched beyond their breaking point on a daily basis.

I woke each morning instantly fearing the daunting quagmires in the day ahead, the ones that could swallow me up in a heartbeat. But I would hold my breath, exhale, and slowly edge my way back to life, back to the expected functionality.

So with feelings hanging up in my bedroom closet knowing they'd never see the light of day or a runway for that matter, I would go through the motions of dressing, showering, preparing breakfast, driving the kids to school. In some alternative universe, I imagined I was a "normal mom," laughing in the carpool line as I listened to the chatter among parents who longingly counted the seconds until their healthy child was sitting behind them safely in their car seat again, eager to enjoy any number of after-school activities—activities with other children—without worrying if there would be a phone call from whoever was in charge to apologetically request them to come back and pick up their child. Again.

Then, almost daily, I narrowly escaped the spiraling depression that continued to twist me inside out, pulling me toward hopelessness. Some days I wondered whether I could trust the happiness and joy to last and to outlast the stormy weeks of craziness and despair. On bad days, life exhausted me to the point where I couldn't comprehend how I would get through the next twenty-four hours.

More and more, I would discover my eyes leaking tears without my consent. "Mommy, why you crying? Is sadness inside you?" Iyal would ask in a keenly perceptive moment. "Am I a bad boy?" A question that became an automatic reflex of Iyal's if he thought he had disappointed us in some way.

"No, honey," I lied, "just Mommy's allergies making her eyes water. You are amazing!"

Still, at eighteen years old, when Iyal is feeling remorse for using some unacceptable language or realizing he made a "mistake," he'll desperately ask us, "Am I a good boy, Mom? Am I a good boy?" I hated that he felt the need to ask all these years! How did that question become lodged in his brain and in his heart and mine? It should never have happened! God damn it!

No matter how many times or years we reassured Iyal that he was a good boy, it was as though Iyal never heard it. It never registered. By the time Iyal was sixteen, I would respond to his broken-record request, "Of course, Iyal. But, honey, you are a fine young man now, not just a good boy any longer." Iyal remained mired in a swamp filled with disbelief that he would *ever* be a "good boy," a boy who would make us proud and himself unashamed. And the truth continued to glare at me despite my best attempts to ignore it or turn away: we could not "fix" Iyal. No one and nothing could change him. We tried medication after medication—antianxiety meds and antidepressants, meds to numb his mood, and pills to soften the chemical riptide eroding the calming signals in his brain. We kept changing doctors, wishing that a new set of eyes and ears would reveal something the last doctor had missed. Who were we kidding?

—

There has always been a deeply buried sliver of panic in my ability to be a good wife or to be a good enough anything—mother, advocate, actress, or writer. And now this splinter of self-doubt plunged deeper as I became nothing more than an encourager, a sounding board, for Harvey and his extremely stressful workload. He proffered few questions about my day, seemingly absorbed in another life, another world, one where there's much less demand on him, where he's married to that other perfect me in the carpool line.

As we approached Iyal's eighth birthday, my world remained colored by some internal nuclear winter. Gray weather inside and out. A real terror of what awaited when I arrived home on those rare occasions when I left the house alone for a doctor's appointment of my own (which, as a result of the cumulative stress, were becoming more and more frequent) or a quick trip to the grocery store. Honestly, and I hate admitting this, but I felt so confused by my own reactions to things in my home—in my life—things that felt so broken and unfixable, I often thought about just continuing to drive. Instead of taking the Roswell exit toward home, I'd just keep driving north—Chattanooga, Knoxville, then through Kentucky and Ohio, on up into Canada, the North Pole. The final destination didn't matter; I just wanted to go anywhere but this airless place where I had to return and manufacture oxygen for all of us.

Either Harvey was there ready to unload that day's temple trauma or Iyal was warming up for the daily neuronal fireworks, or both if I happened to hit the jackpot that day. Of course, I would never abandon my family under any circumstances, but I did know that something had to give because *I* was disappearing. And I didn't know where to find me.

One morning, Iyal told me he had dreamed of being buried alive with no one there to help him. I was alarmed at the glaring call for help and held him so close, unable to fathom my eight-year-old son telling me this. And subsequent night terrors besieged him, leaving him bereft, saddened by loss, and heavy with a grief he could not name.

Then I became more terrified, sinking further into despair because I knew exactly how he felt.

Because of the nature of Iyal's organic brain injury, most medications didn't result in positive outcomes. In fact, they might make his symptoms and behaviors worse. Treading water, we were always looking for new therapies, ideas—anything to help him feel more in control and better, anything to help us manage a routine, consistent ways to handle his outbursts. But no matter what we tried, as Iyal grew older, attachment issues and post-traumatic stress responses became permanent fixtures of our landscape.

By now, I had amassed a library of notebooks filled with pages printed from the Internet, hardcover books, spiral-bound workbooks, training DVDs, and stacks of brochures and flyers that held tight the promise of better futures for children who struggled with FASDs. I also started to attend workshops and conferences about FASDs whenever I could. The first international FASD conference I attended was in 2006 with my dad in Vancouver, Canada. Just having my father choose to be by my side no matter what the expense, where we had to go, or what we had to do when we got there . . . evidenced his devotion to me and my family. And *this* dad loved to travel.

My mom and dad took me with them on some of the best and funniest vacations I had growing up and as an adult. People are blown away when I tell them that the three of us would spend days and nights together traveling in the States or in Europe.

"Wait," a friend would say with a look of bewilderment spreading across her face. "You actually stayed in the same *room* with your parents?"

Undeterred by this question and probably the next ten that followed, I'd answer, "Yeah! We had a blast."

Note: friend's face would now be twisted into a gasp, without sound.

I'd continue, "What, you never shared a five-by-five-foot bathroom in a moderately priced hotel room (depending on the value of the dollar and the AAA travel guide) in London with your mom and dad?" I'd smile broadly, enjoying my monologue. "You *never* stayed in a B and B with your folks, and the three of you fell asleep and woke up at the exact same time because *you* shared *their* DNA and *they* shared thirty years of marriage together?"

My friend would have now sat down so she wouldn't faint. I could go on and on, but would decide I like this friend and don't want to make her hate me with unforgivable jealousy. "Like I said. We had a blast."

After my dad and I checked into the hotel and registered at the conference, we walked around the lobby, looking at the badges people were wearing, saying who they were, what they did, and where they were from, and listening to all the different accents among the twelve hundred attendees. I was truly astonished to realize that *everyone* here had a connection to FASDs. *Everyone* here spoke the same language, F-A-S-D. I wasn't expecting to feel the emotional swell of being among others who understood my son, who spoke his language, which was becoming mine and my family's.

While at this conference, experts on FASDs talked about the benefits of an "external brain." Before the conference, I had discovered that term in an article by Teresa Kellerman, an adoptive mom and FASD expert, who writes and speaks about her hands-on approach to the challenges presented by an invisible disability. In an article that I'd almost memorized, Kellerman cited the work of Dr. Susan Doctor and Dr. Sterling Clarren, medical researchers, who believed that "the person with FAS will always need an external brain—key words are 'always' and 'external.'"[2]

Kellerman claims the rationale behind this assertion stems from the comparison between the external supports and benefits provided to other individuals with physical disabilities, such as guide dogs, hearing aids, interpreters, and wheelchairs. These assistive devices afford individuals a much broader range of function, enhancing their potential for a fully lived life. She goes on to point out how no one "blames" individuals living with physical disabilities for behaviors stemming from their disability: bumping into tables, not seeing, not hearing, or being unable to use their voice to communicate.

However, respecting people living with the physical disability of organic brain damage with the same kind of external support is just as important. The injury affecting the brain, particularly the forebrain or frontal lobes, greatly impacts the individual's capacity to regulate their executive functions. They may look completely healthy and functional, what most people think of as "normal," but they struggle with challenges every bit as debilitating as any of the other "obvious" ones.

Most people, if born healthy and without an injury, don't realize the complexity of how brain functions make simple decisions that typically impact all the other parts of their body. So the important thing to remember is that FASDs are *physical disabilities* (static encephalopathy, to be specific) that don't allow normal functioning of an essential part of the body, the brain. Even if the body itself is healthy, the control center is damaged in people who experience FASDs.

So what does an external brain look like? It's any responsible person (family member, caregiver, teacher) who is willing to function as a processing, thinking, decision-making facilitator for a person whose brain can't complete these functions. Ideally, the external-brain person helps protect an impaired individual from unwanted experiences, including major ones like drug addiction, alcoholism, pregnancy, homelessness, abuse, or accidental death and instead gently guides them into positive choices and experiences.

I realized then that Iyal would always need an external brain, someone to look out for him, to compensate for the organic brain damage that left him vulnerable and unable to make choices for a "happy and healthy life" on his own. I agree with Kellerman that perhaps our biggest challenge as parents is to help our children with FASDs understand and accept their need for an external brain without deflating their self-confidence. Iyal must accept the idea of an external brain based on his past experiences that might not have turned out so well and his understanding of what this kind of support means to him. He can have access to greater opportunities if someone is riding sidecar, pointing out the tricky turns and upcoming bumps in the road.

For our family, everyone in this external-brain gig takes on a role. All of us try to stay one step ahead of Iyal in helping him make good decisions. For instance, I have drilled into Iyal that if he threatens that he wants to blow someone up because that person has pissed him off, and he is making this pronouncement outdoors *so* loud that the police in the next state can hear him, he is going to need someone to help him calm down! Because he *can't*—not won't—but *can't* regulate himself all the time and in all the places where he may find himself. That's just the way it is. It's not about him not trying to do better. It's about recognizing how his brain injury makes it harder, but not impossible, to live.

We reluctantly accepted that while Iyal would grow up like his peers on the outside, on the inside, his development would remain arrested, creating a phenomenon called dysmaturity. The gap would widen as his healthy ("neurotypical") sister, Morasha, soared through her life, unburdened by extreme impulsivity and a lack of understanding of cause and effect.

Research suggests that building a circle of support or community for those living with disabilities strengthens the outcome for the individual. So how could we do this when the disorder rendered Iyal unable to interact with others in a meaningful way? How could we find consistent "external brains" for Iyal beyond our immediate family?

Traditional therapies were not helping Iyal to function in his world, so I decided it was time to get radical. After all, what did we have to lose?

—

Although I reluctantly ruled out psychics, crystal therapy, and medical marijuana (unless it was for me), I continued to struggle with available options to support Iyal. Somehow amid all the confusion that had established permanent residency in my brain, I remembered reading in a magazine about service dogs that assisted children who lived with autism spectrum disorder (ASD). Wow. Why hadn't I thought of this sooner? If dogs were being trained to assist children with developmental disabilities, perhaps a service dog would be helpful to Iyal as well as the rest of our family! For one thing, using a service dog would legitimize his invisible disability and add validity to behaviors that others might misinterpret. And that might be just the beginning.

Thus inspired, in the spring of 2006, I began to research everything I could get my hands on about service dogs (also called assistance dogs). The current law states that service animals (usually dogs) are legally defined as trained to meet the disability-related needs of their handlers/clients, as set forth in the 1990 Americans with Disabilities Act (ADA). The federal laws in place protect the rights of individuals with disabilities to be accompanied by their service animals in public places, anywhere a person who lives with a disability may be. States may differ slightly in the rights of service animals, but federal law always takes precedence. The law distinctly says, "Service animals are working animals, not pets." And don't get me started on this one! The stories I've been told while waiting at the food store checkout line with Chancer on one side of me and Iyal on the other.

The original Seeing Eye dog–training facility was near where I grew up in New Jersey, so I was aware of the work of guide dogs for the visually impaired and blind. Most people probably think of this type of guide dog when "service dog" comes up in a conversation. Guide dogs have had exposure in television and movies for longer than any other kind of service dog. Mobility assistance dogs also have been available and present in our culture for a while. At this time, my service-dog radar included hearing alert dogs and seizure alert dogs. I read several articles illustrating how service dogs were now being trained to assist those with invisible disabilities like psychiatric disorders, including dogs trained for people who experience PTSD, especially veterans. (In these last several years, photos of soldiers and their working dogs have mesmerized me. Their stories have brought me to tears, both on my face and in my heart.)

In all my research into interventions and treatments for FASDs, I hadn't yet seen anything about assistance dogs being trained for this specific birth defect. However, as I learned more about how service dogs were taught to help children who experience ASD, I became more excited about the possibility of a dog helping Iyal. Could this really be possible? By this point, I was so desperate that I felt like my world was going to collapse and we'd "all fall down" and leave London Bridge in permanent disrepair. The more I researched the miraculous work assistance dogs were now trained to provide to a variety of people, the more I knew I had to pursue this option. I was slipping toward the end of my rope and didn't know where I'd land. A service dog might be able to tie a knot so we could all hang on.

I couldn't wait to tell Harvey and bided my time until after dinner, grateful for a momentary lull in the room as the kids prepared for bed. I had mentally practiced my spiel, of course, and tried to sell the idea, but not too hard, show just enough curiosity and enthusiasm that it would spark Harvey's interest, not try to manipulate it. But I didn't even get the match lit. After I stopped talking, handing him a file of information and articles I'd printed from the Internet, he just looked at me like I'd sprouted wings.

"Are you kidding me?" He continued staring at me. "You've got to be joking, Donnie, and I'm in no mood right now—not after the kind of day I've had."

I assured him I was dead serious.

"Donnie, think about it! That's all we need—another creature running around causing chaos in this house—not to mention the expense! Like we have any money left over after we pay a dozen different doctors and specialists. I don't know what you were thinking. I really don't!"

"But, Harve," I said softly, trying to downshift the tension. He looked at me again, and I feared the veins on his forehead might pop out of his head, unleashing a river of pent-up frustration, anger, indignation, and all the grief he had not yet realized. "Just think about it, okay?"

"Donnie, we're through talking about this. Finished. End of conversation."

Chapter Four

"What makes you think a service dog would even help Iyal?" Harvey asked, unable to hide his cynicism. It was probably the third or fourth time I had brought up the topic again that week.

And let me interject an observation here. I believe each partner in a relationship is the gas, the brake, the emergency brake, or the eject button. Guess which one I am? Now, can you guess which Harvey is? And how many collisions can your marriage have as one of you zooms into the future while the other is determined to hold on to the history of a life that feels safe even if it's upside down?

I was nothing if not determined. "Well, families with children who have disabilities are documenting dramatic improvement when the dog bonds with their kids. They help ground the child emotionally in a very confusing world, providing a kind of living, breathing security blanket. I know you've read in newspapers and magazines about people who live with autism spectrum disorder using assistance animals successfully. If it works for them, why can't it work for Iyal?"

"So this service-dog thing has never even been tried for FASDs—is that what you're saying?" He stared at me as if he had suddenly realized the idea was even more absurd than he first thought, as if I were suggesting Iyal rocket to Mars for a quick FAS cure.

"Just because they haven't been used for FASDs before doesn't mean anything," I continued. "You know how complex Iyal's symptoms are—there is no linear path he follows—he lives only in the moment. Harvey, we can't connect Iyal's chemical constellation, and there is no map. He free-falls in his mind all the time, leaving us constantly looking for ways to restabilize him.

"And many of his disabilities are similar to what other individuals experience—like ASD, PTSD, anxiety, OCD, and other mental illnesses. The service dogs are uniquely trained to understand how to help them. What have we got to lose?"

I sensed that Harvey was slipping from emergency brake to the eject button. Our shit was hitting the fan, and no Diaper Genie could contain it.

Harvey shook his head. "Other than the last little shred of my sanity? Other than thousands of dollars we can't afford to waste on something as crazy as this? Other than the unpredictable bedlam of having a dog reacting to Iyal's outbursts? I'd say we have *a lot* to lose."

I felt like we were dueling for power in our relationship, our swords always within reach if one of us crossed the line into the other's self-righteous point of view. Without Harvey's support, my "second" was my dad, who watched my back from a close distance that allowed me to access him for support. But he, too, was struggling not to judge Harvey while he saw us embroiled in this unending, shattering battle.

My mom and dad held their emotions close, perhaps a byproduct of their generation and their parents' values. For better or worse, they rarely expressed anger during my childhood. We didn't fight in my house. We never swore at each other. So when I was around others who were verbally abusive or embroiled in a silent fight-to-the-death marathon, I felt sick to my stomach and wished I were anywhere but where I was. My need for feeling invisible in the midst of relationship conflict, including my own, hasn't changed.

Of course we had an undertow in my house as I grew up. It explains the lack of dark raging red, burning orange, or searing green on my emotional palette. When I was eleven, my dad, at age forty-one, had a serious heart attack. He recovered completely and was a dream patient for his doctors, nurses, and well-wishers. I inherited the Kanter trait: Don't make a fuss, don't ask for extra (anything), be nice, and people will like you more. I find this to be true for the most part.

You might have thought that my dad ingratiated himself in this way. But in fact, he *was* this way. My dad breathed "nice air." And sometimes it drove my mom nuts! And when I became an adult, I understood why. Everyone loved my dad—I mean *everyone* loved my dad. It was actually pretty unbelievable and made me proud. So what did it mean then if I didn't like something my dad said or I felt frustrated by his behavior? What kind of person did that make *me*? An ungrateful daughter?

It was difficult for my mom, my brother, and me to breathe "anger air" in our family. Besides, being angry was *not okay* when my dad was recovering from his heart attack. The doctor told us to "be quiet and don't do anything to make your father upset." Although unintended, those words wounded me over and over again, leaving a hole where I should have had an emotional resource to lift my voice up no matter how it sounded and what it said. I don't think I would have recognized myself if I had shouted.

When Harvey's voice escalated to make his point, I shuddered. I had stockpiled my own ammunition of disrespect, disdain, and disbelief, but I couldn't yell these feelings. After all, I could barely *name* them. I didn't know what to do with them because I lacked the courage to confront Harvey.

My emotions were desperately out of sorts, Harvey and I were horribly out of sync, and I was spiraling downward toward depression while navigating around my elevated anxiety. I didn't see how our communication would improve if neither of us could take responsibility for our part in this relationship détente. We were moving further and further away from any reconciliation. Harvey had always been the voice of reason, which he finessed the longer he was a rabbi. But discussions at home were contentious and wounding, fueled by a passion or stubbornness neither of us could control. Sadly, I would never have imagined that Harvey had the capacity to hurl such disdain at an idea I thought so creative and evidence based. I couldn't think of anything else to say. There was no way to break our stalemate. My partner on our "ship" was breaking away, leaving us rudderless and unstable.

"Mom?" asked Morasha as she was getting ready for bed. "Can I ask you something?"

I turned from leaving her room and stepped back in. "Of course, honey," I said as I perched myself on the end of her bed.

"I was just wondering . . . you know, it seems like . . ." She trailed off, looking away from me. I knew this conversation wasn't going to be good.

"Morasha, what is it, honey?" I asked, turning her face back to me.

Her face scrunched up. "Are you and Dad going to get divorced?"

Oh shit. I can't believe she just asked that. Well, yes I can. Our daughter is intuitive, sensitive, and smart.

"Sweetheart," I mumbled as my face brushed against her just-shampooed hair, smelling of innocence, a blatant contradiction of the words she had just spoken.

"Well, Mom?"

I sat up, trying to figure out what other parents would say in this situation, knowing this kind of talk was much more common in families than it used to be. "Why do you ask that? What makes you think that Daddy and I would get divorced?"

Tears slipped from Morasha's eyes, down her cheeks, into her sweet mouth as she spoke. "It seems like Dad is yelling all the time, and you seem quiet. You seem so sad, Mom. Something feels different."

I sat for a moment so I wouldn't cry also. It wasn't fair for seven-year-old Morasha to sense or feel all the crap that was going on. But she did.

"Honey, we aren't getting divorced. I promise." I could feel her relief travel from her face to her tummy, which relaxed under her nightgown. "You're right that Daddy is yelling more, and I'm feeling sad about that. But it doesn't mean anything bad." I was telling this to myself, too, as I had every night for many weeks, many months. "Daddy and I love each other, and we are staying as a family."

This wasn't Morasha's problem.

We would be fine.

Remembering my conversation with Morasha, I felt even more unsure about how much of my bottled-up emotions to uncork with my husband. Sensing my uncertainty, Harvey put his arm around me and tried to draw me close, clearly thinking he had won, at least for the moment. He said, "I know you're tired of dealing with Iyal's problems, Donnie, and I am, too—"

My momentary confusion at his gesture erupted, and I shrugged him away. In a rare moment of uncontrolled, pent-up frustration, I said, "You're hardly ever here! You have no idea what it's like to deal with him twenty-four seven! You can compartmentalize and shut us out, but our son needs intense supervision all the time. I know you've juggled your schedule to be here more, and I appreciate that, but I dread the weekends when I have to handle all of this craziness, programming Iyal's schedule moment by moment so he doesn't lose it. I've heard professionals say, 'People who experience FASDs don't know what to do when they don't know what to do.' I *totally* get this. It's so draining to run our house like a day camp." I felt myself choking on the truth I needed to say out loud. But I was scared shitless. "And, and . . . I *need* you here with me, but I don't know if that's where you want to be."

My husband froze in place. The silence between us seemed interminable. I knew he thought I had gone too far. But I had nowhere else to go. Why didn't I think I had the right to say something like this? To insist on what I needed?

Then Harvey just shook his head at me again. "I'm going to ignore what you just said because you have no idea what it's like to be a rabbi, to be on call—not just for one person but for hundreds—all the time! I have to be everyone's counselor, confessor, and confidant. You think I like working seventy, eighty hours a week? But I'm the one who provides for our family. You can't possibly understand the kind of pressure I feel!" The issue of emotional and physical resources was like a snakebite—a double wound—which poisoned our respect for each other.

Whenever we had a conversation that turned into the inevitable "you think *you* have it bad?" I felt like a deflated punching bag hanging by a thread. I was *always* in need of emotional resources because there were never enough in my home, in my head, to refill my daily depleted well. I used up all my serotonin by ten a.m., having been sucked dry by Iyal's needs just to get him off to school in the morning!

When Harvey reminded me of the pressure he felt to provide for the family, I immediately went to my "guilty place." I sincerely appreciated how hard he worked for the congregation and to put food on our table. Neither of us expected that the expense of Iyal's medical and behavioral needs would have serious implications for our budget. But I didn't want to feel guilty for doing things the way I thought was best for my family.

I closed my eyes, aware of the drumbeat of pain that had started pounding in my brain. I could hear the TV on upstairs and the sound of Morasha and Iyal giggling together, a rare piece of music. "Look, Harve, I'm sorry I said that. It's just . . . I'm so tired, and I don't know what else to do. We try doctor after doctor, medication after medication. He goes from zero to a hundred in the blink of an eye, and it frustrates him as much as it does us. I just feel like we need to try and give the service-dog idea a chance, okay?"

"I know this is hard on you. Hard on all of us. It's not what we expected when we signed on. I'm in this with you—I really am. I love Iyal just as much as you do. I love our family and remain as committed as that first day we held them in our arms. But a dog is not going to help, Donnie," he said. "I can't do it."

Though spoken gently, his words crushed my fragile hope.

I couldn't understand why Harvey refused to change his mind—and why I couldn't let go of this idea. The more adamant he became that we wouldn't be getting a dog of any kind—let alone a service dog that would cost at least ten to fifteen grand—the more driven I became to follow my instincts. Through most of our marriage, I had been stunned into submission by Harvey's authoritarian statements. I'm certain he didn't know how he came across when he was feeling things spinning out of control—yet he clamped down on every moving piece. Which included us.

And I knew my idea would only work for the family if he were a part of the experience. I needed his buy-in. And his overreaction still didn't make sense. Harvey's family had lived with dogs his entire life. He loved them! What made *this* dog such a negative idea?

My marriage was the most important thing to me, but I had become unable to breathe, fearful of how much space I could fill in the relationship without my husband feeling threatened that it would "just be too much" and walking away. My own fears of abandonment were eroding the pillars of self-assurance I had worked so hard to develop.

He must have sensed how close I was to the brink of despair because he concluded our stalemate conversation with a small concession. "If you want," he instructed, "you may conduct more research and present a report at a time when you feel I can entertain this idea again."

What? Who the fuck was this person? I couldn't believe what I was hearing. Who had taken my husband and replaced him with this angry throwback from another century?

I didn't know whether to be grateful or outraged, perhaps a little of both.

"But do me a favor. While you're doing this research, I don't want to talk about it, and I don't want anyone else talking to me about it. Got it?"

Although I nodded, I couldn't fathom how to accept this demand that would isolate me even further in the marriage. What would I talk about with him if he didn't want to know where my journey was taking us and how I spent my time? Maybe his intended consolation prize was more of an insult after all. Because once again, I felt summarily dismissed by his need to control what went on in our house, in our relationship.

We were both struggling to have our voices heard, but we had already become deaf to each other out of sheer exhaustion and loss of patience. I was convinced that Harvey's anger was displaced but couldn't figure out how to talk with him about it. Now he was becoming someone I barely recognized.

"So," he said flatly, "go ahead. Find your experts and see what they say. It's not going to change my mind."

It wasn't the outcome I wanted, but it was something. If Harvey knew anything about me, he knew I was good at researching, networking, and getting people to rally around a cause.

But now the stakes seemed higher than ever. I had to assemble a credible jury and one that would still rule in favor of trying a service dog for Iyal. Suddenly, I felt more like a character in a John Grisham novel—and all to convince my husband of something that I thought he would be as excited to embrace as I was.

I hadn't floated the dog idea to the kids yet, especially Iyal. I had seen his curiosity around dogs at the park and knew he would be excited about the idea of a dog whose primary job was to help him navigate the daily challenges of controlling his feelings and interacting with the world.

In the meantime, he continued to struggle more than ever, which meant I wasn't doing so great myself. Whenever I watched my son struggle inside his skin, my heart rate climbed, the surge of cortisol signaling my own impending anxiety attack. The simultaneous agony of witnessing his being held captive by his birth defect left me deflated and somber. Catapulting off the walls as if trapped in a room of trampolines, Iyal would linger just long enough to watch his shadow catch up with him before bouncing to the next wall.

At least a service dog would give him something else to focus on, something to distract him and hopefully comfort him. My pledge to obtain a service dog for Iyal rose out of frustration, heartache, and the desire to find a way that he could feel more grounded, more at home inside *himself* as well as with other people. The dog, as an addition to the family dynamics, would provide a positive shift in our fractured framework. As a kind of guardian, Iyal's service dog would be looking out for Iyal's best interests in a unique way. He or she would be trained to protect Iyal from his own behavior by de-escalating rages that could tear Iyal apart inside and often result in Iyal tearing his room apart. I prayed that our constant negative attention on Iyal would diminish and be replaced by respect and encouragement.

But convincing Harvey meant I had to find a way to make this risk seem more of an asset than a liability. Fortunately, one of my oldest friends in the area, going back thirty years, was the former head veterinarian of Zoo Atlanta, and she immediately thought my idea worthwhile and exciting. And I knew Harvey respected her.

She also proved to be an incredible resource in coming up with other names and expert evidence. With her help, I assembled an expert canine advisory council that included one of the top animal behavioral analysts in the country, two professional dog trainers, and the former director of Happy Tails, a reputable therapy-dog organization in Georgia. I'd chosen my jury but feared that Harvey's judgment would be difficult to change.

He seemed impressed with my hard work and reluctantly agreed that my advisory council could come to dinner, which at the time seemed like a step closer to victory. My friends, old and new, understood the gravity of the situation and made their support for my agenda known before the appetizers were out of the oven. From there, the conversation quickly became a steady, persuasive blaze that consumed all oxygen in the room. Harvey spoke about twenty-five words all evening. I couldn't even make eye contact with him. Before dessert, he excused himself from the table while I was left to apologize to our guests, accept their sympathy, and clean up while impatient tears waited to validate my sadness.

The next day, however, a tectonic shift took place in Harvey.

Going for broke, I read him a letter I'd prepared as a result of conversations with my therapist. I informed him that while I had tried so hard to do this dog thing *with* him, I would no longer jump through hoops nor did I need his approval or anyone else's. This was huge for me, because my assertiveness had dissolved to nothing and had taken months of rehearsing versions of this letter in my therapy.

Harvey said, "Okay. I still don't agree with it, but I see this is what you want to do."

I knew deep down that Harvey loved me and respected me. Perhaps he was hoping I could help us find each other again.

My dad saw our marriage dissolving due to years of stress and disappointment—disappointment that we couldn't find a way to connect Iyal to us and to the world around him. Harvey and I became disappointed in each other when we felt lost and expected the other to magically find us.

I called Dad the day I finally told Harvey I was going to get a service dog for Iyal with or without his consent.

"Hi, Dad," I said as the tears began to flow.

"Don?" he said. "Honey, what's going on?"

I took a breath and then said, "Oh, Dad, I just told Harvey I was going to get a service dog even if he didn't agree." I was sobbing. "I'm so worried, Dad."

"Oh . . . honey. You did the right thing."

"I just wanted you to know that no matter what happens . . . to us, I love you and thank you for trusting me to take care of my kids even if I can't take care of my husband." I sighed as another wave of tears washed over me. I couldn't believe I had finally done it. I had finally opened the door for a service dog even if I might've closed it on my marriage.

With begrudging permission to move forward, I already knew the training facility I would call first: 4 Paws for Ability had a comprehensive website that left me thoroughly impressed. With nervous excitement, I called the director of 4 Paws, Karen Shirk, and explained our situation with Iyal and why I thought a service dog would help him. I slowed down to ask, "Have you ever trained a service dog to work specifically with a child living with FASDs?"

"Not that I'm aware," she said, which is what I'd expected. "But it's possible. I mean, so many of our families have members with disabilities similar to what your son experiences. With all the different disorders we've trained for, I wouldn't be surprised if some of our clients' issues were related to FASDs."

Oh my God! Was I hearing her correctly? Was she *not* telling me there was no way in hell they would even begin to consider providing a dog for Iyal? I needed to replay this conversation in my head, right now. And another time, because what I'd rehearsed involved a lot more pleading and bargaining than what might be necessary. I was momentarily stunned—in a good way.

From there, everything fell into place. No pitch to Karen was necessary, just the "prescription" for a service dog from one of Iyal's doctors. The psychiatrist that Iyal was seeing at the time literally wrote a prescription on his prescription pad for a behavioral assistant dog to help Iyal with his FAS.

Just like that.

Filling out the 4 Paws application, I obsessed a little (I'm sure you're shocked) and listed all the dog books I'd been reading as well as the names of my advisory council members.

Prior to having a dog officially matched with Iyal, we submitted our portion of the training fee with the application. Families obtaining 4 Paws service dogs were responsible for raising or submitting one half of the fee for training their particular service dog. This was a unique model for a service-dog agency, since most agencies had their dogs' trainings sponsored by corporate donors or private individuals. Through this model, the clients didn't have to pay for their dogs. However, in some cases, clients would have to "give back" their service dog to the agency after it was retired or fell sick or for some other reason. A devastating scenario.

Because 4 Paws for Ability trained their dogs case specifically, their financial model differed. Each dog was trained to serve the exact needs of one particular child. In 2008, we were responsible for providing $9,800, which was half the cost of training for that particular kind of dog. A search-and-rescue dog trained for tracking a lost child would require a higher fee, as the training would be more extensive.

Fortunately, I knew I had the financial backing. My dad being, well, my dad was determined to help us pay the training fee. He told me early on in our conversation about getting a service dog for Iyal that it was something he and my mom (who had passed away by this time) would want to do. I knew how deeply he meant this. One of the most magical things my parents shared was their love of animals. Animals were officially their second religion. But it was a close race in their eyes!

So my dad already knew how much a service dog cost at 4 Paws, and when I asked if he would help, he immediately said, "I love you and your family," his way of saying "Of course." Besides viewing it as an investment in his grandson's future, it was an expression of his adoration for and commitment to my children. My spirituality is defined by finding God in the brokenness of life. My dad's connection to Iyal displayed a vast expanse of devotion and a love brimming with compassion and unconditional acceptance. And somehow I felt my late mom's deeply life-affirming love for my whole family, something I so desperately needed to feel illuminating this arduous path toward another chance for us all that only an animal could offer.

The application was complete, the prescription written, the check filled out, and the video of Iyal's behaviors recorded. All was submitted and certified, with a returned receipt—I couldn't be too sure. And it was only a few days until I received the phone call from a 4 Paws staff person saying they were ready to train a dog for Iyal! All alone in the house when the call came, I wept with relief, with the grief that was always the underpinning of trying a new intervention, and, this time, with more hope than I had ever dared to feel. But something felt different this time.

The success of the "match" with a specific dog to a child was based on the way in which the head trainer, Jeremy Dulebohn, interpreted the behavior of the client on the submitted video. 4 Paws requested a video from each family that showed all the child's behaviors that needed to be disrupted or supported. The behaviors would be linked to a command or cue for the dog so the dog could be trained when the command was said or shown with a hand signal. For clients who were medically fragile or unable to express behaviors on demand, dogs were trained to perform interventions based on the history of similar clients and their dogs.

This was the beginning of the magic. And it would only get better. Now we would just have to wait.

Ten months was the minimum amount of time possible before our new furry friend would be ready for us. I was struck by the extent to which 4 Paws trained the dogs for their clients. Since they trained the dogs case specifically, and because no one had ever asked about an FASD dog, we were in new territory. But their willingness to understand and to take this risk with us was one of the things that set 4 Paws apart from most of the other service-dog agencies.

Also, the trainers at 4 Paws had tons of experience training dogs for kids living with autism and were, in fact, the founding agency of autism-assistance dogs. 4 Paws is still the only service-dog facility that trains dogs with tracking skills for children who elope as a result of their disability. The dogs can track up to an hour and a half after a child goes missing. As a result, they had become the go-to agency for families whose children experience ASD and want service dogs. This skill and being tethered to a trained dog was key to parents who lived in constant hypervigilance, worrying about the child or children disappearing almost in front of their eyes. And I could personally relate to the clench of fear in the gut. That fear seemed to follow me around everywhere I went.

Our dog would experience a similar training process because the training is based on "behavior disruption." The trainers interpreted the child's behaviors and then translated them into commands or cues for the dog to respond in the best way to assist the child in various situations. More than one thousand dogs and handler teams have graduated since 1999, with more than one hundred dogs placed for a variety of disorders per year.

We also had legal hurdles to jump, and 4 Paws obviously knew how to clear these. In the United States, a service dog can only be certified for public access as mandated by federal law by receiving a minimum of 120 hours of training over a period of no less than six months. Once certified, the animal can accompany its human owner everywhere that anyone else can go—the subway, the mall, the library, wherever. The dogs trained by 4 Paws receive upward of five hundred hours of training, with the handlers themselves being trained for at least sixty hours.

Iyal's age was another factor. Very few agencies even allow dogs to be placed with individuals under the age of eighteen, and most have a minimum age of twelve. Iyal was only nine at the time, but fortunately 4 Paws had no minimum age. However, because of the laws pertaining to this field, an adult must be the "handler" and accompany the dog and child at all times when the dog is out in public "working." We would be a three-person team.

Iyal was unable to grasp most of what was entailed in this whole application process. He understood why we were taking video of him (everywhere we went for a month!). Sometimes recording his tantrums and total meltdowns caused more tantrums and total meltdowns, but that was actually a good thing. When he was self-conscious of the videotaping, he would certainly let me know by screaming, kicking the wall, or running around hysterically, some of the many behaviors we hoped Iyal's service dog could disrupt.

Once I told him about his new service dog, Iyal asked continuous questions, many of them repeated on a daily basis. Ten months never seemed so long! But now I at least felt like there was hope, a goal, a light at the end of this confining tunnel of fear and anguish. Morasha and I visited the 4 Paws website every night to look at all the puppies and dogs. We were so excited wondering which of the darling faces would become part of our family. I would've liked to share this with Harvey, but involving him wasn't meant to be. I was trying to respect his wishes and not include him. However, I knew the fence I straddled couldn't hold the weight of our conflict forever.

Harvey removed himself from the process, and we rarely discussed anything relating to the service dog. Thank God I had friends and family members who enthusiastically participated in my anticipation of this unique intervention. However, when he finally asked how much the dog cost and I told him my dad was covering the $9,800 fee, he went ballistic. "How could you do this without talking to me? We should have discussed this. That money could have gone for more therapy, or camp, or, or . . . something! How dare you make this decision without consulting me?"

Since Harvey pretty much took care of our finances, this was a particularly sharp blade he was facing, and I needed him to see that it couldn't cut both ways.

"Harvey, you don't have veto power if I wasn't supposed to tell you things about the dog." I continued softly, hoping he would recognize the catch-22. "You specifically told me you *did not* want to discuss anything having to do with the dog. This was my idea, and Dad was in agreement about how to spend his money. And you know he was thrilled to be able to help us out." It would be difficult for Harvey to "go up against" anything relating to my dad. Harvey loved my father with all his heart. And my dad couldn't have loved Harvey more. So this was an impasse, and Harvey retreated. But only a little.

When Karen called to give me the date for the training session with our dog, I asked Harvey if he would go with us. He checked his calendar and informed me that he had work commitments that would prevent him from going. With his calm, matter-of-fact tone, he might as well have been trying to schedule a dental appointment. I hid my deep disappointment but didn't allow it to dampen the enthusiasm Iyal, Morasha, my dad, and I shared.

Our match for Iyal wasn't revealed to us until ten days before we left for Ohio. 4 Paws does this intentionally so they can be absolutely sure they have chosen the right dog and so that families don't become attached to the face of another dog on their website. Iyal received a photo and a note from a dog named Chancer, introducing himself. The picture was of a gorgeous, generous, huge, blond golden retriever with a coal-black nose and deep reflecting eyes. Something in his expression made me suspect he harbored an old soul inside. He was lovely, somehow sympathetic- and playful-looking at the same time. I started to cry just looking at his photo. It meant that we were that much closer to having Iyal's buddy.

We needed two adults to accompany Iyal to the training. As backup, which I felt was critical, my dear cousin who was like a sister, Adair, flew in from Missoula, Montana, to help and videotape our training. Morasha and my dad would come with us. Finally, the date approached, and we packed and began the drive to the small town of Xenia, Ohio, about halfway between Cincinnati and Columbus, where 4 Paws was located.

We would be there for ten straight days, being educated on all we would need to know about our new family member and his ability to help Iyal. Between 10:00 a.m. and 4:00 p.m. each day, we would learn the commands and cues needed to train and handle our dogs in public. Eight other families from all over the country would also be in our class to complete their training and acquire their respective service dogs as well.

I could hardly wait, as anxious as I had ever been, eager to exhale after swimming underwater for so long.

Chapter Five

"Hello, sweetheart!" I said, gazing into the deep, dark eyes sparkling back at me from the other side of a two-by-three-by-three-foot dog kennel. I had anticipated this moment with an almost painful joy, like opening a present and wondering if what I knew was inside would really live up to my expectations. Now, though, I trusted the joy would come alive with the promise this new member of our family would offer.

Not so joyful was the way *eau de dog* permeated the air, and the impact was breathtaking to say the least. There in the warehouse-like kennel building at 4 Paws, we were finally meeting our Chancer face-to-face. Even though a canine symphony of yapping and barking played in the background, all I could see was the smiling face of this giant golden boy in front of me.

With thick fur the color of summer wheat, blond going lighter at the ends, he was as regal as a lion and as adorable as a pony. His alert eyes belied a keen intelligence, softened by generous eyebrows moving up and down like some canine Groucho Marx. He wasn't barking like the other dogs around him. From the way his head cocked quizzically, I could tell his question was the same, just from a dog's perspective: "Are you my human? Are you the one I've been waiting for?"

Iyal, within an inch of the kennel door, grinned into the face of his new best friend and said, "Hey, Chancer! Good boy, good boy!" and then up at me, "Let him out, Mom! Let him out!"

As soon as he was liberated, Chancer expressed his gratitude with much tail wagging and many slurpy kisses for Iyal. I quickly attached our brand-new leash to his collar before he decided to have a play date with the collie next door, and we bounded into the training area. As if eight other families with children didn't provide enough chaos, we had just added nine dogs to the mix.

Nervous and excited, relieved and expectant, anxious and uncertain—we all shared the same unspoken question: *Can this service dog really help my child?* As I looked around at the other parents and caregivers, I knew we were each wagering more than the ten-thousand-dollar cost of the dogs. We were betting on our family's future well-being. We were betting on hope.

Our class of nine families met every day as a group. The large training room was split, half classroom for the adults and half indoor game room for the kids. Before we all migrated to our respective halves of the room, each family introduced themselves and proudly announced the name of their new service dog. As for the children, they varied in sizes, shapes, ages, and levels of function and ability.

Children from the various nine families ranged from ages two to fifteen. The majority of them lived somewhere on the autism spectrum, while others battled additional challenges such as seizure disorders, intellectual impairment, psychiatric illness, and immobility. The youngest, a two-year-old named Rachel, who was the size of a six-month-old infant, lay on a baby blanket on the floor, immobile and nonverbal. Requiring a feeding tube, she looked so fragile that I worried about her dog accidentally crushing her. However, the match between Rachel and a sweet male collie named Dallas couldn't have been more perfect. I watched, mesmerized, as the dog gently lifted Rachel's teeny arm with his nose as she produced a tiny giggle.

Soon it was our turn, and despite my career in theater and vast experience as a public speaker, I wasn't sure what to say. How could I condense years of struggle, disappointment, and uncertainty into two minutes? How could I communicate how much I deeply loved and adored my son?

“I’m Donnie Winokur,” I began, “and this is my son, Iyal, and my daughter, Morasha. My husband, Harvey, wasn’t able to join us—he’s a rabbi back in Atlanta, where we live. But I have recruited other family members from New Jersey and Montana to help us.” I introduced my dad and Adair, and they all beamed at the other families.

“And this is Chancer!” I announced as my little blond pony stood right up on cue. “He’s going to help Iyal with some of the difficulties he faces with FASDs—fetal alcohol spectrum disorders. Some of you may be familiar with FASDs and its similarities to autism and ADHD. Uh, I’ll be happy to tell you more about it, and our story, while we’re here. I’m really looking forward to comparing notes and learning from each of you during our training time. Thanks!”

We had so much information to absorb in a relatively short time. Each day was going to be a cross between summer camp, finishing school, and a daily field trip to the pound. Despite feeling overwhelmed, I knew I would love it.

Our instructor, Jeremy, began by giving us a general overview on how a service dog thinks. Basic obedience instructions were next on the agenda. Jeremy taught us how to correct the dogs and reward them with the appropriate motivators, often a treat or a toy, and, most important, genuine praise for the dog. We learned basic commands like “sit,” “down,” and “stay” by the end of that first day, with each of us able to put our dog in a “down” and walk away without him stirring for at least ten to fifteen seconds. Most dogs—trained to remain close to the person they’re assisting—actually would get up and follow their person if not told to “stay” in a “down,” especially if a treat bag was attached to their person's hip! Chancer had no problem whatsoever and seemed a little bored, a star pupil held back by the rest of his class.

The hours flew by, and I was amazed how quickly we had bonded, both with our respective service dogs as well as with each other. As parents, we instantly understood each other in ways that I hadn't anticipated, sharing familiar knowledge of how our family's orbit could continually be eclipsed by one member's disability. And it was equally astonishing how the individual canine chosen for each child seemed to match them and their family's needs so perfectly.

I had assumed Iyal would need a big dog to help him adjust and control his behaviors and was proved right. But I wondered about the other criteria for this significant partnership, and when I asked Jeremy about it during one of our breaks, I was fascinated by his explanation.

"We really try to match temperaments, personalities, and breeds of the dogs to each child's needs," he explained. "After watching the videos you sent me of Iyal and reading through your application, I knew he would need a large dog with a gentle temperament and really high ego strength. Your son needs a service dog that won't take it personally if Iyal pushes him away or ignores him." Smiling, he said, "Chancer's the best boy for the job."

"Has Chancer been here since he was a puppy?" I asked, curious to know his history.

"No," Jeremy answered, "he came to us kind of late, actually."

I asked, "What does that mean, Jeremy?"

He said, "Well, a family had bought him from a breeder and, after a year, realized how much time it took to care for a dog like Chancer. The family felt they had neglected him, not providing enough exercise or watching his diet. I think most of all they felt badly that they weren't there for Chancer."

Jeremy paused as he gazed at Chancer, who was lying close by on the floor, taking up a considerable amount of real estate. I noticed that every time Jeremy said Chancer's name, our furry friend looked up with his lovely brown eyes as if to say, "Yes, that's me he's talking about! So listen . . ."

Jeremy said quietly, "The family offered him no relationship, a horrible thing for a dog—especially a golden."

I heard myself gulp back tears that were so close to becoming part of this conversation. I knew it wasn't just about Chancer's neglect but also Iyal's. And maybe even my own in this particularly painful time in my relationship with Harvey. So many reasons to cry at this moment.

Saving me from myself, Jeremy said, "At least per their contract with the breeder, they returned Chancer so he could have a better life." Jeremy smiled, as Chancer was now offering his own irresistible smile that beckoned petting and kisses, which I provided as this conversation came to a close. "And that's how he wound up at 4 Paws. I know you're as happy as we are that this is how the story goes."

"So he's a second-Chancer?" I couldn't resist.

"Exactly." Jeremy nodded. "Don't we all need second chances?"

"He'll fit right in," I said, holding back a deluge of emotions. "Our family is full of second chances."

—

The second day we were allowed to take our dogs to our hotel with us, which felt a little like driving a new car off the dealer's lot and knowing that Chancer was really ours now. We had been loaned crates and all the supplies we would need to care for our service dog for the duration of the training.

That first night with Chancer was uneventful even though I didn't sleep well—too many thoughts running through my mind, along with the dregs of too much caffeine and the overflowing adrenaline. I must have drifted off, though, because before I knew it light was streaming around the edges of the curtains. I crept into the next room, where Iyal lay sleeping next to my dad, an image that rests peacefully in my heart, while Chancer sprawled inside his crate.

While I was showering, everyone else began to stir. By the time I was finished, Adair had let Chancer out of his crate, and he had wasted no time jumping on the bed next to the sleeping Iyal, spooning him with big front paws, literally holding "his boy." Chancer then greeted his new favorite boy with gentle good-morning kisses. Iyal, typically quite cranky most mornings, smiled awake and seemed to enjoy his canine wake-up call, which relieved me because Iyal didn't always respond to unexpected changes so easily. But apparently, he liked all this attention from Chancer, a good sign.

Our third day passed with more classroom instruction and interaction, including what each family had experienced their first night with their new canine collaborator. This routine became the first thing we did every morning in class. Each family would share what the last twelve hours with their new service dog had been like, giving us the chance to learn from the experience of others and allowing us to vent embarrassing moments. Some of the family members who were learning to become our dog's handlers cringed about what had happened, but everyone usually ended up laughing about the silly things that the "dog made us do" that dissolved any humiliation anyone might have felt.

That afternoon after training, I planned to run errands—groceries for us and gas for the van—while Adair and Dad made plans to meet some of the other families back at our hotel pool. The kids were eager to unleash some of their pent-up energy from being inside all day, and I was grateful for a few minutes by myself.

But as a result, I missed out on all the excitement.

As planned, Adair had taken Chancer out to go potty while my father accompanied Iyal and Morasha to the indoor pool area. Adair had just turned the corner with Chancer and was about to approach the chlorine-scented oasis when Chancer lunged, pulling the leash out of Adair's hand. The tiled floor was wet, of course, and she couldn't catch up with the golden blur soaring into the hot tub where Iyal sat with Morasha.

By the time they all got out of the hot tub, figuring out who thought they were rescuing the other was difficult. But as everyone's laughter subsided, we all marveled that Chancer had thought he needed to rescue Iyal out of the water—something we soon learned Chancer hadn't been trained to do. Already Chancer knew that Iyal's well-being was his number-one priority.

Yep, our hotel room smelled like wet dog for the next two days. But I didn't mind and actually memorized the smell. My son had a new lifeguard.

"Can I help you find anything, ma'am?" a young man in a blue vest asked me as I stood pretending to peruse an aisle of electrical switches, wires, and fuses. Chancer waited patiently at my left side as instructed. It was our fifth day together, and we were making our public debut at a nearby Lowe's home improvement store, a field trip I'd both eagerly anticipated and dreaded.

One of the trainers accompanied me and two other family handlers from our group as we took our service dogs for a test-drive. We "heeled" the dogs around the store, stopping to shop and talk with other people a few times to make sure the dogs would respect us just as well outside the classroom as they were during our training.

Chancer was brilliant. He would check in every few seconds by looking up at me to make sure he was doing the right thing. I praised him with a "good boy" and a pat on the head.

We were already communicating well, with many of the commands implied by my expression and our context, a common phenomenon and good indicator of the bond between us. Over time, Chancer would become accustomed to my shopping style in that I didn't make quick decisions when purchasing an item (in my family, this was a birthright). He soon learned that I would have to obsess about the price for a while, which sometimes meant a return visit to the same store at a different location so I felt confident I had covered all my bases. These excursions and my expressions, both verbal and facial, were just part of Chancer's conversion to Judaism. Considering he was becoming the service dog for a rabbi's son, we found interesting ways to envelop him in Jewish traditions and culture (while a bark mitzvah was obvious, I was now curious to see if he could also be immersed in a mikvah while we said the Hebrew prayers for him).

I was encouraged to see Chancer responding so intuitively to my leadership. After only a few days, we had already started to drop off vocal and hand commands for certain tasks. Such natural chemistry seemed too good to be true, and I only hoped Chancer would prove just as reliable relating to my son.

Because we still had a long way to go.

—

As soon as we returned from our successful shopping expedition, we learned how to "tether" Iyal to Chancer using a different harness on the dog and special vest that Iyal wears. If the handler thought their child was about to dash out into traffic, he or she would cue the dog into a "down" and the dog wouldn't move. Thus, neither would Iyal.

Jeremy used Chancer as the example for the class. He literally pulled, tugged, and then dragged Chancer across the linoleum floor of the classroom to show how Chancer wouldn't budge. Watching was hysterical but also deeply reassuring. When necessary, I could now tether Iyal to Chancer and know his golden anchor was more than strong enough to restrain the boy from running. Similarly, should I see Iyal take off, I could immediately heel Chancer by my side, and the two of us together would serve as a human monument. Iyal would be attached to Chancer's harness with a tether, linked to his vest. I would be attached to Chancer by a separate leash. Chancer literally had two humans to whom he was connected. Iyal would also have his very own two-foot leash to use whenever he walked Chancer, but an adult handler would still be leashed to Chancer as backup.

When people ask why Iyal doesn't walk Chancer alone, I explain that the reason Iyal has a service dog is that Iyal doesn't always make good choices. He might become distracted by something and drop the leash to follow his nose, so to speak. Chancer might follow him, as Iyal's scent might take over Chancer, which could put two living creatures in danger. Chancer's instinct to protect Iyal might override his own skill set.

Plus, we were constantly reminded that we couldn't take the dog out of a service dog. A barbecue grill with sizzling steaks in the next neighborhood could easily engage any one of the 250 million scent glands in Chancer's nose. Unlike a human, who has about five million scent glands, Chancer could not only smell my homemade spaghetti sauce, but he also could sift each sniff into individual ingredients. I was wondering if I could train Chancer to pick out the basil from my fresh herb pot on the deck and then shred it for me like a sous chef. Little did I know Chancer probably could have been trained to shred high-security documents for the Secret Service!

After another successful night back at the hotel, the next day in the classroom, we covered many topics, including travel, the laws pertaining to service dogs, and several other relevant issues. After lunch, we took another outing—this time to an indoor mall near our hotel. Jeremy spent about twenty minutes following each handler-and-dog team and then offered suggestions and corrections.

Even though Iyal wasn't with me (he was back at the hotel with Adair, Morasha, and Dad), my stress level was higher than when we had visited Lowe's, especially when we met the other eight family handlers and service dogs at the food court. The place was mobbed, and the food court stood in as Disneyland for dogs! Their noses didn't stop twitching. The food court was the ultimate training ground for practicing obedience and exercising our repertoire of commands and reinforcing the dogs' respect for us.

Once again, Chancer was exemplary, but I realized we would now have to allow an extra fifteen minutes whenever we went anywhere just to give us time to answer people's questions and allow them to pet Chancer. Many people are confused when we allow them to pet Chancer, because they've heard you should ignore service dogs in order to not distract them from doing their job. However, part of Chancer's role as a service dog for Iyal was to provide "social lubrication."

This term, coined by social scientists R. A. Mugford and J. G. M'Comisky, describes the phenomenon by which the presence of animals increases positive social interaction among people. Studying these interactions, other researchers suggest the attractiveness and uniqueness of a child's pet (or service dog) may, as a secondary gain, enhance the attraction to the child as a potential friend or playmate.

In other words, the sheer presence of this huge, handsome, smiling golden retriever would lure people over to where Iyal might be. Some of Iyal's quirky behaviors or repetitive motions regularly put off kids, especially when he was younger. But Chancer distracted other children from such tics and Iyal's nonsensical babbling and invited people to talk to Iyal about his dog. This was a huge deal because it offered Iyal a chance to feel included in social settings. And from the start, Iyal *loved* telling people about Chancer. A lot.

Over time, I realized that Chancer would be the best advocacy vehicle for invisible disabilities. Ever. He provided an educational opportunity when people inevitably asked, "What does he do for your son?"

Besides my describing some of the commands for which Chancer was trained, he allowed others to talk about things they might never have said out loud. Chancer could hold their secrets as they petted him and whispered doggy things in his ear.

Even after all these years, I'm enthralled watching the uptight demeanor of some individuals fade as Chancer's fur and face pulls them away from whatever stresses froze their feelings and stole their joy. Chancer had an impact on children and adults, which always started with them smiling. Many times, a person would tell me that he or she was deathly afraid of dogs. In these instances, I certainly would respect that fear and keep Chancer close by my side. I would offer an explanation of how Chancer helps Iyal and how other service dogs help their humans. On occasion, that individual might ease forward into Chancer's space and reach out a hand tentatively to touch him. The person would gaze at Chancer's eyes and look up at mine as I stayed quietly by them both. On several occasions, seeing the transformation on the person's face when she or he moved from fear to ease was amazing.

Once I made an appointment at our pediatrician's office specifically to spend time with a nurse to help her overcome her fear of dogs—especially big dogs. Magic happened between Chancer and the nurse that left us both in awe and tears.

Chancer opened the door to a conversation that was awkward and difficult for many people, especially when I talked about how Iyal came to live with a hidden disability. He gave room for people to stop for a moment in their busy lives and think differently, think thoughtfully about people who lived with disabilities. I like to think that moment lasted for many people.

I couldn't have foreseen how, in the next several years, Chancer would have a global influence in introducing the world to FASDs and other developmental disabilities.

The days flew by as our confidence soared. Finally, as "graduation day" approached, we reviewed everything we had learned. By far, the most important lesson was appreciating how Chancer was motivated, either by food, a toy, or praise. (In my case, it was food, a new purse, or praise.)

Jeremy taught us the difference between high motivators and low motivators. On the high end, a hot dog in any shape, cooked, nuked, grilled, or freeze-dried, was like caviar for dogs. (I was not a bit repulsed by *this* kind of caviar.) A low motivator might be less exciting, like a piece of zucchini—not to be completely ignored, because it is, after all, human food—but understood even by a dog to be a "healthy treat." It turned out that broccoli became a high motivator for Chancer. Who knew? Soon I wondered if Chancer could tell the difference between kosher and nonkosher hot dogs.

After we left 4 Paws, I found dog treats in just about everything I had taken with me in case I needed to correct or reward Chancer. It took about a year to remove the scent of bacon, chicken, peanut butter, kidney, and fake cheese from the pockets of my pants, my rolled-up sleeves, my socks, and even my toiletry bag.

We learned that for service dogs, competitive games, like tug-of-war, wrestling, and roughhousing, were never a good idea. The only exception was if the dog's child was involved and the child knew the bounds of play. In that case, the competitive game could be a form of bonding. Toys had to be plastic or rubber, and if they were stuffed animals, they couldn't look real, because we didn't want to arouse the dog's primal instincts unnecessarily. Similarly, no real bones, hooves, or pig ears (which I found disgusting even before we became a kosher-style home), as meat products bring out the carnivore in their canine nature. Rawhide was forbidden because it could cause life-threatening problems if not properly digested.

Timing was critical. At home, Chancer would actually offer a specific bark when he was about to get in trouble. He was warning us that he was planning to destroy something important. If we ignored the warning . . . well . . . he could do an "I told you so" or "I tried to warn you guys."

Appropriate treats and happy talk, the almost silly-sounding, chirpy, over-the-top, ridiculously happy positive-reinforcement language, also helped train Chancer to be childproof. To increase Chancer's tolerance of possible tail pulling, shoving, and yelling by Iyal, we practiced being "not nice" to him and then praised him up with treats and lots of "good boys." In essence, we rewarded him for being patient and forgiving of any possible trespasses by Iyal during a tantrum. This lesson was important for Iyal to learn as well, including the necessity of always having treats for his new best friend. Unfortunately, Iyal took this idea way too far so that everything Iyal was about to put in his *own* mouth was considered a treat for Chancer as well.

Looking back, I'm struck by the similarity between dog training and understanding individuals with special needs. And I make this comparison with the utmost respect. When an unusual behavior occurs with Iyal, I've learned to ask myself, "What does he need right now? What is his behavior telling me?" I would try to remind myself over and over again that in a person living with FASDs, the disability is about the *brain*—not the behavior. "How can I reward his strengths and attempts at self-control?" I knew this was key to bolstering his self-esteem.

With dogs, you learn that you correct *the thought* before *the action.* If you motivate the thought, then you can praise the action. And of course, you must follow the golden rule of dog training: *be consistent.* Repetition and consistency are crucial in dog training as well as child rearing. Iyal, like the majority of kids with special needs (or kids in general, as many parents have told me), thrives on consistency and predictability. It keeps his anxiety levels lower, which helps everyone else stay calmer and reduces my therapist's bill and consumption of chocolate.

Already I could see how Chancer would not only serve Iyal but our entire family, especially me.

Chapter Six

Our time at 4 Paws felt more like ten weeks than ten days as we consumed an overwhelming amount of knowledge about service dogs. In truth, I would've stayed another ten weeks because I didn't want to leave such a place that offered me a spiritual healing I could only find in animals. I drank in the adoring love that immediately grew between the dogs and the children. Even when a child was unable to reciprocate love for his or her dog in an understandable way, you still felt the love blooming.

The forever connection I have with the eight other families in the training class and the mystery of witnessing the bond between dogs and humans will remain one of the most extraordinary experiences in my life. Looking back, I now realize that Chancer not only brought his healing into our home, he also shaped a holiness out of the chaos that was threatening to tear apart our family. Coming off such a high, though, I was physically and emotionally drained and anxious about Harvey's reaction to Chancer.

Our newest family member was perfectly behaved the entire eight-and-a-half-hour drive home and pottied on command during our pit stops. Iyal did fairly well, clearly in the honeymoon phase with his new best friend. Finally, we pulled into the driveway, and the moment of truth was staring me in the face. Was I ready?

Chancer bounded into the house, reverberating pent-up energy as his huge paws drummed on the hardwood floor. There was no sniffing about or waiting for Iyal to direct him. Chancer immediately went to Harvey as though he knew that he still needed to fold one other family member into his pack. Rubbing his golden head against Harvey's leg, the dog waited for the petting festivities to begin.

Harvey seemed equally eager to get acquainted and gave Chancer a hug. "Hey there, big boy. Wow!" Then, smiling at his son, "Iyal, you finally got your boy! Do you love him?"

"Yes, Daddy, I do." Iyal was about to burst with the giddy joy of having Chancer with him here at home. I still watched Harvey out of the corner of my eye, assessing how authentic his reaction was, which wasn't easy, because I tend to project my own emotions on significant people and events in my life—sort of *willing* them to think and act like I would. I find doing so makes life easier to deal with.

And then Iyal went flying down the stairs to see the room he had missed over the last two weeks. He called out, "Chancer! Come here, boy. I want you to see your new kennel. Come, Chancer!" The big dog dutifully followed Iyal's voice down to his bedroom and immediately jumped on his bed, rolling around playfully until Iyal joined him in a fit of giggles as bubbly as a glass of champagne.

Harvey hugged our daughter and asked, "Did you have fun, Morash?" We both used this nickname for her.

"Dad, you should have seen all the dogs and puppies. They were so cute! I got to hold lots of baby goldens that were just a few days old. They were so adorable." Then she disappeared into her own bedroom, longing to be surrounded by her familiar stuffed animals and girl things.

I finally hugged Harvey and told him I'd missed him. We had spoken on the phone several times while we were away, but the brief conversations we'd had felt a bit tense, as if we had chosen to go on vacation without him and he didn't seem at all disappointed. But I was. Painfully.

By then, my dad had settled into our house, allowing us some space for our family reunion, yet still curious to see his son-in-law's response to the new addition. Harvey seemed genuinely glad to see us.

We had been home for fifteen minutes, and so far, so good.

All evening, I shared details with Harvey, wanting desperately to convey the miraculous transformation I had experienced during the ten days of training. He listened closely, nodding as if he understood before he began to catch me up on temple news and visits with mutual friends. Before bed, we both went down to check on the kids and show Chancer his new bathroom. Fortunately, we had a door on the bottom floor outside Iyal's room that opened directly to the downstairs deck, with steps leading into an enclosed pen. Years before, it had held toddler play equipment that transformed into imaginary castles and dungeons (the promised land where Zipporah and Moses often lived, respectively), and now it was the perfect place for the purpose of doggy doo-doo elimination.

I have to mention that within Chancer's five hundred hours of service-dog training, he learned to "hold it" until someone asks, "Chancer, do you need to potty?" Seriously, he was more like a camel than a dog. No matter how much he drank, he just never had to go! In fact, the entire time that Chancer has been with us, we've never had to worry about getting back to the house to allow him to relieve himself. This part of his anatomy was truly a gift, one of those things we came to appreciate as an extra benefit of having Chancer as our dog.

That first night, Chancer did his business and returned right away as he had been trained to do before making a beeline back up to the living room to explore. By the time Harvey and I climbed the two short sets of stairs, Chancer was prancing all around the living room with what looked like a big grin on his face. The grin was filled with something he'd just discovered on our coffee table.

"Shit!" Harvey yelled. "Get the remote out of his mouth!"

"Oh my God, why's he doing that?"

While I scrambled to grab the remote from Chancer's jaws, he loved this game of keep-away with his new humans and began to prance faster and higher than Rudolf Nureyev. Later we would label this his "happy dance," but we weren't so happy at this particular moment, especially when he won our tug-of-war and charged into the kitchen to celebrate with a loud *crunch*.

"Oh no!" I gasped. "I can't believe he just did that! He's not supposed to put things in his mouth!" Cringing, I pulled out pieces of black plastic and oval buttons with numbers and a tangle of small wires from his mouth and peered at the drool-covered mess in my hand.

"Oh, great . . . ," moaned Harvey. "Just what we need! Now we'll have to get a new remote. I thought service dogs didn't do things like that!"

"He's never put anything in his mouth that didn't belong there before. I swear. So far, he's been an angel." Our first night home and already Harvey was pissed. Big-time.

"I sure hope he doesn't do that again." His threat was implied but icicle clear. "Or else" were the words hovering overhead, threatening to trigger my next panic attack.

Harvey stormed out of the living room and into the bedroom, grumbling to himself, "I just knew it . . . I just knew this was going to be a train wreck." He didn't say he was going to bed or offer me a "good night" or anything. Chancer's first offense and it didn't seem like the punishment fit the crime. But I knew better. Harvey could be very irrational whenever something ignited his anger.

I threw away the remote pieces and walked Chancer downstairs to Iyal's room. Iyal had been getting into his pajamas by himself, and I told him, "Look, honey, you got into your jammies by yourself! That's great, and don't forget to brush your teeth, sweetheart."

"I won't. Mom, can Chancer sleep in my bed with me?" Iyal gazed at his new best friend.

"Oh, I'm sorry . . . honey. Remember what Jeremy said? Chancer needs to sleep in his brand-new crate." And a gargantuan crate it was, a canine castle in which Iyal and Chancer would have sleepovers for years to come. Per our contract with 4 Paws, we agreed, for one year, the dog must sleep overnight in the crate as well as be crated whenever we were out of the house. It was a one-year insurance policy to cement the crate training, and it offered the additional respite the service dog might need after a hard day with his child.

I let Iyal hug Chancer good night, and then I kissed Iyal and tucked him in. When I opened the crate door, Chancer walked into his new spot without prompting, circling a few times before coming in for a landing with a little cartoon-sounding harrumph.

Within seconds of kneeling in front of Chancer, I began sobbing, keeping my back to Iyal so he wouldn't hear me. I couldn't believe how shitty this first night ended. Everything I didn't want to happen seemed to cut right into me, picking my bloom of hope right off the vine, so I just sat in front of the crate crying, feeling dismissed and wounded.

"I love you, Chancer," I whispered. "You are here for good, I promise." Funny that I often spoke these same words to Iyal from time to time, depending on how insecure he might be feeling if his attachment disorganization was front and center.

I didn't want to leave Chancer. *I* wanted to sleep with him inside his crate, wrapping myself up in his warmth, paws around me, and breathing with him in the mystical synchronicity of species to species. But I wiped my eyes and dragged myself upstairs, emptied from the car ride, the ten days of intense training, and the emotional letdown upon arriving "home sweet home."

But I didn't sleep for most of the night.

I felt bereft. For me, nothing had changed.

The next morning, when I came down, Iyal had already let Chancer out of his kennel and was running around the house like a whirling dervish, repeatedly asking who would feed his dog. I didn't know how long they had been up, but I took Iyal by the hand and walked him as slowly as possible to the downstairs kitchenette outside his bedroom, which would also serve as "Chancer's Café."

Sensing something jubilant was about to occur, Chancer trotted several paws ahead of us. Aware of the 4 Paws service-dog product preferences prior to our leaving for Ohio, we had stocked an award-winning inventory of dog food, training treats, toys, chews, and Nylabones. Preparing for Chancer's arrival had reminded me of the anticipatory exhilaration I felt back when buying clothes and nursery-room decor personalized for the babies. I'm sure Chancer's bounty appeared equally excessive to others, but it gave me that special joy a mother feels waiting for her new family member. Before we fed him, though, I told Iyal we had to let him out to potty. When Chancer was finished with his business, they both came back inside, with the dog's nose clearly leading him to breakfast. Which lasted all of two minutes as he, like his ancestors before him, wolfed down his kibble, turning his big head side to side to capture every morsel before slurping from his water bowl. Iyal seemed fascinated by his new best friend's breakfast habits.

From upstairs, I heard Harvey asking if anyone had seen his cell phone, an exasperated refrain at least one of us called out, not unlike "Did you see my keys?" on a daily basis. Morasha shouted from her room, "I don't know, Dad. Haven't seen it."

Heading upstairs, I called out, "When did you last use it?"

Harvey started to answer, "I think I left it on the—" Then a torturous absence of sound.

No. It wasn't possible. I tried to breathe through my skin as the horror of silence ripped wide open.

"Damn it! He *ate* my cell phone!" roared Harvey. "Now what do I do? That's no service dog. A service dog wouldn't eat a cell phone! I can't believe this!"

"Are you sure?" I asked, entering the room in measured steps.

"Am I sure he ate the cell phone, or am I sure he's not a service dog?" He didn't wait for my response as he grabbed his briefcase, *New York Times*, and keys and rushed out the door and off to work. I was still holding my breath.

Everything was going wrong. In less than twenty-four hours since we'd been home, I knew the chaos created by Chancer didn't bode well. I followed Harvey into the garage, hoping for a divine intervention. Then from the car, he yelled, "You better call your trainer guy and figure out what to do. This is totally unacceptable."

The car door slammed. Another implicit threat.

Somehow, in a trance, I helped the kids get ready for school and snapped the leash on Chancer, and the four of us walked to the corner of the subdivision to wait for the bus. Chancer tilted his nose and sniffed, the scent of rain in the air. Or maybe he sensed the torrent waiting to pour from behind my eyes. I began shaking, holding back my rage and my sadness that I was determined not to reveal to my children. The bus finally arrived, the kids boarded, and I waved good-bye, attempting a cheery but frantic smile.

I stood there with Chancer at the intersection, feeling so disoriented, as if dropped into a bad dream already in progress. How could this be happening? From when I'd first discovered that a service dog might help Iyal until that moment, three excruciating long years had gone by. And now, the unthinkable: *What if Harvey was right?*

I didn't mind being wrong as much as I hated feeling my hope evaporate from solid form to a mist of bewilderment. On autopilot, I started walking the mile toward the Starbucks near our neighborhood. Once there, I sat in one of the metal café chairs out front and frantically scrolled through my phone contacts. By the time I found Jeremy's number at 4 Paws, I was crying hysterically. We had been given carte blanche to call him 24/7 if we were having any problems with the dogs. Miraculously, he answered right away. Thank God.

"Jeremy . . ." I sniffed, composing myself. "This is Donnie Winokur, from Atlanta. We have, you know, I . . . Iyal . . . Chancer, um Chancer . . ."

"Okay, Donnie, take a deep breath," he said soothingly. "Tell me what's going on."

Just hearing his voice began to calm me. "Oh, Jeremy . . . we haven't even been back twenty-four hours and Chancer chewed up our remote *and* my husband's cell phone . . . and, and . . ." Then my tears began streaming again.

"Donnie, it'll be okay. Remember, Chancer just turned two—he's still a puppy. Even though he's an amazing service dog, he's still a dog. And goldens tend to be mouthy—you know, like a toddler. Everything winds up in their mouth. He's exploring his world."

"Yeah, but—"

Jeremy continued, "I promise you this won't last long."

"Neither will my marriage!" I blurted out, immediately embarrassed by my impulsive candor.

We paused a beat, and Chancer looked up at me as if aware this was all about him.

"Oh. That bad, huh?"

I swallowed a crying hiccup and said, "Yes."

"Listen, Donnie, I'll call you back this afternoon with some ideas on how we can help Chancer make better choices about what he puts in his mouth—and what you guys can do to manage and protect your environment. It will be all right. I promise. There is a learning curve for everyone."

Walking away from Starbucks with Chancer, already embarrassed by the way my Trevi Fountain of tears had transformed my face into a gargoyle's, I plopped down onto a grassy area to collapse and regroup. Chancer lay down next to me with a paw over my lap, his version of holding my hand. I was beginning to wonder if I needed Chancer to be my service dog more than Iyal did.

Shelving my fear and grief as best I could, I went through the motions and began checking off items on that day's obsessed-over to-do list. I pondered how exactly I expected Chancer to help Iyal, and therefore help the rest of our family. Was this just more magical thinking on my part, as if Chancer would just take care of us all like Nana in *Peter Pan* or Lassie pulling Timmy out of the well? I know, everyone thinks this actually happened in the TV series, but I think we all made it up as we *needed* to believe that dogs could be the reliable rescuer, the safety superhero. I know I did. As Jeremy had reminded me on the phone, no matter how amazing Chancer might be, at the end of the day, he was still just a dog.

After lunch, while Chancer enjoyed an hour of crate time, I ran to the grocery store before the kids got home. Like most moms, I had learned over the years that shopping goes twice as fast, and often costs half as much, when done alone. Besides, I knew too well how easily a visit to Kroger with Iyal could turn into an incident of global proportions.

In fact, the memory of our last visit seemed fresher than the produce section where I now stood. We had just completed day five of our training at 4 Paws. My dad was driving us back to the hotel while I collapsed in the front passenger seat, euphoric but utterly drained from a long, fascinating day of full engagement in Chancer's world. My cousin Adair, Morasha, Iyal, and Chancer squeezed together in their designated seats behind me.

Knowing we needed a few items from the grocery store but unable to imagine summoning the energy, I pointed out a Kroger to my dad and asked Adair, "If I bribe you with a Starbucks, would you mind going in to get a few things? My list is short, but I feel so wiped out."

Before the last word was out of my mouth, Iyal piped in, "I wanna go with Adair! Please, Mom, please—let me go with her! Let me go, okay, Mom? Please!" His voice grew louder and more insistent with each repetition.

Barely able to put two thoughts together, I turned to look at Adair and asked if she was okay with it. "Of course," she said, and even as I saw her loving commitment to us on display, a voice cut through the fog in my weary brain. "You have no idea what could happen," it said. "Iyal can ignite over anything—*anything*—and explode with more collateral damage than you can imagine."

Thanking Adair, I added a safeguard and said, "Morasha, honey, would you please go in with Adair just in case she needs some help with Iyal?" With Starbucks promised for all, the three of them jumped out of the van. Chancer stayed with my dad and me. Because Adair didn't know all the specifics of handling Chancer in a public environment, I didn't want to overwhelm her. After only a couple of preliminary outings, I still wasn't comfortable with handling Chancer along with Iyal just yet.

Dad and I talked a bit about the day, but he could tell how tired I was and encouraged me to stretch out and close my eyes for a few minutes. With fading sunlight washing over me, I drifted away. Soon my weary mind had dropped me into a dream, probably of what my last trip to Kroger with Iyal had been like.

There I was, in the produce section, trying to corral Iyal, keenly aware of the avalanche of oranges, apples, and bananas that could careen down on top of us at any minute. He was in a meltdown of epic proportions—I'd say about a nine on the FASD seismograph.

Other shoppers scurried by us quickly, some with downcast eyes to avoid witnessing the horrific tornado unleashed inside a pint-sized boy while others stared with curiosity or curt judgment. Replacing the heads of lettuce Iyal tossed at me must have looked like a basketball drill. After we turned the corner to canned goods, I juggled cans of beans like a cartoon character, restocking shelves as fast as my son cleaned them out.

Twenty exhausting minutes later, I gently maneuvered the tornado through a checkout lane to the store exit. Lest I feel too successful, Iyal jerked his hand out of mine and raced into the busy parking lot, throwing himself down on the pavement in a convulsive tantrum of tears. Cars entering and exiting the busy lot screeched to a halt, drivers' faces gawking as Iyal screamed to no one in particular for an ice cream cone, you know, the one he saw *thirty* minutes ago in the freezer section! Funny how his short-term memory works so selectively at times.

"Mom, Mom!" Morasha was suddenly shouting.

My dream was about to become a real nightmare. Opening my eyes, I saw my daughter careening through the parking lot, weaving in and out of the cars and shopping carts, hysterically calling me. I opened the van door and jumped out.

"Honey, are you okay? What's wrong?"

Breathlessly, she sputtered, "Mom! Adair needs your help. Iyal is screaming and running around inside the store. Come quick!" And she took off again, desperate for me to follow.

I gave Dad an "oh shit" glance and chased after Morasha into the store.

I found Adair with Iyal in the center of a growing circle of concerned and confused bystanders next to the Starbucks in the front section of Kroger. Adair was beside herself. "Oh, Don, I'm so sorry. I didn't know what to do. He won't listen to me, and I had to chase him up and down the aisles until he collapsed here. I'm so sorry!"

This was a big deal for Adair. My cousin is an earth mother: calm, soft-spoken, and intelligent. She loves animals and adores my family.

Adair and her husband, Bruce, are some of my favorite people. Ever. Adair isn't easily rattled and has a deep vested interest in my children's well-being, which is why I asked her to join us for the training class.

While 4 Paws requires a minimum of two adults to accompany the child for whom the dog is trained, I brought in backup, sensing that two adults wouldn't be enough to wrangle Iyal during a ten-day break from his normal structured routine. Looking back, this impasse in Kroger would have been a point of surrender for the entire Russian Army.

I hastily excused myself, pushing through the thickening crowd to find Iyal spinning around on the floor. If this had been an episode of *So You Think You Can Dance*, then his performance would have won hands down. Instead, he was writhing, slithering, and yowling as though someone were exorcising a demon from his tortured soul. This was a big one.

A few people yelled out, hands waving like in a contest, "Is there anything I can do? Do you need help?"

I attempted to speak loudly but nicely, "No, but thank you!"

We were in deep doo-doo here. During such neural storms in Iyal's brain, reaching him is nearly impossible because his hearing shuts down, the first sense to unplug during a flight-or-fight response, which is why if a person falls overboard from a boat and you shout, "Swim! Swim to the float!" you might as well be delivering the Gettysburg Address to kindergartners. In a real crisis, people can't hear you. Their brain has turned off audio, singularly focused on either fighting or fleeing.

Despite the fact that I knew shouting at Iyal was pointless, I still did it as an instinctive reaction to my own helplessness and need to control. So then I moved on to a more effective response. Carefully getting down on my hands and knees, I began crawling around with Iyal, pretending to be his dance partner and soothingly talking to him. As his flailing continued, I can't even understand what he is saying between gasps of constant tears.

Once again, I had no idea what was happening inside my little boy.

Well, that's not exactly true. I understood the objective, scientific explanation: organic brain damage as a result of the fetal alcohol exposure and the impact it has on his ability to regulate his arousal system and emotions. But this didn't help either of us as I tried to calm him until the chemical storm subsided, desperately trying to come up with my strategy of rescue.

"Honey. Iyal. It's okay. What do you need? How can I help you?" I don't know how Iyal could even identify his needs drenched in this hurricane of anguish, an unrealistic expectation on my part.

His torrent of tears slowed to a trickle as he scanned the disseminating crowd around him, sobbing, "Why is everyone looking at me? Why are they making fun of me?"

I quietly said, "They're worried about you. People worry when they see children upset. They want to help."

"No, they don't!" shrieked Iyal. "They see my broken brain and are laughing at me."

My stomach contracted as though the wind had been kicked out of me. Suddenly, I was on the verge of tears and had to try with all my might to contain my own emotions. "Oh, sweetheart, that just isn't true! No one is laughing at you."

It was all I could do *not* to reach out to Iyal. To embrace him. Stroke his cheek. Kiss away his tears. I knew I couldn't, though, because doing so might only set off another outburst. My maternal heart felt as though it were under water, drowning in the sorrow I had to keep swallowing.

I waited as Iyal gradually calmed down. *This* storm had passed. Slowly, the people around us began to recede into the aisles like an exhausted tide no longer trying to reach shore.

Remembering that meltdown in Kroger left me feeling foolish—foolish for hoping that Chancer or any service dog could do what a mother couldn't, foolish for believing that this solution really could make a difference for my son's quality of life. Nonetheless, I had to try and keep some spark of hope alive. Something in me refused to give up entirely. Maybe my usual optimism colored my expectations, but that didn't mean miracles couldn't happen.

—

When Harvey later asked about my call to Jeremy, I tried to make Chancer's "accidents" sound like natural, one-time occurrences. "He's just excited and getting used to new surroundings," I explained.

"Right," Harvey said, clearly unconvinced.

But seeing Iyal interact with Chancer definitely fanned my feeble spark of hope. Some moments I would temporarily forget everything I knew about FASDs as I relished the joy that came from watching a little boy romp with a big dog. "Come on, Chancer!" Iyal would shout as the two bounded up and down the stairs in a larger-than-life game of chase.

—

We then experienced a turning point in which my spark became an actual flame. The second week we were home from our training, I had invited over dear new friends with their service dog. An Atlanta family had received a service dog a year before we were due to get Chancer. Karen Shirk, the 4 Paws director, had given me their name. The mom was a doll—spiritual, enthusiastic, funny, and bright. She came over with her freckle-faced six-year-old daughter and eight-year-old son, who was small, curious, and intelligent and who experienced Asperger's syndrome. He had been placed with a 4 Paws autism-assistance dog.

Jen had become my mentor as we tried to wait patiently over the ten months after being placed in our training class for the end of January 2008. We would take our kids to local playgrounds, and she would show me commands that had been developed by 4 Paws to help Ajax, their service dog, assist Matthew. I had a gazillion questions, and Jen had a gazillion answers. Bless her heart, she never tired of me squeezing out information from her that helped me through another day of waiting for our service dog.

Ajax, a boxer–Great Pyrenees mix, was enormous, built like a machine, and playful. His fur wasn't fluffy and long but was more like that of a boxer, short and trim. And although Ajax wasn't white like the Pyrenees, he sure had the "Great," as he was exceptionally tall! He was *so* tall, in fact, that Chancer could walk right underneath him, which we thought was hysterical! And in time, our own cats would amble or zoom underneath a standing Chancer like he was the Brooklyn Bridge.

During their visit this particular day, we heard rumblings—the kind that precede full meltdowns—coming from Iyal, down two levels in our den. As his distress signals became louder, I looked over at the two service dogs in a heap together lounging on the floor. Suddenly, Chancer stood up, fully alerted, his ears lifted along with his back and tail. For a moment, he stood like a beautiful golden statue, with only his nose twitching almost imperceptibly, getting ready for action.

Then it happened.

Iyal erupted into a total meltdown, sobbing and muttering unintelligible words, but clearly the result of some internal or external incident he was experiencing. I stood up and looked over the balcony down the two flights and saw Iyal sitting with his legs straight out in front of him, arms crossed fiercely and deliberately over his chest. He hollered through his tears, "Mommy, I need Chancer! I need him to nuzzle me. Where is he?"

"Nuzzle" was a response command Chancer had learned at 4 Paws specifically for such situations with Iyal. Proving to be the most important way in which Chancer would help Iyal, nuzzling combined this robust but intimate technique of calming and de-escalating the limbic rages that plagued Iyal.

Before I could respond, Chancer was there with Iyal. I stood watching in awe as Chancer, having descended the two short flights of stairs, was already burying his long snout between Iyal's crossed arms and gently but firmly pushing them apart. He was already licking and kissing Iyal's face by the time I sprinted to the landing where the two of them were intertwined in an interspecies living sculpture.

For the first time ever, Iyal had asked for his "medicine," and it had arrived in an instant. And it had worked!

I stepped back quietly and watched as Chancer licked Iyal's tears and Iyal began to giggle. "Mom! Look at Chancer! He did what he was supposed to do!" Iyal had his arms around Chancer now.

"I know, honey." I sniffed back a few tears. "Isn't he wonderful?"

Chancer and Iyal were now lying together on the floor and looked inseparable. I peered up to the foyer between the den and the living room and caught Jen's expression. Tears were flowing down her face as her thumbs were going up.

I only wished Harvey had been there to witness our minor miracle, which in my mind was evidence of how Chancer could drastically alter our family for the better. But I deeply feared that Harvey wasn't even willing to give Chancer a second chance, especially after the remote and cell phone. He seemed resigned to the fact that the best we could do was simply manage Iyal's FASD-related challenges, not actually remediate or improve them. I wondered if Harvey was still stuck in our quicksand, unable to realize that we didn't necessarily have to drown. I think so many years of feeling flung against a wall that never seemed to budge had worn down any resilience Harvey may have had.

Ever since we had returned—or ever since Chancer's "mouthy" first impression—Harvey had once again seemed distracted, immersed so deeply in work and the many demands placed on him. I couldn't decipher if he had returned to his all-consuming schedule because he hadn't yet seen anything brilliant that Chancer could do or if believing in a positive change for Iyal and not having it materialize was just too painful to bear again. I wanted to believe the latter. I felt Harvey's distance increase further, which made me rant and wail inside. Something had changed. I couldn't put my finger on it, but it didn't feel good.

He seemed to maneuver himself around me and the kids and Chancer so he wouldn't have to engage with us. *God!* I was hoping that horrible feeling was going to *change* after we came back from Ohio. I just couldn't conceive that he and I would continue this out-of-step waltz one more day. I didn't know anything else I could do to bring him back into my arms or my heart.

I was out of ideas.

We both knew parenthood would never be easy. And it was clear at an early age that attachment disorganization would fracture the frame of Iyal's ability to feel intimacy with his family and others. Ironically, however, our son's need for connection and engagement with us would only intensify as he grew older.

Iyal's often-suffocating neediness and our inability to be a team with a shared strategic plan often became the elephant in our family room.

Whenever I considered Iyal's needs and neediness within this framework, I always remembered how much I love elephants. Maybe I'd watched too many shows on Animal Planet or thumbed through too many *National Geographic* articles in doctors' waiting rooms. But I'd learned a few things about elephants that endeared them to me.

Baby elephants, calves as they're called, are born blind with little to no survival instincts. They must rely on their mothers and other older family members to teach them how to behave within the herd. Baby elephants stay extremely close to their mothers with bonding as the priority over exploring or self-sufficiency. They drink their mothers' milk for about four years, sometimes longer. Often traveling in single file while holding their mothers' tails in their trunks like some kind of external umbilical cord, calves remain dependent on their mothers for at least ten years.

The innate structure of the elephant hierarchy establishes the autonomy and ability of a calf to mature within the safety of its family, herd, and then the larger group. A mother elephant will lay down her life for her baby. Mother elephants have been observed grieving over stillborn calves, and some elephants have even been spotted returning to, and lingering near, areas where their family and pack members died.

While mourning the death of their relatives, they may place grass, dirt, or branches over the body. They stay with the body for several days. I compare it to sitting shivah—the Jewish ritual of being with the family of a loved one who has passed, by visiting with them, sharing memories, telling stories, eating (of course), and offering prayer to help honor the loss and mourn the deceased within a healing community.

Perhaps what I find most poignant in the elephant world is that an elephant with an injury, a disability, will never be left alone. Others in the herd may nurse an elephant back to health or wait together as in a vigil until its death. They create sort of a unique pachyderm hospice. They won't abandon their own, and there are touching accounts of elephants exhibiting these behaviors with other species as well.

So considering Iyal's FASD challenges as the elephant in the room always proved more than a cliché, because *these* elephant images rumbled past the backdrop of our world, reminding me of the significance of developing the mutual attachment among our family members.

Unfortunately, another more figurative kind of elephant was never far from our marriage either. It would creep into the room silently when Harvey and I weren't well connected, unable to help each other when one or both of us were stressed beyond belief. Occasionally, we would lose the ability to hold ourselves together, or hold the other one up, when the gravity of our life threatened to pull us down and under. Although invisible, these elephants left enormous footprints that would become the cavernous pits we would fall into and climb out of year after year.

Whenever Iyal's disability brought Harvey and me to our knees and we had nothing left to offer him or each other, we would spew out accusatory, angry, irrational, and hurtful words at each other. Because I felt as though I could never do enough for Iyal, I expected Harvey to feel the same way. I also believed I was never doing enough for Morasha.

When I wanted Harvey to try harder to understand Iyal, exhibit greater patience, see past Iyal's behavior, and recognize his injured brain as the culprit, I would only feel disappointed and want him to be a different husband. At times my compassion for Iyal upstaged my compassion for Harvey. I felt torn, unable to evenly share my heart between the two. Frustrated, I would then soliloquize about how Harvey should change. Be better. Step in deeper. Expand his capacity for Iyal's ever-intrusive and enveloping needs. I knew my expectations were unrealistic of *any* husband, but it didn't change the fact that I was requiring so much more from Harvey to refill my own empty well.

These vulnerable times left the wounds wide open for the elephant to pad in and settle under the carpet. Then we would navigate an unspoken, unacknowledged path around the hump, believing that if we didn't talk about it, it wasn't really there. Often addressing our own insecurities while attending to Iyal's and Morasha's was just too much, so we swept our problems under a flying carpet. Magical thinking that I had mastered as a little girl came back in force, delivering me into a pretend world I created where I could feel in control of others or me.

The dreaded wrath of the "if onlys" took over. Many marriages probably develop this fairly common internal language when a disconnect occurs between spouses and one always thinks the *other* is the one who needs to change. But here is what my skipping CD sounds like:

If only I said something to Harvey in a way that wouldn't make him defensive, he'd change.

If only I used the word *we* instead of *you* in discussing how to help out Iyal by giving him a mere seven seconds more to process what we have said, Iyal might understand something.

If only Harvey knew how often he upset Iyal by barking orders at him, Harvey somehow thinking that this militaristic method would jump-start Iyal's uncooperative brain into compliance.

If only Harvey, when his patience hadn't yet arrived, hadn't remarked to Iyal that he probably wouldn't *ever* change if his dad had to remind him to brush his teeth for the eight hundredth time, which begs the question, if one is asking someone to change *anything* eight hundred times and he *can't*—not he *won't*—then who is the one who needs to change?

If only Harvey didn't repeat himself over and over when he talked to Iyal, which wasn't unlike Iyal talking to us, except that we wanted to think we knew better.

None of this ever felt good. Thinking it and not saying it. Saying it and then wanting to take it back. Never knowing if after a ceasefire we would land in the same country.

I allowed my fantasies of a different kind of marriage to keep me together when I didn't believe that the one I was in would survive. This ongoing sense of uneasiness left me feeling disoriented, outside myself, separate from living in the moment. I remained hypervigilant looking for the splintering cracks in our foundation or preparing to psychologically duck when a loose cannon destroyed a marital promise gone AWOL.

Invisible elephants paraded in and out of our marriage, sometimes offering me nurturance and hope and other times reminding me how fragile a relationship can be when under the crushing weight of a shared burden.

Healing our wounds was a slow process. I wasn't sure that when or if Harvey realized how much hurt had rendered me silent, he would even connect his part in this painfully raw time in our marriage, our family. When I felt unsure where he and I were in our relationship, I'd take a few steps out to test the water, but sometimes ran back to shore before even the tiniest waves would reach my toes. I felt so achingly fragile that I feared that my broken heart might not ever feel whole again. I think he felt the same way, too.

Somehow, a little bit at a time, Harvey came back to me, to us. The entire first year after Chancer came to live with us, I was afraid to believe that we were okay. As soon as I let myself feel confident and let my breath out a little, a backslide would occur. "Donnie!" Harvey would holler from downstairs. "I thought we agreed that Chancer was *not* going to go with Iyal to the doctor if it wasn't a long appointment! Didn't we agree to that?" I was never clear about what constituted a "long" appointment. Christ. I'm not even going to go there.

I thought deep down that Harvey was trying hard to "undo" some of the damage that had occurred. When Harvey felt unguarded and gave in to the great joy that Chancer had brought Iyal, Harvey became a different father. A different husband. And a different son-in-law. Though nothing was ever said between Harvey and my dad during these difficult years, I know they both felt the absence of something important. They missed each other. And now, all the scattered pieces of our life started to come back together, and the new picture was even more magnificent than the previous one.

I remembered again why I first fell in love with Harvey. That barometer of our marriage had fallen off the crumbling wall several years ago, and I had stopped looking for it. Now, his laughter reinvigorated me. Harvey's recognition that Chancer might be a gift greater than any of us could have imagined made me giddy and light. I began to trust Harvey again.

Chancer's magic was working on all of us.

Chapter Seven

"I'm sorry, ma'am, but you'll have to put your dog under the seat in front of you." The flight attendant glared down at me, making it clear she wasn't joking. I looked down at the golden carpet, a.k.a. Chancer, outstretched across my feet. Already wedged into a middle seat in coach, I suddenly felt claustrophobic, trapped in a new kind of disaster movie—*Secret Service Dog at Thirty-Two Thousand Feet*—as I processed her ridiculous command.

"*What?* You can't be serious—he's not a purse! He's a service dog. A *ninety-pound* service dog. I don't think he'll be able to fit under that seat any time soon." I started to meditate to keep myself from flying off without the plane, wishing I could be half as calm as Chancer, who raised those expressive eyebrows of his, one at a time, looking up to see what had my cortisol level skyrocketing.

"We have policies we have to follow, ma'am." She dramatically pushed a blond strand of hair behind her ear and crossed her arms. And the dull, glazed look in her eyes and fixed expression on her face told me I wouldn't be having a rational conversation with this Stepford stewardess.

"May I please see your supervisor?" I said.

She nodded, rolled her eyes, and turned sharply into the passenger waiting to board behind her. I muffled a laugh, shook my head, and muttered "Jesus Christ!" under my breath. Thinking to myself, I ran through all the possible scenarios of flying with service dogs we had discussed during our training at 4 Paws. I couldn't remember that this particularly insane situation had ever come up. It was just way too fucking weird! Part of me wondered what little gem of aviation wisdom would come trippingly off the edge of her tongue the next time she opened up her carefully-applied-gloss-covered mouth. I was actually waiting to see if her lips themselves would just slide off her face. I had better sit out of the way just in case.

Looking down the aisle, I saw Miss Stepford's supervisor headed my way, looking like *she* had just escaped from Madame Tussauds wax museum of aviation history. I may be petty, but in my humble opinion, she was well on her way to a pink Cadillac from Mary Kay. Her face grew taut with authority (or maybe just Botox), and her eyes locked with mine as if spotting a covert terrorist. She forced her way past embarking passengers and stopped at my row, her stance suggesting some foreign object might be stuck in her orifice.

And to think I was worried about how Chancer would behave on the flight.

We had been taught all about bringing the dogs on airplanes, and I was confident that I would have no problems. I had called the airline, which in this instance shall remain nameless to protect the innocent, ahead of time as instructed, informing them I would be traveling with a service dog and confirming a seat in the bulkhead area. The airline didn't charge additional airfare for service dogs, but of course they don't get to sit on a seat. Fair enough, I thought. At 4 Paws, we had practiced walking our dogs through rows of chairs lined up close together with their backs about three feet apart, to simulate walking through an airplane aisle. And despite the reason Chancer was making this trip back to the big house, he instinctively knew when it was time for a "down" or "under."

He was a champ going through airport security. I was somewhat anxious, which was nothing new, as I had built up a reservoir of flying phobias over the years that became a catchall for many of my neuroses. Fear of flying was common and didn't make people speculate about all the other craziness that lived in my head. But I knew I had to rise above this particular fixation to be there for Chancer. Just as I did when I flew with my kids.

I removed his collar containing metal and his leash before I could send him through the security machine. I wasn't allowed to walk with him. Anxiety alert. He had to go before or after me. This part was tricky. I opted for sending him first. As soon as he walked through, I told him "sit," which he did as I rushed through to him. Seeing me move so quickly, his eyes lit up in hopes of a game of chase. I gave him a stern look in return.

When I'd called to make arrangements with the airline, I'd decided we would be the last ones on and the first ones off to lessen the possibility of a traffic jam on the plane as people would then want to stop and look at or pet Chancer. My plan made sense to me and was also an issue of safety for all. I kept envisioning this scene of calm, smooth obedience on Chancer's part, but that vision assumed the people we encountered would be just as well behaved.

Without fanfare, Chancer and I had walked onto the plane single file, me first, the flight mostly full. When I asked about the bulkhead seat I'd been promised and assigned when booking my ticket, I was informed that this model of plane didn't have the same number of bulkhead seats so I'd been automatically reassigned. *Fuck. Okay, it'll be fine,* I thought.

So I reluctantly led Chancer through the aisle to row 22B, where two elderly people occupied the window and aisle seats; they didn't appear to be traveling together. I tried to focus on how this was going to work while keeping a lid on the brain chemicals simmering to a full-boil panic typhoon. Both seniors seemed hard of hearing and unsure of what exactly was happening. They looked at us as if we were part of the in-flight entertainment. They didn't visually or verbally react to seeing a miniature, furry, pony-like creature standing in the aisle. Maybe it was their failing eyesight.

Chancer and I attempted to squeeze in between them, which is when it went from kinda funny to unbelievably crazy. I knew I was doing it just to prove the sheer impossibility of such a feat, which had led to my lovely flight attendant telling me to *put my dog under the seat in front of me*! I tried to hold it together, just a little longer, as the flight attendant's supervisor, in all her shiny and waxy glory, stood above me. Our exchange went something like this:

"Can I help you?" Madame Tussaud asked.

Oh, come on! Was she really as stupid as the other one? Tragically, I believed she was. Did she think I just wanted extra pretzels or the faux-sophisticated Biscoff cookies?

"Yes, please—here's the situation," I said. I explained and remained as calm as possible and politely requested her assistance, despite the chemicals combusting in my brain.

"Wait here. I'll see what I can do," she said. I nodded and, by this time, did indeed feel like the in-flight entertainment. Would I be up for an Emmy? I realized I was smiling and nodding at the other nearby passengers, most of them eager to see what would happen next, when our waxed dummy returned.

"We have two seats available in first class . . ."—I started a rabbinic-wife's silent prayer of thanks and felt my hand unclench the death grip on Chancer's leash—". . . so if you two kind folks will come with me, I'll get you reseated up in first class. I think you'll both be much more comfortable up there."

Stunned, I realized that she was addressing the two seniors! She was moving them to friggin' first class, not me and the ninety-pound service dog? *Breathe, just breathe,* I said to my inner Yoda . . . *It's going to be fine.*

"Uh . . . I'm sorry, but is there any chance my service dog and I could move to the first-class section?" I asked.

"*Oh* no—that wouldn't work with our policy. Your seat is here in 22B. Here, sir—let me help you with your belongings."

At that point, I began looking around for the cameras—this had to be an episode of *Punk'd* or *Saturday Night Live* or—or maybe both. So while Chancer panted, patiently standing in the aisle, I tried to organize the one carry-on I had and put it above me in the bin. I contorted my body as if in a Cirque du Soleil performance, pulling a hamstring as I twisted around and over the seat. Of course. There's no room left. The Stepford stewardess is nowhere in sight—probably serving piña coladas to Grandma and Grandpa up in first class.

I looked around but couldn't find any open bins. Where were the Good Samaritans willing to offer their kind assistance to the woman with the service dog? At last, a nice young man noticed us, grabbed my backpack, and placed it several bins down from us. He smiled broadly at Chancer and me, and I offered to have his firstborn child in return for his kindness.

The decision to be on that flight wasn't an easy one. As we neared the end of our first year with Chancer, he clearly needed some do-over training. It wasn't just the remote, Harvey's cell phone, and the three pairs of Iyal's prescription glasses. Several variables were at play here, but the biggest setback was how Iyal had untrained Chancer—not deliberately of course—but mostly due to Iyal's impulsivity and inability to remember anything that happened before his "now." The past, present, and future were a moving target in my child's brain. I don't think Iyal even knew where he would land at the end of a thought, the end of a sentence, let alone the following day, week, or month, which made it hard for him to understand the need to be consistent in our commands and interactions with Chancer.

We had learned service dogs are motivated to follow a command by being rewarded with food, toys, praise, or any combination of those. Service dogs are specifically trained to resist people food, unless they have a specific reason to come in contact with it—for example, bringing certain foods to their human who is challenged with some kind of immobility. On the other hand, goldens are known for nonstop eating and tend to dance through life like a toddler devouring cupcakes.

At the time we acquired Chancer, 4 Paws had working relationships with three correctional facilities that had developed high-level dog-obedience-training programs. Inmates at Lakin Correctional Center in West Virginia trained Chancer in basic obedience. Along with two human roommates and one other dog in training, Chancer learned a solid foundation of everyday commands. All 4 Paws dogs went through prison. Well respected for its innovative impact on both inmates and canines, many service-dog agencies are incorporating correctional facilities into their training program. Those inmates who excelled in the program advanced to training service dogs for special skills. I have watched videos of inmates being interviewed, and as they emote their devotion to the dogs that they're training and express the importance of this relationship in their life, I honor their work with tears.

While in prison, green tennis balls definitely became Chancer's choice of motivation. So during training, I had more tennis balls in my pockets than Serena Williams at Wimbledon. And they worked, ideal for "luring" or "targeting"—having Chancer follow me to a specific spot or to set up a specific task. We used them successfully this way while training Chancer to tether with Iyal. I must admit that early on when Chancer lived with us, I watched him eye the slit tennis balls that were used under walking devices. One time when my dad was in the hospital, Chancer ambled over to the walker standing in the corner of the room, stared for a minute, and actually barked, willing the tennis balls to zoom out from under this contraption and play with him.

After we initially brought him home, we quickly figured out that food was Chancer's ultimate motivator, which convinced me he must be Jewish and would fit right in with our family. However, because he had been trained to ignore people food while walking through supermarkets and restaurants, if he paid even the slightest attention to a crumb on the floor, a quick reminder of "leave it!" refocused his attention.

Unbeknownst to us at first, Iyal was offering human goodies to Chancer, which was a *big* no-no. Even now, seven years later, we still can't break the habit of Iyal gifting Chancer with food. Their system runs like an inside job at a bank heist. Chancer will go under our kitchen table with his tail sticking out, but his head rests on Iyal's lap, awaiting manna from heaven. Chancer will go into a "down" as he should, but he is so tall that he can rest his head on Iyal's lap to catch the tasty pieces "falling" from Iyal's fingertips.

Iyal has always been transparent, and it's a good thing he can't lie. Well, if he does, he will tell me he did and why within hours of the suspected incident. We always know the truth, eventually, about Iyal's day-to-day life; his ability to consistently repeat himself over and over is another clue. Once he was caught, Iyal would say, "But, Mom, look at Chancer's face, his eyes—he wants some food. I have to give him some!"

Gently but sternly, I told him, "Iyal, remember how Jeremy explained that we couldn't give Chancer people food? It messes up his training." Okay, I know, a really dumb explanation because Iyal's short-term memory is impaired and he would have no recollection of the number of times I have said anything!

"But he looks so sad. I *have* to give him something!" Iyal mastered pleading with me, while I practically made refusing a religion.

I'd remind Iyal that Chancer—like all dogs—was born with that loving expression that says, "Feed me and I'll be your best friend."

After we discovered their little secret, we had countless conversations about why Iyal should *not* display the food on his plate to Chancer before he sits down at the table. I would come into the kitchen, and the look on both of their faces said, "Busted." So Iyal untrained Chancer in the ultimate experience of food. Like I said, Chancer was becoming Jewish. And fast.

We also discovered within the first few months that Iyal loved to hold up a Nylabone or toy for Chancer, and inevitably Chancer would jump up for his treat. A behavioral assistance dog is rarely supposed to jump up, unless used for a behavior disruption. However, neither Chancer nor Iyal knew jumping up for a bone wasn't part of the training repertoire. Because Iyal was unable to understand that an action would lead to a consequence, convincing him to stop holding up the bones and toys was extremely difficult. I was worried that Chancer might jump up in public and knock someone down, or at the very least be mistaken for a dancing bear.

Then there was the issue of who was in charge. And in a way, *I* was responsible for this transgression. 4 Paws doesn't subscribe to the alpha dog theory of animal behavior control that became popular years ago with celebrity trainers and so-called dog whisperers. Furthermore, the agency never uses punishment, only positive reinforcement. When Chancer was paired with Iyal, the trainers also had to take into consideration pairing *my* petite size with this massive ninety-pound golden retriever. Chancer weighed almost as much as I did!

Consequently, Chancer was trained with a Gentle Leader, a type of simple headgear that gently strapped around his snout and attached to a regular leash. It wasn't a muzzle, and Chancer could eat with it on. Thank God. The premise of the headgear: where Chancer's head turned, the body would follow, which totally made sense to me. After all, Chancer's head was fifteen pounds all by itself, so I trained Chancer using the Gentle Leader, which worked great . . . until it didn't.

About nine months after Chancer started living with us, he had figured out that I was basically an emotional marshmallow when it came to correcting his mistakes. Even though I could use verbal reminders, I couldn't physically correct the wrong choice with a training collar because he and I weren't trained with one. On walks, without his vest on, Chancer realized he could win a tug-of-war with me, paws down. Even though he wasn't "working" on these walks, it still showed a lack of control on my part. Walking together had become a contest of wills.

He decided if we should go right or left. If he sniffed a chicken bone three hundred yards away in a parking lot, he was off like a wild mustang, with me trying to hang on, often twisting on the ground like a rodeo cowboy, kicking up the dust behind us. Nothing says "I can't control my dog" like being dragged behind him like a kite tail in a tornado. Can you imagine how humiliating it was?

He would "heel" nicely on my left side, his shoulders correctly aligned with my hips, until he decided he was done and would plop down wherever we were. He'd stretch out in his full golden glory, kicking his legs around, flopping his head back and forth in ecstasy, eyes wild with excitement, maybe flipping over and rolling in the grass, and I was reduced to spectator. Unable to redirect the strength of his decisions with my five-foot-two, 110-pound body, I was left feeling demoted in rank.

As soon as Chancer realized he could call the shots in one area, he inevitably began to act like he was auditioning for a sequel to *Marley & Me*. His height gave him the precise altitude to cruise our kitchen counters and of course anything below. Nothing was safe if it wasn't pushed out of reach or perched above six feet. One embarrassing moment transpired when company was getting ready to leave our home after an elaborate dinner. With so many leftovers, I had prepared a wrapped plate for our friends. As our backs were turned, Chancer stretched up to the counter and grabbed his doggie bag to go.

Everything was fair game. Sandwiches tucked safely in their baggies disappeared in one gulp if they were within reach. Chancer was a cheese connoisseur with an insatiable appetite. Entire cheese balls, blue, Brie, Gouda, Gruyère—with or without crackers, it didn't matter. Leftover toast wasn't safe, nor was the last doughnut. In fact, one time when we were in New Jersey with Chancer, my dad was home alone with him. Dad had just returned from Dunkin' Donuts with his favorite, a jelly doughnut covered with powdered sugar. While the coffee was dripping, Dad began making an omelet. Waiting to flip it, he took his doughnut from the bag and placed it on a plate and set it next to his newspaper on the kitchen table.

Dad retrieved the omelet from the stove, poured his coffee, and turned toward the table. Hmmm. Jelly doughnut was MIA. He put down the coffee mug and omelet and retraced his steps into the kitchen only a few feet away. No . . . the doughnut wasn't there or in the bag. Hmmm. Again.

He turned back to the table, where Chancer now stood, head slightly tilted, looking up at him. Then my dad noticed something red running down Chancer's chin. He freaked out at first and thought Chancer must be bleeding. As he picked up his phone to call me, he realized the truth. That wasn't blood—it was raspberry jelly! Unfortunately, this wasn't the last time Chancer created his own drive-through when we brought home Dunkin' Donuts.

Clearly, something had to be done.

Between the food issues, jumping up at the bones and toys, and Chancer's insistence on being the self-appointed leader on our trips together in public, I knew that he needed to go back for "advanced" training at 4 Paws. The agency's policy was generous because ours wasn't an uncommon experience. The initial training that worked with a child might no longer be appropriate if the behaviors that the dog was trained for significantly changed. Family members can't predict everything their child might do as he or she grows, so there's no way to anticipate different commands that the child might need over time.

Certain cues could remain the same, say, if a child was medically fragile, hard of hearing, or lived with a seizure disorder. But children on a spectrum of FASDs or ASDs might have distinctively different behaviors as they develop. Therefore, the policy at 4 Paws was that a family could send their dog back for additional training as many times as they wanted without additional fees. However, the handler would need to return to finish the new training with the service dog, which would require a few days of practice.

So late in December of 2008, I flew with Chancer back to 4 Paws to leave him for seven weeks of retraining, or as we came to call it, Chancer's return to the big house. I dreaded his absence both for Iyal and for me. Despite the various offenses, Chancer was clearly having a positive impact on my son's FASD-related behaviors. And it was more than just his physical presence and always-positive disposition.

Since Chancer's arrival, Iyal's self-confidence had also grown, and his social skills were slowly morphing into more appropriate choices. Most amazing of all, his formerly primitive vocabulary improved dramatically. Instead of saying "I want OJ," he would ask, "May I please have my orange juice in that medium-sized glass I like?" Iyal was now using multisyllabic words in more sophisticated sentences. Even more startling and fulfilling was how Iyal began to express feelings about himself. "Do other people have FASDs? Why don't I know them?" This was a new level of abstract thinking. At last my son was making his inner life more accessible.

Perhaps one of the most surprising "untargeted behaviors" was how Iyal would use Chancer as his mirror. Often Iyal would talk about Chancer's feelings, which I believed were reflections of his own. A typical exchange might go like this:

"Mom, I think Chancer is feeling sad today."

"Why do you think that, Iyal?"

"Well, he just doesn't seem to be his playful self."

This kind of projection never occurred before Chancer. Iyal also expressed concern for Chancer's feelings, indicating Iyal's attempt to imagine the impact of his actions. He might say to me, "Mom, do you think Chancer will be upset if I go bowling without him tonight?" Chancer was clearly providing Iyal with a crucial emotional touchstone he had been lacking.

One morning, in the kitchen while I was preparing breakfast, Chancer and Iyal were hanging out on the floor together.

Thoughtfully, Iyal asked, "Does Chancer have fetal alcohol syndrome? Do you think his mother drank alcohol while he was in his mommy's tummy? Did it hurt his brain, too?"

Oh. My. God. This was a huge advance in his thinking. I softly replied, "Iyal, dogs don't drink alcohol, so no, he doesn't have fetal alcohol syndrome because his mommy didn't drink any when her puppies were inside her."

Another opportunity to recognize the change in Iyal's thought processes happened when Iyal asked me out of the blue, "Mommy, will Chancer's *babies* have fetal alcohol syndrome?"

The internal ocean of disbelief washed over me as I realized how Iyal's understanding of his disability had changed. The fact that he was even thinking about his disability exploded my expectations of the total arrested development I feared in my darling son.

"Sweetheart, Chancer can't have puppies because he is a boy, and if he could, they wouldn't have fetal alcohol syndrome." Before Chancer, Iyal never talked about having a disability. If he had any thoughts, they would evaporate before becoming words, let alone sentences. Now Iyal would often project ideas and feelings onto Chancer, using his new furry friend as a way to objectify and untangle the knots inside his brain.

These projections of feelings and understanding that Iyal channeled through Chancer became a way to gain significant insight into my son. And all of this occurred within the first year of having Chancer, so clearly I was ambivalent about sending our precious service dog back for more training. I relished these monumental shifts of Iyal's self-concept and knew that seven Chancer-free weeks would seem like an eternity. Even to me.

Any concerns Harvey and I had about Chancer's naughty antics were offset by seeing him on the floor beside a calm, smiling Iyal, their paws and hands intertwined in a gentle solidarity. Whenever we were going somewhere, Iyal always asked if we could take his new best friend with us, and usually we did. With Chancer in tow, suddenly I was able to grasp what other moms meant when they said a "quick Home Depot run" or understand the convenience of "fast food."

Before Chancer, such routine trips were a race against time—would we make it home before the emotional detonator triggered inside Iyal? Usually, we didn't. Within seconds of entering a fast-food joint, Iyal would begin running around and talking loudly about what he wanted to order. He didn't have an ability to modulate his voice and had never distinguished an "inside voice" from an "outside voice," which most children learn in kindergarten.

The rest of us typically huddled together like football players before a game and tried to be invisible while waiting in line for our turn. Inevitably, we'd have to punt. Then it would happen—his fuse was lit and the clock was rapidly ticking—and we'd have to run interference.

Iyal would fly by and zero in on his target, suddenly screeching about which kid's meal toy from the latest movie promotion he wanted with his lunch. "Unhappy meals" had become a whole nasty experience in and of themselves. McDonald's, Burger King, Wendy's—I hated them all for promoting movies with items of mass emotional and physical destruction, because in just about every restaurant, the toy Iyal wanted was out of stock at the time of our visit. Crap.

Chancer's presence didn't magically transform such trips into nirvana, but the contrast was pretty amazing. Instead of running all over the restaurant or store, Iyal remained anchored by Chancer and preoccupied with all the attention the golden beauty attracted from those around us. He was so proud of Chancer and would immediately begin telling anyone who asked that the vest on Chancer meant he was a working service dog.

I remember waiting to enter an exhibit at the World of Coca-Cola here in Atlanta when Iyal spontaneously introduced Chancer to the family standing next to us in line.

"Chancer is my service dog and my best friend . . . my brother. He makes me feel better when I'm upset. And if I'm crying, he comes over and gives me kisses all over my face! I don't feel as lonely with Chancer," Iyal said with a grin.

What Disney movie had Iyal stepped out of? I swelled with pride knowing I couldn't have written a better script for him. How thrilling to hear him say these words to folks he had just met instead of shrieking about why we had to wait so long.

Chancer didn't just provide social lubrication; he was a bridge between Iyal and other people, something that had been sorely lacking. But we knew such progress would deteriorate if Chancer weren't retrained to obey commands and unlearn the bad behaviors we were unintentionally reinforcing. Iyal seemed to understand—at least that Chancer had to go back for some more training—but that didn't make it any easier for him to say good-bye. For my son, without a sense of time, seven weeks felt like forever.

Arriving at the Dayton International Airport, I rented a car for the hour-and-a-half drive to Xenia. I called to let Karen know we had arrived and would see her and the team first thing in the morning. Chancer and I spent a blessedly quiet, uneventful night in an older hotel a few blocks from 4 Paws. I dreamed about Chancer and me fighting our way through a plane full of smiling, makeup-plastered mannequins trying to shove us into submission. I know—I need to let it go.

The staff at 4 Paws was overjoyed to see Chancer again and poured on some major love and kisses. They also hugged me, who probably needed it more than Chancer. As my emotions got the better of me, I wavered in my purpose and felt tempted to say, "Oh, never mind. Really. He's not that bad . . . We can handle it . . . He doesn't need to stay. We just made those things up so we could come and visit. So, how are things?"

It didn't work. They had experienced this kind of last-minute handler desperation before. We discussed my list of "fixes," and I hung out for a few hours, cooed over the newborn puppies, asked about changes in dog food, treats, or anything else to keep me from leaving without Chancer.

But then I couldn't stall any longer. Shortly after lunch, I had to leave to drive back to catch my flight. Even though I knew we would be in touch over the seven weeks he would be there, I cried all the way to the airport.

Chapter Eight

"How's my boy doing? Is he making all A's? Has he been getting stickers?" Iyal's voice bubbled with the love and excitement of a proud parent checking up on their kid at camp. I smiled at his questions as we talked on the phone while I was in Ohio to retrieve our new-and-improved Chancer.

Seven weeks after I had deposited Chancer into the loving arms of the 4 Paws trainers, I was more than eager to bring him home to Iyal and our family. During those seven weeks he was gone, I forced myself not to think about Chancer. I imagine that's how a parent feels when the first child goes off to college. You know that leaving the fold is the right thing, but you ache inside from your child's absence.

In February of 2009, I flew back to Ohio with the plan of spending a few days to learn new commands and give my training a tune-up. I knew Chancer was not the only one who needed a refresher. And when the staff brought him to me, I almost wept with relief. Chancer rubbed his face against my legs, first one and then the other, just to make sure I knew the reunion meant as much to him. I crouched down to kiss his adorable muzzle over and over again. Chancer's tail wagged so fast, like a propeller, that I thought we might take off in a flight of joy!

During the seven weeks of advanced training, I told myself that it was as though Chancer were being groomed for the Navy SEALs or as a black ops spy for the CIA. He had a mission, and now I was going to test his knowledge and performance before we went back in the field—okay, more like a suburban home. The difference was astonishing—I couldn't believe the change in Chancer!

The staff had retrained Chancer to not jump up for a bone if anyone (meaning Iyal) offered him one. They trained him well, because now when Chancer saw a bone in midair, he immediately went into a "down." It was like watching a soldier take cover from a grenade—how's that for a do-over!

The food issue had been the biggest offense, and now he seemed to ignore any food available to him and obey his command. I was told I had to either put Chancer in an "under" below the table whenever food was available, at any height, or tell him to go to his "place." This second command was one we had learned earlier, but we hadn't reinforced during our first year with Chancer. "Place" could be used to detour a dog's wrong decision for just about anything. The command served like a La-Z-Boy recliner, something that held a lure, in this case, an especially nice dog mat big enough to accommodate the size of the specific service dog. If told "place," the dog had to go to his special mat, and as long as two paws were touching the mat, he was successfully obedient. At times I wish *I* could've been told "place" and had a custom-sized mat appear for me to rest on!

Maneuverability was another area where I could see a huge difference. Chancer was initially trained with a Gentle Leader and was now wearing a training collar, a silver link chain collar that had two circles intertwined for closure. My main task was to learn how to use the new collar for corrections when Chancer wasn't focused on his job.

For me, that was easier said than done, but not so much for Chancer. He was good with this training collar thing! I wanted to cry every time I had to quickly pull up just a tad on the collar with my leash to make the zip sound as a correction. I was sure this was my penance for not intervening sooner when Chancer was becoming untrained.

However, Jeremy assured me that what felt like a major yank, Chancer experienced as a gentle tug, a reminder to pay attention. With Chancer's head turning right or left or up or down, every tug felt like I was doing resistance training at the gym. Somehow I wasn't easily convinced that this pulling thing was a normal part of obedience training. Because I grew up with cats—the pets that put their *humans* through obedience training—I wasn't used to being in charge.

During Chancer's seven-week training period, I found myself deliberately trying *not* to think about our wonderful dog. I hadn't expected to feel this new kind of sadness while he was away. Suddenly, I understood why people would say having a dog in your life was a unique joy you couldn't know until you had one. I got it now and would never be the same. And I was grateful. I couldn't wait for our family to see the new-and-improved Chancer.

In advance, Harvey and I had planned that I would participate in a training class to make sure I felt comfortable and secure in using Chancer's new training collar. I'd only need to be there for the last five days out of the ten because both Chancer and I already knew the basics. The thought of participating in a new class and meeting new families and dogs was one of the best things in life I could imagine! The whole aura of being at 4 Paws and training with your service dog became such a lure to me I couldn't get enough of this unique and magical experience.

After the retraining session had ended and I was packing up to head home to Atlanta, I felt reenergized with feelings of being in control again, a rare phenomenon. The return trip was uneventful and, believe it or not, actually enjoyable. I guess the Stepford-wife stewardesses and their friends, with their perpetually waxed eyebrows, mustaches, and legs (I don't even want to *think* about any other body parts), were away on vacation or picking up their pink Caddies. But the real test would be when Iyal started up his shenanigans with Chancer and I saw how Chancer responded.

Iyal and Chancer's reunion was something out of a fairy tale. Iyal was jumping up and down like a pogo stick as Chancer bounded into our foyer, where a boy and his dog were reunited like something out of *Homeward Bound: The Incredible Journey*. It was a lickfest of joyful recognition. Chancer immediately flung himself over Iyal, who had rolled himself onto the floor, licked Iyal all over his face, and began rolling around beside him.

This reunion was one of the happiest moments.

The phone rang—it was 2:23 a.m. I bolted upright, swirling toward Harvey and the nightstand next to him, where the phone continued to detonate. He grabbed it, turned on the light, and looked at me with a face fresh from REM sleep, a face that doesn't seem to register the panic of impending doom. Time stopped, and I felt both the calm and the storm happening at once.

"Hello?" he said, awakening the frog asleep in his throat as well.

By that time, I had already played out one thousand scenarios in my head, and none of them was good. What if something had happened to my dad, who was my entire world, my anchor for fifty-seven years? Air evaporated, and I gasped as the sweeping flush of an anxiety attack washed over my skin, descending from my head down to my toes and ricocheting back up again. What if it was my brother? Someone from New Jersey was calling with dreaded news—what had happened to my family there?

Or what if Buffalo was calling? Oh shit! It's Harvey's sister Randy calling about my mother-in-law. Maybe she's been in an accident. Unlikely at 2:23 a.m. Oh God, maybe it's his other sister Ilene calling from Kuwait! What the hell time was it there right now? And what about my father-in-law—is he okay?

Whatever the news, I was definitely not ready. Harvey placed the phone between us to his right ear, and my left, connecting us to what must be a harbinger of doom.

"Hello, Harvey? It's Denise." I recognized the voice of our neighbor from a few streets over. Her voice sounded normal and calm like it always did, one of the things I admired about her. Also, she was from New Jersey, which automatically gives her extra points. However, I was used to bumping into her at Publix or chatting at the pool, not receiving calls in the middle of the night.

"Harvey, Donnie—everything's okay. Everything is fine," she near-whispered. Unable to hear her clearly above the drum solo of my heartbeat, I released the breath I'd been holding. Denise continued softly, "Hey, guys, Iyal is with me and he's fine. It's okay."

I thought about exhaling again and looked up at Harvey. Everything's fine? Really? Then why are we having this surreal conversation at two thirty in the morning? *Fine?* No, I don't think so. Not if our ten-year-old son, Iyal, has just happened to drop by Denise's house instead of being downstairs in his room in his bed soundly sleeping!

"I'm actually with Iyal in my car, in your driveway right now, and I just told him to go back into the house the way he came out and quietly get back in bed." She sounded so reassuring and serene that I wondered if she had ever considered being a 911 operator or maybe a crisis hotline counselor. I didn't know where to begin to untwist the tornado spinning through my imagination as it leveled any security I had about how to keep my children safe.

Denise paused, and we heard a car door open and close in the background. By this point I was about on top of Harvey, crawling into the phone to make sure I hadn't missed anything. "Denise? *What happened?* How did Iyal get to your house?" Harvey looked at me with his levelheaded, stay-calm expression, one of his tricks-of-the-rabbi-trade.

"Well, do you have a minute?" Denise said. She actually asked if I had a minute to hear how my son showed up on her doorstep in the middle of the night? This entire conversation felt like an out-of-body experience. It was just too weird and awful to think our son had left the safety of our home. What was he *thinking*? Fortunately, Denise didn't wait on me to respond and jumped in.

"I heard a knock at the door—I must not have been sleeping very soundly. So I get up, go to the door, and peer through the peephole . . ." My impatience threatened to interrupt her casual pace, but I concentrated on breathing and counting to ten. And then twenty. I was counting fast. Denise continued, "And I see Iyal standing there in his pajamas."

Oh my God! It was freezing outside, and he didn't even have a robe. I mean, not even in his closet! I have failed miserably as a parent. Someone should just handcuff me and take me away.

"So I opened the door and gently guided him inside and asked him, 'Iyal, are you okay? Do your mom and dad know you are here?'"

Right. Like we're the kind of parents who let our son walk through the neighborhood in the middle of the night—which apparently now we were.

She added, "'Honey, is Chancer with you?' I asked, and Iyal shook his head no and asked me, 'Does Dennis live here? Is this Dennis's house?'"

Harvey and I squinted at each other, puzzled. Dennis? Who the fuck was Dennis? Maybe that kid who always talked with Iyal at the pool? The one with the freckles?

"I told Iyal, 'No, Dennis doesn't live here. He lives across the street.' And then Iyal asked, 'Why isn't he here? We were supposed to walk to California today.'"

California? Did she just say *California*? Like the friggin' state? Did Iyal even know California was a place, never mind that it was more than three thousand miles away? To my knowledge, my son didn't know the difference between a village and a city, let alone a state. Did

Iyal have any idea of what was *in* California—you know, Disneyland, Hollywood, and all that sunshine?

Denise continued, "Donnie, Harvey, this is when I noticed Iyal was holding a brown lunch bag in one hand and a crumpled map in the other. His school book bag was over his shoulder."

I envisioned our sweet son looking like a poor little hobo, or maybe like Tom Sawyer with a fishing pole bending ever so slightly under the weight of the knotted kerchief holding whatever it is that Tom Sawyer held in that little kerchief bundle of his. That's when I began to cry.

"What was he *doing* in the middle of the night?" I croaked. But I know because Denise just told us. He was going to California with Dennis, the kid with the freckles.

"Maybe he was sleepwalking," Denise said. "I think he's fine, though. I'll let you go now so you can tuck him in. We can talk tomorrow. Good night."

Again, I was struck by how calm and pleasant she sounded. If my kid had to wander to a neighbor's door in the middle of the night, he couldn't have picked a better one than Denise's. Realizing I was still glued to the phone, Harvey pried it away from me and handed me a tissue. Manhattan and Eilat, our two cats, joined us on the bed, awakened no doubt by our unexpected after-midnight conversation. I tried to relax a little and meditate with Yoda (he's available 24/7). Manhattan and Eilat were trying to figure out what they should do to help their freaked-out parents. Their default was to start kneading our stomachs to make muffins that we all know are considered comfort food in the cat world.

We waited to hear any sound convincing us that Iyal had reentered the house and made his way back to bed. Ah—footsteps! He was home. We then heard him say, "Good night, Chancer." Harvey and I looked at each other, sharing the same simultaneous question: *Where was Chancer when Iyal was going out the door?* Of course, my mind continued exploding with follow-up questions as well. Why didn't our golden guardian try to stop our little boy? Wasn't that what a service dog should do? Did they cover anything about this at 4 Paws? Wasn't this what Ajax, the Plunks' first dog, was trained to do?

That's when we heard the thump, thump, thump of our Tom Sawyer climbing up the stairs to our room. Iyal entered and stood by our bed and asked, "Am I grounded?" We had never grounded him—where did he even learn that word? Like a four-legged Huck Finn, Chancer then bounded into the room beside our son and looked at Harvey and me quizzically like, "Why all the fuss?"

It turned out that Chancer wasn't trained to know the difference between night and day expeditions. Even though service dogs often remain alert and responsive to situations for which they haven't been trained, which we had witnessed multiple times, Chancer was unaware that Iyal had a curfew. He must've thought Iyal was just going to the bathroom or upstairs to the kitchen and fell back to doggie sleep in his kennel.

Needless to say, this entire escapade elevated our concern for Iyal's safety to a whole new level. The thought of our child walking through a subdivision to a house that was streets away, in the middle of the night, still isn't funny. It's scary as shit. I had to *make* it funny to survive my real fears. Iyal had no idea that he was outside in the middle of the night. He didn't recognize that it was dark and he was in his pajamas. He had no fear of danger, because he couldn't process what danger might be.

To tell Iyal not to go outside in the dark might prevent him from going outside on that particular day, but he couldn't generalize this statement to another circumstance. His thinking is concrete. Knowing and doing something once doesn't mean that he would remember it again or realize that the same rule applies, say, every Wednesday. There is no carryover. Every day is a new beginning for Iyal. But not like a religious greeting card kind of new beginning. Unfortunately, we can't assume that yesterday's activities will inform his choices today. We simply can't take that chance. However, Iyal *did* know how to slip out the back door, climb down the stairs to the backyard, and navigate the neighborhood almost to Dennis's house.

After that night, our doors were alarmed on the top where Iyal couldn't reach. We explained to him that the doors would tell us with a noise when he wanted to go out and play. We hoped not again after bedtime and before the crack of dawn. After we were convinced that our night owl had returned to his roost, Harvey and I finally began to sleep through the night again.

How could we teach Iyal what might've happened? Using natural consequences as a lesson is dubious when the person may not remember or understand that *this* action causes *that* reaction! And he could get into big trouble. Sometimes a person doesn't get a second chance to teach that lesson. I was devastated over and over to realize how difficult it was for Iyal to survive in our world.

Thank God for Denise. And neighbors like her.

Both sets of grandparents continued to dote on Iyal and Morasha even as they grew older. Harvey's parents, Miriam and Doug, called Meemie and Papa Doug by the kids, visited us from their home in Buffalo as often as they could. So when the kids were little, having them fly down to see us was easier because Harvey's rabbinic duties rarely allowed him to visit them for any length of time. They loved every moment with the kids and never seemed fazed by Iyal's meltdowns, not outwardly anyway. Harvey's mom and dad had already helped raise five grandchildren, so they were accustomed to the duties of grandparenting. They relished bringing two adopted children into the Winokur fold.

My parents, Gig and Herb, a.k.a. Giggy and Pop-Pop, visited often because they were both retired. I usually talked to one of them almost every day, reporting the latest achievements, milestones, or charming stories of their precious grandson and granddaughter, which made it even harder when the life I knew completely fell away from me.

On February 14, 2002, my mom was diagnosed with myelodysplastic syndrome, which after four months converted to acute myeloid leukemia. Her illness left me unanchored and bereft. This desperation demanded and armed me to be involved on every level of her care. I felt like I would only breathe if I stayed active in her care. An intrusive anxiety but also an understanding of patient care in a situation like my mom's forced me to try and get her into clinical trials where the newest medicines might hold promise for a better treatment, a better outcome. She participated in three trials, knowing these protocols wouldn't save her but they might save someone else. I was frantically desperate to keep going, for her. And of course, for me. I didn't know how I would ever live without her.

The kids were only three and a half when she became ill. When she passed away, they were five. So much sadness surrounded us, knowing she wouldn't be alive to watch her most cherished grandchildren grow up. But something grew poignantly between my mom and Morasha. Despite Morasha being so young, she and my mom had an unusual connection. The fact that Morasha was an old soul helped them both understand and accept something impossible.

For almost two years as a long-distance caregiver, I traveled back and forth from Atlanta to my parents' in New Jersey every few weeks or so. When I was in New Jersey, I wished I could be in Atlanta. When I was in Atlanta, I wanted to be in New Jersey. I missed the kids and Harvey, and I missed my mom and dad. I never felt present in any one place.

My dad's devotion to my mom steadied his grief. All our family and friends rallied over that year and a half, pressing forward despite the always unspoken.

During this time, Iyal's symptoms began to evince themselves, and I passed through one grief time zone and back to another.

As the High Holidays approached in 2003 and my mom's death was imminent, being a rabbi's wife wasn't anything I could think about. Bereaved and exhausted, I clung to my mom's life until her last breath. She died between Rosh Hashanah and Yom Kippur, the two holiest holidays in the Jewish tradition.

While expected, losing my mom deadened my newly unwrapped joy of motherhood and left me feeling even more adrift. I wondered if I would ever fully function again without her. How could I? She had taught me all I knew about what it means to be a mom, and I still needed her. I still yearned to be my mother's daughter.

Spending even more time with Morasha and Iyal put a new, clean dressing on my wound most days. Other times, mourning the loss of my mom left me panicked, wondering where she was. Honestly, I wondered where *was* she because she wasn't on the earth anymore! Where could I find her? I felt unmoored, as though I would sink into my depression and not be able to find my way out.

The weight of my sadness consumed me, yet then I found myself feeling guilty that my emotional state left little to offer my family. I just couldn't figure out who I was supposed to *be*. Was it okay to be a mourning daughter at the same time I had to stabilize my household when Iyal began to wreak havoc? Was it okay if I didn't feel up to being "the rabbi's wife"? Members of the temple were caring and reached out to me in my grief, but I didn't know how to be available to them when I wasn't even available to myself.

I knew moving through bereavement would take time. Who could know how long, especially when the path of grief is seldom linear? Of course, no one knows these things. When Mom died, I already had an expectation that grieving wasn't a finite thing. Sometimes waves would come crashing in, pulling me off my feet, off the earth, and sweeping me back out to temporarily disappear at sea. There were moments when sadness tapped me on the shoulder, reminding me of the empty spot at the back of my heart that ached. I felt myself pulled apart wanting the time to feel my pain, to cherish a memory, or to talk to my dad about losing Mom.

At three, Iyal was barreling through the house, careening through my brain, and giving me no free moment to do anything but keep him safe. Harvey and I each had a twelve-hour shift of guard duty that exhausted us, wringing us dry of understanding or patience.

And Morasha needed us, too! And we wanted to be needed by her, but only after one of us had enough sleep to enjoy her adorable charm. I hate that sometimes I can't remember these parts of her childhood without watching an old video or taking out a scrapbook. I'm resentful that I felt emptied by the energy it took to take care of Iyal. And when I already felt empty, it only compounded the vacancy my mom's death left inside.

Harvey's support for me was steadfast. He understood my ache and stayed present with me in my sorrow. He found his place as a son-in-law through my mom's death, and this loving concern solidified his relation to my dad and me.

My dad had begun to grieve many months before my mom passed away. He adored his wife, and everyone knew it. Within his grief, he knew his life with my mom was the best he could've lived. Having no regrets in the world he shared with my mom was a given for him. My mom's love for my dad and the gift of their long life together was all he needed for happiness.

Even if I didn't know how long it would take for me to heal, the smallest thing—easing Morasha's comb through her tangled hair while she grimaced, then smiling into a mirror, or tying Iyal's little shoelaces, his fingers entwined with mine—created new memories. Braiding together both the present loving feelings toward the kids with the loving feelings I felt for my mom became a way to help ease my mourning toward healing.

I especially remember returning home with the kids one late October evening. We had been to a classmate's birthday party, and as the four of us emptied out of the van, we gathered all the little-kid-party paraphernalia that had seemed to follow us home like stray cats. Coming down from a mild sugar high of cake and candy, Iyal giggled and chatted nonsense to no one in particular, as he often did when he and Harvey disappeared through our garage and into the house. Morasha and I lingered on the driveway, a rare moment with just the two of us, watching the last strands of twilight melt into darkness.

Morasha, in her darling top and matching navy tights, intently peered up at the night sky, also navy blue. As we spied the moon emerging from behind a cloud, I smiled at the illumination of my daughter in profile, grateful for all the joy she provided our family, dispelling shadows wherever she went. So I just stood there, a few feet away from Morasha, quietly adoring her.

Then she slowly lowered her head and thoughtfully asked, "Mommy?"

"Yes, sweetheart?" I replied, already accustomed to the serious tone of voice coming out of this little girl's body.

Morasha regarded the pink helium balloon anchored tightly in her tiny hand, guarding it from takeoff. "If I let my balloon go, would you make sure that God finds Giggy and gives it to her?"

The daily armor against my grief slipped from my grip so easily. I held back my tears but wasn't surprised at how quickly they sprang forward. "Oh, sweetheart, of course I will ask God for you. And I'm sure he'll want to help you."

Stepping closer, I gently reached for her other hand and suddenly felt as though I were holding a smaller version of my mom's hand. Morasha looked upward with all her childlike curiosity for a glimpse of this God she had heard so much about.

Breathing in this image, I sealed it in my memory, pulling her so close that I could smell her little-girl fragrance scenting the air. She nodded at me, confirming we were both ready for our tandem purposes, and then carefully let go of the string as we watched the balloon begin its ascent to God—and Giggy. When neither of us could see any trace of the balloon up among the faint stars, we turned together and walked hand in hand into the house.

—

Prior to my mom's death, our family had spent the previous two summers with my folks in New Jersey so the kids could attend a day camp there while I helped to take care of Mom during her illness. Each summer after, Morasha continued to attend the same day camp until she aged out in eighth grade.

After Iyal was diagnosed in 2002, he also continued to attend the same day camp with Morasha for a few more years until the camp no longer met his needs. At that time, his symptoms had become all-encompassing. Although the brain damage itself was invisible, his behaviors stemming from the brain damage were not. They had become neon bright. Even in the daylight. By the time Iyal was nine, we had discovered a sleepaway camp for children and young adults who lived with developmental disabilities.

Round Lake Camp, a New Jersey Y sleepaway camp, was located in the Poconos of Pennsylvania. A session of four weeks coordinated with our stay in New Jersey over the summer. So that first summer after obtaining Chancer, we decided that Morasha, Chancer, and I would keep my dad company while Iyal took a bus up to Pennsylvania for a fun-filled month. All by himself, he boarded the bus not far from my dad's house and headed three hours north to his camp. Harvey stayed in Atlanta, working for most of this time, but did take some long weekends to come up and visit.

For several years, Morasha would spend part of the summer at Camp Coleman, the Southeast Reform sleepaway camp in Northern

Georgia. The camp helped to give her fun and educational experiences that also strengthened her Jewish identity. (Now in college, she's teaching Hebrew at a religious school and quickly becoming a leader in the Charlotte Jewish community.)

At home in Atlanta, Harvey was a camper at the Cat's Meow Sleepaway Camp. Of course, our cats were in charge—of everything. If Harvey was well behaved, Manhattan and Eilat (notice that the cats are named after cities) would offer him tuna treats melted in between graham crackers and marshmallows. You know that chocolate is bad for cats (and dogs). But not for Harvey, so he negotiated the treat issue by giving his counselors catnip in exchange for Hershey's chocolate.

I sincerely believe that Dad and the kids and I were not the only ones whom Harvey missed. Quietly, he and Chancer had already begun to explore their relationship. I watched from the sidelines, not making a big deal, but absolutely felt a difference as Harvey's resistance faded away and Chancer's love moved in.

We were able to bring Chancer to see Iyal at camp on family visiting day, which was a blast and allowed Iyal an opportunity to show off Chancer to his camp friends and counselors. Of course, they all wanted Chancer to stay as their mascot.

But we had already thought through the decision about not sending Chancer to camp with Iyal. Chancer didn't accompany Iyal for several reasons. Chancer needed to have a trained handler with him. Furthermore, the days were extremely hot, which Chancer wouldn't have tolerated. Besides, the ratio of counselors to campers was super: two campers for every one counselor. This afforded Iyal the one-on-one attention he needed. The counselors were well trained to care for campers with special needs. Not sending Chancer to camp also provided a reprieve for him to catch up on the well-deserved opportunity to just be a dog.

When a service dog wears his vest or jacket, the dog understands that it's time to work. The dog's demeanor changes, and some trainers call it the halo effect. The dogs know instinctively they are "on," and it's an amazing thing to experience. What made our situation even more unique was that most of the work Chancer was trained to do remained inside our own house. Allow me to explain.

If Iyal had been at school for six hours, he had adapted his behaviors to his environment to the best of his ability, but at a cost. His cognitive fatigue, the stress on his brain to "keep it together," was taxing, which resulted in Iyal's need to let it all out by the time he came home. That was when Chancer really went to work.

We anticipated that Iyal would fall apart when he returned home after school. His yelling reverberated throughout the house, interspersed with angry muttering, and inevitably tears connected the two. Somehow Chancer knew when Iyal was to return home and remained situated by our glass front door, watching keenly for the school bus to arrive at our cul-de-sac. He probably heard the bus coming down the street, which was his cue to get ready for work.

As soon as he was inside the front door, Iyal instantly plummeted to the ground so that Chancer could begin licking and kissing before Iyal emotionally spun out of control. Chancer had quickly learned the timing and the behavior that accompanies Iyal's reentry into the house. Sometimes this interaction was enough, and Iyal quickly deescalated from his meltdown.

Other times, Iyal bolted out of Chancer's reach and ran up the stairs to continue the tantrum in the hall or kitchen or dashed downstairs to his bedroom, where he'd slam the door behind him. Undeterred, Chancer wasn't far behind. On rare occasions, Iyal would push Chancer away, saying, "Go away, Chancer! I don't want you. Go away from me, dog!"

In this kind of meltdown situation, Chancer moved away and waited quietly nearby until the storm passed on its own. He recognized that sometimes Iyal didn't want his help throughout the de-escalation process. Smart dog. In most cases, after the worst part of the chemical storm peaked and Iyal's arousal level began to descend, Iyal felt such remorse at excluding Chancer that he would share tears and terms of endearment with his forever friend. Then Chancer usually flopped on top of Iyal (in response to the "over" command), and the lovefest continued while Chancer gently pinned Iyal's legs to the floor, offering ninety pounds' worth of deep pressure to calm my son's overloaded sensory memory.

One particular summer in New Jersey, I took Morasha and her girlfriend, along with Chancer, to a local outdoor amusement park, one that the kids had enjoyed every summer when they were little. The park held many good memories for me as well, some rites of passage, as I had grown up in the area.

The four of us entered the park after paying the outrageous price of the tickets. Once inside, the girls flew off to explore the rides and promised to physically check in within fifteen minutes. I made myself comfortable on a bench, with Chancer lying by my feet, enjoying a humid but not unbearable summer evening.

Virtually all our experiences with Chancer in public until then had been positive; we hadn't yet experienced the human ignorance of misunderstanding about service dogs. That was all about to change. Out of the corner of my eye, I noticed a dark cloud blowing our way. Trying to be my naturally optimistic self, I thought maybe it was one of the popular costumed characters that often roamed the park for photo ops with little kids. Only this character looked like a lost cast member from *The Lord of the Rings*. Or maybe Darth Vader. Possibly even Voldemort.

It was the park manager. *Oh crap, what have the girls done now?* I wondered. Plastering on my best fake smile, I said, "Hi, how are you?"

He glared down at me and replied, "Ma'am, I'm sorry, but you'll have to take this dog out of our park. No animals allowed."

"I'm sorry, sir," I said, keeping the fake smile in place despite the fact that I had stopped breathing. "But this is a certified service dog, and they're allowed to be in the park. It's federal law."

"Well, you see, then we have a situation." The manager had clearly given up a career in the military. Hmmm, I wondered if he might be involved with training a certain couple of flight attendants with whom I had shared a similar delightful exchange.

"Oh?" I asked innocently.

"Yes. You see, there's a family over there whose child is afraid of dogs." He pointed about a quarter mile away, past several rides in another part of the *outdoor* park. "So you'll have to take the dog out of the park. Besides it's Saturday, and we're really busy here tonight. If it were a different night . . ."

I looked at him like he was a politician because there were probably less than thirty customers in the entire park. Or maybe he was in marketing—some profession that made him think he could spin the truth into what he needed in the moment.

In my kindest, sincerest voice, I said, "I'm so sorry that the child is afraid of dogs. I can appreciate that. However, this is a service dog, and the law allows him to accompany me, his handler, wherever I go. So we won't be leaving." All the while, I thought to myself, *Listen, bozo, we're outside here, and people can go wherever the fuck they want, or away from wherever they don't want to be. No one's being forced to stand within a hundred feet of me and the dog—or the Ferris wheel, for that matter. What if I had a phobia about roller coasters? Would you take the coaster out of the park? Come on, mister.*

Besides, how could anyone be afraid of Chancer? Okay, so he's a big dog—big deal. But he was about the mellowest fellow around. As if on cue, Chancer smiled, because he probably sensed I needed him to look even more adorable than usual.

The manager folded his arms and replied in a low, menacing voice, "I guess I'll have to go speak to my supervisor then."

"That's a great idea!" I said with a genuine smile this time, thinking I could psych him out. "Why don't you do that?" And of course, I thought of a few other things he could go and do, with or without his supervisor.

He left, and I started organizing my action plan as he walked away. By this time, the girls had returned out of breath and excited. But Morasha sensed the uncomfortable aura surrounding Chancer and me. Searching my face, she asked, "Mom—what is it?" I calmly explained that the manager had asked us to leave the park, because of Chancer.

"He can't do that!" Morasha, who had been at 4 Paws with me for our original training session and, as my little fifth-grade deputy, knew the rules. She pleaded, "And, Mom, we're not ready to go yet—we just got here! They can't make us leave. It's illegal!"

"I know, sweetheart, and I have no intention of leaving. I'll get it straightened out—don't worry about it. Why don't you girls go back to the rides, and I'll take care of this."

"Okay," the girls chimed in unison. They disappeared again into the nearly deserted amusement park. Morasha looked over her shoulder to see the worried expression on my face, but I nodded, and she let her friend drag her to find a ride that they hadn't yet experienced.

Yep, there were no two ways about it—this place was *empty*. Maybe a couple dozen families were there at most. I assumed the place had outpriced itself and now competed with the franchised water and amusement parks such as Six Flags. I felt a momentary twinge of sadness as I recalled the many summer romances that had once brought me to this place. The laughter, the disgustingly greasy pizza, the flirting, pretending to be scared on a ride so I'd have to snuggle in next to whomever my date was at the time. I remembered clearly the summer I humiliated myself while playing miniature golf, hitting the ball so hard it broke the paddle off the decrepit windmill, ricocheted off the ridiculous-looking laughing gorilla, and proceeded into the algae-covered moat. Miniature golf was not my strong suit.

Neither was dealing with unreasonable people.

I returned from my reminiscing and watched as *two* dark clouds of evil approached the bench and hovered in front of Chancer and me.

The new taller, gaunter, more *Despicable Me*-ish supervisor said, "I hear we have a problem."

I smiled with my best effort. "We don't have a problem." Chancer wagged his tail.

"Ma'am, I believe my associate here made it clear that pets aren't allowed in the park. You'll have to remove him."

I knew it was time to pull out the big guns. No, not a lightsaber—something better. A document from the federal government. I unzipped a pocket on one side of Chancer's vest and pulled out a small, typed laminated card with the pertinent paragraph from the 1990 ADA. It stated,

> A person with a disability cannot be asked to remove his service animal from the premises unless: (1) the dog is out of control and the handler does not take effective action to control it or (2) the dog is not housebroken. When there is a legitimate reason to ask that a service animal be removed, staff must offer the person with the disability the opportunity to obtain goods or services without the animal's presence.

I gave them a moment—okay, quite a few—to digest what this meant. Then I said, "So you see, sir, we have every right to be here."

"Ma'am," repeated the supervisor, "the dog still has to leave the premises."

Wow, I thought, *maybe he doesn't understand English.* What part of "cannot be asked to remove his service animal from the premises" didn't he understand? I repeated, "We have a legal right to be in this park."

He smirked, or maybe it was more like a snort, and said, "I'm asking you nicely to take the dog and come back when you don't have the dog with you." After a beat, he added, "And why is this dog even here?"

I was becoming accustomed to strangers asking if Chancer was my service dog. I'd explain that Chancer was my son's dog; however, I was Chancer's trained handler. By law, I have the same rights that my son has and cannot be denied public access. Educating the public about service dogs was another tool to advocate for people living with disabilities.

Even though I didn't want to answer his asinine question, I considered whether doing so would relieve some of the tension. Throughout this conversation, the cartoon bubble over my head said, "If my son, Iyal, were here and you told us to leave, then you'd really understand why he has a service dog!" I couldn't even begin to imagine the size of the earthquake his meltdown would have produced. The aftershocks would've reached California. Yes, *that* California. See how easily I don't let go of things?

He planted himself in front of Chancer and me, clearly not moving from his position. I put the ADA law card back into Chancer's vest and took out my cell phone. "Look," I said, "I can either call the police or the local TV station. Which would you prefer?"

The supervisor contemplated his choices just as the girls reappeared. Morasha instantly froze in place, taking it all in. Prepared for disappointment or embarrassment, she looked at me, trying to decide how to deal with a mother who had fire coming out of her mouth and horns where her ears should be.

"Mom," she implored, "it's okay. Please don't do this. Let's just leave. I don't want to make a scene and ruin the night!"

We were already in act two. It was too late. The supervisor didn't seem at all threatened by my ultimatum, which prompted Morasha again. "Can we please just *go*? This isn't worth it!" Her girlfriend had been staring at all of us, clearly new to this kind of drama. I was caught between not wanting to back down, prepared to call the police or TV station, and concern that Morasha would be traumatized if I forced my point. The last thing I wanted was for her to become reluctant to take Chancer out in public.

"Okay, we'll leave your amusement park, but you need to know that I'll be writing a letter to the editor of *Courier News*."

The supervisor, sensing blood in the water, gave a shark grin and said, "How's this? We will refund the cost of your tickets."

I couldn't even believe he thought this helped. "Okay, thank you," I muttered.

"We'll mail you a check." He then wrote down my address and gave me his business card. The girls, Chancer, and I took our time strolling out through the decrepit gates of the park. The girls dragged me the way Chancer usually did.

In the parking lot, Morasha exclaimed, "Oh boy. If Iyal had been there and this happened, there wouldn't be a park left after his nuclear meltdown."

"I know, sweetheart. I'm so sorry about this. Let's go across the highway to TGI Fridays and try to have a nice dinner."

Inside the restaurant, customers and the staff quickly acknowledged Chancer's presence and rolled out the red carpet. The servers were falling all over themselves wanting to serve the section where we had been seated. The waitress actually lay down on the floor to talk to Chancer. The fact that this huge service dog was a customer in their restaurant was celebrated. It offset the scrim of anger and frustration from the most unamusing park across the street.

Chapter Nine

The Bowcraft incident, as it's come to be known in our family lore, wasn't the only time that we encountered unexpected turbulence from Chancer's presence. Bowcraft never responded to my letter, which didn't surprise me, but what did catch me off guard was finding a similar attitude in New York of all places—you know, the city where no one looks twice at a performance artist standing on a bustling street corner in Manhattan, dramatically ripping old New York City phone books in half while reciting soliloquies from Hamlet—when we had a door literally slammed in our faces.

Before penning this memoir, I had the unique and inspiring opportunity to write and publish two books (one with Morasha when she was eleven years old) with the award-winning author, advocate, and publisher Jodee Kulp. Now you may better appreciate my ability to be self-deprecating without completely drenching everyone in my fascination with emotional weather patterns. Not to mention the uncompromising wit resulting from my sometimes-warped interpretation of events that leave me stunned. What? Okay, I'll stop. Even *I* know when I've had enough of myself.

Even so, this memoir isn't my first time writing about our family's story. When we were preparing to go to 4 Paws the first time, I had been referred to Jodee Kulp through the National Organization on Fetal Alcohol Syndrome based in Washington, DC. She is considered one of the first "warrior moms" from the late 1980s to become by default an educator and expert in the support of individuals living with FASDs and their caregivers. The term FAS was first published in 1973, and its consideration as a lifelong birth defect was slow to be recognized by the medical community. Jodee was determined to bring this "invisible disability" to light for families created through adoption and foster care and those where mothers had consumed alcohol while pregnant. She provided reality-based guidance for an international community that desperately needed a better understanding of how to live with family members affected by fetal alcohol exposure. Jodee and her daughter, Liz, who experiences FASDs, have published several award-winning books. Their books, brimming with "how to mitigate real-life challenges" for both fetal-alcohol-affected people and those who care for them, became my FASD bibles, factually based but spiritually healing in a way that served me well.

After my first phone call with Jodee, in which I explained my family's upcoming journey to 4 Paws to meet Chancer, she decided to meet us in Ohio and, as she said, "audit" our training. I cleared it with Karen Shirk just to confirm that Jodee would be welcome as a student of service-dog training. By this time, not only was Jodee paving the way for families struggling with the impact brought on by FASDs, but she also had already trained more than eight hundred dogs. Our visit to Xenia was within eight days of when we spoke on the phone, and I couldn't believe that I was meeting my own version of the Madonna. Jodee's books written about FASDs had truly become my bibles. My Jewish affiliation aside, I needed to believe in some kind of miracle that would address Iyal's turmoil and save Harvey and me from dissolving into each other's anguish.

And Jodee understood "the marriage thing," too. I didn't have to say anything. She saw it in my tired and hurt expression. With this unspoken understanding, our lifelong friendship was cemented.

Her insight into our family's emotional roller coaster ride gave me hope when I had little. She deeply understood what I needed from a service dog that would anchor Iyal. With Jodee, I never had to apologize for Iyal's behavior or *mine*! During lunch on one of the training days, she and I began talking about the importance of having a "circle of support," people who understood the complex variables in the life of someone who experiences FASDs. A circle of support was the idea of a village that would never outgrow that individual's changing needs and would also serve as a safety net for the family.

As our conversation continued, Jodee offhandedly mentioned that I should write a book about Chancer to help others learn about invisible disabilities and service dogs. She said she'd be glad to coach me through the process and help in any way she could. At first, I thought she was kidding, not being able to fathom working on a book with this nationally known expert. But Jodee never says something she doesn't really mean.

Her suggestion took root, and my imagination grew so quickly that I had trouble keeping up with it! We discussed this book idea on and off over the next four days until we had graduated Chancer from his training. By then, the book concept had expanded into a trilogy of books: a children's book from Chancer's perspective on how he befriended a boy with an invisible disability; an older (middle school) kids' book from the vantage point of a sibling, a.k.a. Morasha, of a family member experiencing this kind of birth defect; and some kind of autobiography written by me as an adoptive mother of a son diagnosed with FAS.

We left 4 Paws after graduation, promising to stay in touch about developing the books, which is exactly what we did. Within a few short months, we had strategized the order of the books and published

Morasha's book, *My Invisible World: Life with My Brother, His Disability and His Service Dog*, in November 2009.

My Invisible World came together when Jodee invited Morasha to visit her for a week. Jodee interviewed Morasha with real-life questions, based on raising her daughter Liz, who was now around twenty. This fluid exchange of questions and explorations into Morasha's hidden world became the narrative and manuscript for Morasha's book. Besides, raising Liz, who was adopted at birth by Jodee and her husband, Karl, and their history of fostering seventeen children, Jodee knew just how to navigate Morasha's initiation into the world of writing.

Nuzzle: Love between a Boy and His Service Dog came next and was composed from the perspective of Chancer, who had channeled the book through me. The story was delivered mostly through illustrations, photos, and graphics, and told in a way aimed at ages five and up. Both self-published, *My Invisible World* and *Nuzzle* went on to receive numerous national and international awards, including the Mom's Choice Gold Award.

So in late May of 2010, Chancer and my dad accompanied me to BookExpo America (BEA), the annual publishing trade show in the United States, being held at the Jacob Javits Center in New York. The Mom's Choice organization had a booth and offered to sponsor a book signing for us as well as produce a video we could use to promote the book. I had been eagerly looking forward to the show and couldn't wait to mingle with thousands of book people in hopes that someone else's success might rub off on me or that I'd meet a literary agent or famous author.

Regarding logistics with Chancer, I had to consider the safest way to transport him without tiring him. I was concerned because even though Chancer was only four years old, he had developed premature hip dysplasia, and I knew he could only walk so far at one time before needing to rest.

So Chancer and I left Iyal with Harvey, and we flew to Newark Liberty International Airport from Atlanta—this time in a plane with humane (and human) attendants and a bulkhead area! Yeah, we dodged *that* bullet. We knew that Iyal would be okay without Chancer for a few days, although things might be a bit bumpy, but I was willing to take the chance.

In New Jersey, we stayed with my dad and took the local Berkeley Heights train into Penn Station in Manhattan. I was worried about Chancer climbing up the stairs into the train itself because they were ridiculously steep! My dad climbed up first, which also made me anxious, then Chancer and me. No one was left behind.

We turned right into the train car and looked for the kind of seats where you could move the whole long seat back and forth to accommodate passengers. We found one and pushed the middle seat back to one side so we had two benches facing each other with about a foot and a half between them. So far, so good.

Chancer followed me in and lay down by my feet, seemingly quite comfortable. My dad sat across from me, and we spread our stuff out, hoping to discourage anyone from sitting with us amid all the paws and feet. Sure enough, our imaginary force field worked, and we made it all the way to Penn Station without anyone attempting to join us. Chancer was fine with all the starts and stops, the lights going on and off, the sounds of clanking, metal rubbing against metal, and the squeal of the train on the railways.

Most people didn't even notice Chancer was there.

This wasn't going to be so hard after all.

Or so I thought.

Penn Station is a busy place. It's a train station with tunnels, elevators, and escalators moving people in and out of all the trains that come and go. Naturally, it's chaotic, with announcements of the tracks where trains will be leaving from, one person's words falling on top of another's over the loudspeaker, sort of like the people during rush hour, which, in NYC, is every hour! Don't let anyone tell you otherwise. And of course, you can never find the right track until having asked at least five people, all of whom smile broadly but only nod in agreement, even though it wasn't a yes or no question.

But thankfully, we had my dad! We would confidently follow him anywhere and know that we would never be truly lost. Occasionally late, but never lost. My dad was a man who would rather inch along one-way streets in the theater district until midnight, muttering about just missing the spot ahead, than settle for a spot in a parking garage.

Bronx born and raised, my father loved New York City as if he had built it himself. He regaled us with stories about snaking through the ticket lines at Yankee Stadium, getting ahead of the crowd to score the best seats. With Chancer and me in tow, Dad helped us navigate our way to the chartered buses that would take us to the Javits Center and BEA. Because service dogs aren't allowed to ride on escalators because of too much risk for injury, we were used to looking for elevator icons and signs wherever we went. From the train platform, we found the elevator and rode up to the main level. Chancer behaved, but I couldn't begin to imagine all the smells accosting his olfactory glands—coffee, bagels, perfume, sweat, garbage, and who knows what else.

The terminal was beyond busy. Just like I knew it would be. We began asking where to find the buses to BEA and finally landed on someone who knew the right answer. We walked to another part of the station, went headlong into the thick humidity that left us feeling wilted, and crossed the street. We spied four charter buses, head to toe, looking like a line of toy buses waiting for little plastic people to board. But plastic people would have melted in this heat.

Within a few minutes, we boarded the bus. Chancer, completely unfazed, acted like he did this every day on his commute to work.

Within the first few rows were two empty seats together and one across the aisle. I sat next to the window while Chancer jumped up onto the seat next to me, like he did this Monday through Friday and couldn't wait to read his *New York Times* and drink his coffee. Dad sat across from him.

This was when the fun began. People filed onto the bus. Because most people in Manhattan tend to move rather quickly, they walked right by without noticing the unusually tall, golden-haired, ninety-pound business dog taking up an aisle seat. Not until the bus was full and people were getting their laptops, briefcases, and assorted crap settled above them did the first person look over and stare at the huge furry head with the drooling tongue.

From that moment on, the inside of the bus resembled a baseball stadium doing "the wave" at a home game. First, one row stood up to look, and as they were sitting down, the next row of four seats behind them stood up as the wave rippled all the way to the back of the bus. A concert of phrases began as well: "What the *hell*? Is that a dog? Or some kind of *bear*? Oh my God, that is the biggest golden I have ever seen! Where did it come from? Is he an author? Some kind of PR stunt, maybe?" I found this hysterical, and of course Chancer had no idea what all the fuss was about. This author clearly was a showstopper.

After a short ride to the convention center, the three of us disembarked and walked down the twenty-two rows of cement steps (yes, I counted) and stood in a patio area outside this monstrosity of a building. I knew it was big but hadn't expected it to be a complete borough in and of itself! Armed with a directory of the locations of all the booths and the special areas where authors and other celebrated people in the book industry would be speaking, I knew we had quite a walk, maybe even a mile, to get to the Mom's Choice booth. I still worried about Chancer's hips and hoped he'd make the trip without too much discomfort. After all, what would I do if he plopped into a "down" and refused to budge?

I imagined my dad and me dragging Chancer across the convention floor like cavemen back from the hunt with a woolly mammoth. Actually, that vision wasn't funny. And besides the fact that this is no way to treat a dog, let alone a service dog, I knew that Chancer might find it humiliating!

At BEA, almost all books are free giveaways—purchasing books is a no-no. I was ecstatic and calculated how many I could lug around (in one of the free book bags, of course) for the rest of the day. It was a wonderful way to peruse the new books and talk with authors, illustrators, publishers, and other book people.

Another reason for attending BEA was because Chancer would be featured in an upcoming book, *Devoted: 38 Extraordinary Tales of Love, Loyalty, and Life with Dogs*. Written by Rebecca Ascher-Walsh, this book would be published by National Geographic in 2013. Consequently, I kept swinging by the National Geographic booth, hoping to meet someone with whom I could make a personal connection, but I never seemed to time my visit right.

We stopped along the way, not just because we needed to rest, but because about every fifteen yards, people would flank us, asking about Chancer. Answering questions about Chancer was a good publicity opportunity, but I was anxious to get Chancer settled somewhere so he could rest his body after such a hike. We finally arrived at our booth and were graciously received by the staff and other authors who had won Mom's Choice awards.

Until I knew we needed to be "on," I wanted to tuck Chancer under one of the skirted tables out of the way so he could rest but also so he wouldn't detract from anyone else's time in the spotlight. "Tucking" a small-pony-sized golden requires good visual-spatial reasoning, which isn't my best skill, but we managed to move some book boxes around under the tables and make room for him to nap. And nap some more.

The Mom's Choice booth was located in front of the "autograph corral," a coveted area where people would line up, sometimes an hour before an author was to appear, to have an autographed copy of their newest book. Depending on the popularity of the book, the lines would move quickly or slowly and be shorter or longer. When it was my turn to be the autographing author for Morasha's book, I left my dad and Chancer at their strategic positions to walk through the green room, where authors lounged until it was time to go to their assigned spots to receive their fans.

As I entered the green room, I spotted Bernadette Peters, whom I knew would be there. She had just written and published a book about New York dogs, and I was eager to meet her.

As a devout fan since I first saw her on Broadway in the eighties, I was armed and ready. I immediately captured her attention with a warm Evelyn-Wood-speed-reading introduction and a polite handshake and then shoved Morasha's book into her hands at warp speed as I explained about Chancer. She was gracious and attentive but also clearly preoccupied with trying to work her way out of the authors' area. Mission accomplished—I was thrilled.

I made my way over to my table and climbed up on the stool. Next to me, my "assistant" would hand me a book, and then I would sign it. A few yards before the signing table, BEA staff would offer the person in line a piece of paper where he or she could write their inscription, so I wouldn't misspell it as I wrote it in the book.

The cavernous exhibition hall had a lot of ambient sound because of the high ceilings and cement floor. By then, I had already left Chancer with my dad several times at the show so I could run around looking at books and trying to rub elbows with anyone I thought might help market our book. I never worried about Chancer's behavior with my father because they shared a special bond with each other and with a singularly special boy.

Busy signing books with a genuine smile on my face, I darted my eyes around the crowded area to confirm Dad and Chancer were still stationed at the right spot, which they were. Then, above the steady and loud cadence of the crowds, I heard a colossal bark. *Oh please,* I thought. This just wasn't possible! Chancer had never barked without a command. Ever. In fact, we never even heard his "bark" (an event all by itself) until five days into our training when we learned the command "bark." Chancer's diaphragm must be developed like an opera singer's, because one bark would reverberate for twenty seconds!

I smiled and pretended nothing was wrong until a few minutes later when Chancer launched another even more thunderous bark. This one reminded me of the MGM lion roaring in the film company's logo. I cleared my own throat rather loudly, trying to make it seem like this unbelievable loud rumble came from *me* rather than Chancer, who was yards and yards away! Again, I called upon all the frogs in my throat and made a sound that was more like I was retching with dry heaves. I'm not sure I was convincing. I didn't know what to do. Ignore it? Act like this was Chancer's way of introducing himself to the crowds? No one seemed to react to it either way. But a service dog isn't supposed to bark in public unless he is trained to bark as an alert to indicate his person needs immediate help.

Neither my dad nor I ever figured out what caused Chancer to bark during the book show. However, as Chancer has matured, he has informed us with the occasional dog- yodeling soliloquy when he feels like we aren't giving him enough attention. His ability to melodically traverse two octaves in a matter of seconds often leaves Harvey and me doubled over laughing.

During the afternoon, a staff member from Mom's Choice interviewed Chancer and me. I could then use a provided video of the interview for promotional purposes. Fortified with more books than I needed, I was elated but completely exhausted. Finally, after nearly seven hours, it was time to leave and manage our transit segments for the return to Berkeley Heights, New Jersey, and my dad's house.

The three of us walked the mile at Chancer's much slower pace to the entrance of the convention center and found the queue for the charter bus back to Penn Station. Several buses were already running, and diesel fumes in the late-afternoon heat were unbearable. Everyone was bushed—I even overheard one woman say, "Boy, are my dogs barking!" and wondered if Chancer would find her comment offensive. We stood in line and tried to wait patiently to load onto the bus.

At last the line started moving, and after a dozen or so people ahead of us had boarded, it was our turn. Only it wasn't. When the bus driver looked down and saw Chancer, he started yelling expletives in his native tongue that I didn't need translated. In a thick accent that was difficult to identify, he screamed, "No dog on my bus! Do you understand? No dog!"

Really? I looked at my dad with an "OMG, I'm too tired to deal with this asshole" look. But I sighed and screwed on a happy face and then politely clarified that Chancer was a service dog and, by law, was permitted to accompany us onto this bus. The bus driver shook his head empathically and then marched out of the bus. Standing inches from my face, he yelled as though we were three city blocks away, "No, lady, no dog! I drive bus for thirty-seven years, and I never have dog on bus! Not now, not ever!"

I'm thinking, *Never say never. There's a first time for everything. Aren't you lucky?*

So I explained again that the law allows my service dog on his bus. By now the people behind us in line were getting energized and vocal in our favor. Seeing I wasn't going to get anywhere with this disaster of a driver, I calmly asked to speak with his dispatcher.

He glared at me with an expression of "Lady, who do you think you are?"

So I repeated my request as the crowd behind us cheered me on. Adrenaline submerged my exhaustion, and I became a woman on a mission. Again. Super Donnie and Chancer the Golden Wonder! Defeating biased misconceptions and overcoming ignorant assumptions about service dogs everywhere!

Just then, another bus pulled up behind us, and its driver emerged to see what the commotion was about. I immediately sensed good karma from him and elucidated our situation. He nodded his head enthusiastically and said, "Yes!" He even gave the crowd a thumbs-up and motioned for us to proceed onto his bus as if we were royalty entering a regal carriage. The crowd, quite sizable by this time, cheered as my dad, Chancer, and I made our way to our new bus. Before we turned, though, I would swear I saw Chancer give the first bus driver "the paw."

Not long after returning from BEA, I received a call that alarmed me more than any nasty bus driver. I was just about to have my first cup of coffee, a critical juncture in my daily attempt to rise and shine, when I received a call from Iyal's categorical assistant, a one-on-one aide at his school.

"Oh, hi, Robin!" I answered brightly (this was the "shine" part) but tentatively (this was the "rise" part—it's really very difficult for me to rise at 8:45 a.m.). And please understand that I *loved* Robin. I *adored* Robin. She was a perfect fit for Iyal, a total godsend, and remained an "external brain" for him for three consecutive years.

"Hi, Donnie, did I catch you at a good time?" Robin asked. "Everything is okay. Iyal is fine and having a great day."

When your challenged child is under the care of another adult in a supervised setting—whether school, after school, preschool, camp, or social skills program, all of which Iyal participated in—you learn quickly that "everything is okay" means that it's probably not. In fact, it's the universally understood preamble to "Get ready—the shit has hit the fan."

"Hi, Robin. So what's up?" I tried to sound just as casual, but probably equally as unconvincing, as she had.

"Well, we have a situation."

See, what did I tell you? Here it comes.

Robin continued, "I was walking around the classroom and overheard Iyal telling Sam that he had something special to show him. When I looked back over my shoulder, I watched Iyal pull a check out of his backpack."

"A check?" I asked, dumbfounded. "What kind of check?" I placed my coffee cup on the counter and anticipated needing something stronger than caffeine to get me through this phone call, let alone the day. Did Iyal even know about Harvey's desk drawer where our checkbook resided safely in "the checkbook place"?

"Looked like a personal check. It was filled out and made payable to Iyal Winokur."

I shook my head, almost expecting it to rattle with the sound of my disbelief.

"It was filled out to Iyal?" Why was I parroting back everything Robin was saying?

"Yes, and it was for one thousand dollars. And it was in Iyal's handwriting."

I'm incredulous but also mystified. "You mean Iyal wrote himself a check for one thousand dollars? On whose account?"

"Uh, well, it was from your joint account. So I just wanted to touch base with you before I moved forward."

"Sure," I agreed like a ventriloquist's dummy. "What did you have in mind?"

I began imagining Iyal being jailed, but not in a minimum-security, white-collar institution. I knew he was too young to be imprisoned, even in the juvenile justice system. But I also knew what might lie ahead. And it could be a very frightening prediction, one that plagued me like a potentially devastating virus lying dormant, just waiting for the right environment to trigger an outbreak.

"I didn't want to cause Iyal any anxiety. You know, I just wanted to keep this low-key."

I nodded my head, thinking that on the one hand, I was *so very proud* that Iyal even knew that a check had something to do with money. That was actually an amazing, profound connection for him to make! But then I was sobered by the thought that Iyal could write a check to someone else for God-knows-what amount and give it to that person—who might actually try and cash it! Even the thought of this thousand-dollar check floating around his elementary school sent shivers down my spine.

"So the plan?" I asked, trusting that Robin did indeed have one.

"I'm thinking I'll just explain to Iyal that a check is a special thing, so why don't we keep it in his backpack, which we'll then put in his locker for safekeeping. Sound okay?"

"Oh, Robin, that would be perfect! If I don't hear back from you," I said, "I'll assume everything went okay. I really appreciate how you're handling this! Thanks for calling me." We said our good-byes, and I sipped cold coffee, reflecting on the possible ramifications of Iyal's first foray into high finance.

Her call would have been humorous except for the fact rattling my own brain: 60% of individuals older than twelve years of age living with FASDs will be charged with a crime in their lifetime. What if my son simply became upset and acted impulsively in a violent manner? What if he lashed out and hurt someone? Or what if that someone hurt him? There was no easy answer.

Poor judgment and faulty reasoning collide in the minds of those who experience FASDs or cognitive impairment, setting them up to commit a crime. Many people affected with FASDs may never mature beyond the level of a six- to twelve-year-old, with that of a sixteen-year-old sometimes the highest level of social maturity reached. This dysmaturity makes it more difficult for people like Iyal to set "smart" long-term goals and opens them up to manipulation and coercion into criminal behavior or false confessions.

Imagine someone with intellectual impairment being asked if she wanted to waive her Miranda rights. First, she may wonder, *Who's Miranda? Am I supposed to know who Miranda is? I'd better say yes so I can go home and so my mom won't be mad, because I think it is late. And I don't want to make her mad.* Imagining my son at any age facing such a situation still terrifies me.

Judges and attorneys wearily view a revolving door of people battling disabilities; those who experience cognitive impairments, mental illness, or FASDs often repeat the same mistakes multiple times due to their disabilities. You and I might have learned from our mistakes not to commit a crime in order to stay out of jail. Because he doesn't understand the relationship between cause and effect, Iyal could easily wind up "holding the bag" for someone who views his disability as an opportunity. Many experts agree that research generally speaks to the prevalence of full FAS because the distinguishing facial characteristics are visible. Unfortunately, those who live with fetal alcohol exposure without the legitimacy of a medical diagnosis may be held accountable for their actions without exception. What looks like oppositional behavior viewed as implicit choice can, in fact, reflect organic brain damage. Explosive episodes may cause an insurmountable frustration because the person is unable, not unwilling, to respond appropriately. The catastrophic fallout of misunderstood FASD experiences denies those "unseen" individuals a fair chance for compassion and support.

Bruce Ritchie, an expert in FASDs, explains, "Only extreme cases would be diagnosed. Often the neurological damage goes undiagnosed, but not unpunished."[3]

In most cases, someone who doesn't understand FASDs will interpret that person's impaired memory as lying. That's where the phenomenon of confabulation, when a brain-injured person tries to fill in the blanks in understanding a situation, can come into play.

For example, when Iyal was in fifth grade, I received a report from his teacher stating that Iyal was "lying and making up excuses" when he said he didn't understand his homework assignment. His teacher reported, "Iyal told me he understood it in school that day, so why couldn't he complete his assignment when he got home?" And of course when she accused him of lying, Iyal felt under unimaginable pressure and began to confabulate to placate his teacher. I was livid and sent a note explaining to his teacher why Iyal had given her inconsistent answers.

Picture the injured brain looking like a sieve; random information stays in the sieve, but other understandings fall right through the tiny holes. Without having all the information to consider, the person who lives with the brain injury is trying to find *something*, *anything,* to fill up the holes! The core of confabulation is that a person can't remember something he's never heard. However, this laborious attempt at giving an answer that may make no sense at all to, say, a police officer or a judge could prove disastrous, especially if the person with impaired judgment sincerely believes with all his heart that superheroes can help him fix whatever he did wrong, and tells them so.

I live with one of those persons.

So I could just imagine it: some "friends" of Iyal's see an opportunity to steal something from a store. The friends suggest that Iyal go into the store, take, say, the video game when no one is looking, and run back out of the store, fast, to give them the loot. Iyal thinks, *Sure,*

I can do that! They're my friends, and getting a video game for them will make them happy. They will be my friends forever!

You know where this is going.

Or Iyal happens to witness someone *else* committing a crime. He watches a person rob and beat up an older man. Iyal absolutely knows this is wrong, and when the police show up, because police often just "show up" at the scene of a crime, they interrogate Iyal as a witness.

Now here is where there is a debate among the disability community. Some might say that just because an individual may have a developmental or cognitive disability doesn't mean he or she can't be a good witness in this scenario. I understand (and know I'm stating this simplistically) that this mindset is born of wanting disabled individuals to live in an "inclusive community" just like others without disabilities. And yes, of course I want this as well, but I can't see it as an all or nothing. I love Iyal with every part of me, and because of that, I would never want to put him in that situation. Because of FAS, he may never be a reliable witness. And this doesn't make him any less of a person.

When Iyal is cognitively fatigued and has tried so hard to keep up with the auditory pace in his classes, we may see his behavior spiral downward the minute he walks in the door. His teachers may have seen this defeatist attitude in school when Iyal says, "I can't do it!" without even looking at the assignment. He isn't just rebelling; he is also avoiding the possibility that he may fail again. Just like the last time and the time before that, because Iyal just cannot process the instructions. Who wouldn't want to explode? I see this chain reaction in Iyal almost every day. Handling enormous frustrations without any sense of it ever getting better can certainly take its toll.

People think I am overprotective or that I'm not letting Iyal spread his wings when I talk about his ongoing need for an external brain. However, if Iyal unintentionally forgets the "rules of engagement" in a social setting or misinterprets someone's actions and/or intentions, his impulsivity and lack of clear judgment may override his ability to make positive decisions. He will always need another person who can be one step ahead of him. I've told Iyal that he can have access to more opportunities if someone (an external brain) is riding sidecar, pointing out the tricky turns and upcoming bumps in the road.

I know you're wondering, Well, is Chancer an external brain for Iyal? My answer is yes, and no. Because I'm both female and Jewish, I like to weigh things fairly. So Chancer isn't able to actually predict the outcome of actions and understand their consequences. If Iyal is thinking of jumping off a cliff and diving into a river, more than likely Chancer won't throw himself in front of Iyal to prevent him from doing a Butch Cassidy or a Sundance Kid scene stealer. And yet Chancer, in fact, likely saved Iyal's life when he pulled him off the edge of the railing of our three-story deck. In other words, I don't think we can guarantee that Chancer's brain and four furry paws can always save Iyal from being arrested, stolen from, or simply being in the wrong place at the wrong time. After Robin's call, I realized that as much as Chancer did for Iyal and our family, it ultimately wasn't enough. There were more possibilities to worry about than I had first imagined. Despite my best efforts, I wouldn't always be there to protect Iyal, no matter how hard I tried. Sometimes he would not have an external brain and would be forced to rely on his own faulty operating system.

Some things Iyal would face alone.

Chapter Ten

"Mom?" Iyal asked one afternoon while he and I walked Chancer in the neighborhood. Iyal would often talk to me while he was several steps ahead, not realizing that I couldn't hear him if he was facing forward and I was behind him.

"Honey," I said. "Iyal, you have to turn around and talk to me. I can't hear you."

"Okay, Mom," Iyal answered and then continued to keep walking in front of me, facing forward.

I scooted up a few steps with Chancer, trying to hear what he said.

"Mom, can someone switch from FAS to autism?"

In our training class at 4 Paws, several of the kids there had obtained autism-assistance dogs, so autism was a word that Iyal heard more frequently as we became involved in the disability community. I liked that Iyal was considering these kinds of questions, and I believed it showed a tremendous gain in his ability to think in the abstract. He certainly wasn't able to manage this cognitive complexity BC, before Chancer. Although we don't know for sure why specially trained service dogs help make this connection, some animal-and-human scientists say that the service dog lowers the debilitating anxiety level of children so they can access parts of their brain that had been "unavailable" before.

For almost a year, Iyal thought that he also had ASD and, in fact, had been given that diagnosis by a pediatric neurologist years before and displayed many symptoms associated with autism. After thinking for a moment, I answered, "Well, Iyal, that's a great question! I think what might happen is that kids may act a certain way and their parents ask a doctor if their child has autism or FASDs." I wasn't even sure if Iyal was listening or if he had already flown to a different planet in his head. But I continued anyway on the off chance he might have done a cosmic U-turn and returned to this planet. "The doctor may want to do a bunch of tests to see if he can help the parents understand what might be going on with their child."

I heard a muffled "Uh-huh . . ."

Wrapping it up, I said, "So I'm not sure about the switching part, but I believe some people have both."

"Okay." And then Iyal was off babbling about something else.

Being diagnosed with both ASD and FASDs is common and contributes to confusion between these diagnoses. As an educator, I continually stress how FASDs are misdiagnosed or undiagnosed because the behavior seems so similar to ASD or ADHD, but the etiologies are vastly different. Tens of thousands of individuals living with FASDs who haven't been diagnosed are struggling without appropriate interventions. Then when those individuals who have been misdiagnosed or undiagnosed don't improve, it only compounds their frustration and their family's. Left unchecked, this painful cycle only gains momentum, a tornado of tragedy disrupting everything in its path.

About a year after we obtained Chancer, Iyal asked me if kids were born angry. I couldn't help but be astounded by the philosophic turn in Iyal's musings. And of course astonishment was followed by my projections of what meaning lay behind these questions. This theme of anger concerned me as he grew older and we saw displays of Iyal's own anger on a more frequent basis. I truly believed that much of Iyal's anger was born of an awareness and frustration he experienced as more challenges evidenced themselves due to FASDs.

Before Iyal was seven years old, Harvey and I purchased or found books in the library that approached sex on an extremely elementary level, preferably with illustrations. We both talked about sex on Iyal's developmental level when he would ask questions, always aware in the back of our minds that Iyal's physical maturation was years ahead of his intellect. Harvey and I kept it basic, on a need-to-know basis, but we were concerned that Iyal know enough about his body and about sexuality to satisfy his preadolescent questions. We were committed to making sure that he could understand enough so that he wouldn't be susceptible to exploitation or sexual abuse by others. We taught him (and Morasha) to honor their body and respect its unique functions. And if they were ever uncomfortable with someone's interest in touching their body, they were to tell an adult.

The enormity of our responsibility to keep Iyal safe is burdensome. I remain frightened for him every day. Morasha, thank goodness, is grounded and not easily deterred from taking care of herself. Harvey and I are astounded at how mature and solidly centered she has become. We didn't worry about her making unwise decisions, which we knew wasn't the common experience for most parents who had eighteen-year-old daughters heading off to college. Iyal could always shift my worry when he would ask a million-dollar question like, "When you come out of your mother's tummy, do you have clothes on?" It made me smile in the moment. And then it punctured me with the reality of his belief system, far less developed than that of a typical twelve-year-old.

One day after school, Iyal raced off the bus before the other kids and ran up to me where I waited and immediately whispered that he needed to talk "in private." When I asked if he was okay, he said, "I need to show you something!" His hands moved toward the waistband of his pants, and right then I instinctively knew what was about to happen. Shielding Iyal away from Morasha and her friend Gaby, we swiftly crossed the street as I said, "Honey! Wait—not yet, okay? I want to talk about this, but let's get inside the van."

As we were climbing in, my mind was doing its third lap around the Indianapolis 500 without pit stops. I knew that he had natural questions and hoped I could make good on this teachable moment. I had pressed the button to close the side door just in time as he finished lowering his pants to show off his erection.

"Mom, why is my penis pointing up? It doesn't usually do that!" he said, once again displaying the object of his attention. I was just proud that he had used the anatomically correct word!

"Well, when you get to be a bigger boy or a man," I explained, "your body changes. And if your penis is tickled"—I know, but what other word was there?—"or touched a certain way, then this is what naturally happens. It's called an erection, and it's totally normal and happens to all boys and men when they get older."

He thought for a minute, nodded, and then pulled his pants up, thank goodness, just as Morasha opened the door to join us. I motioned for her to let me finish, garnished with an arched eyebrow of "please don't join in this conversation right now."

"And, Iyal, even if you *think* about certain things, your penis might get like this," I continued. "For instance . . . if you think of a girl and you like her and maybe you want to hold her hand or kiss her, then you might have an erection. Sort of like in *WALL-E* when he wanted to hold EVE's hand because he liked her." Oh my God, I was grasping at straws to find something he would recognize and understand.

"Does Chancer ever get an *instruction*?" Iyal asked, not questioning my movie reference. I debated on whether or not to correct his pronunciation but let it go.

"Well, the veterinarian did an operation on Chancer so that he wouldn't get an erection and make puppies with any girl dogs he might meet. He needs to focus on you and on his service work, not on pretty poodles that happen to walk by." I smiled.

"So *instructions* are what make babies . . . ?"

Morasha finally stopped rolling her eyes and began giggling uncontrollably. I shot her a look. From there, Iyal and I discussed all male animals and mammals and what needs to take place for reproduction. We didn't just talk about the birds and the bees—it was the dogs and cats, horses and hippos, circus lions and elephants. Basically, every animal Iyal could think of! But it ended on a light note, and I was grateful that we could talk about puppies and kittens and cubs and calves without it being something shameful or dirty.

—

Four years later, the "instruction incident" seemed pure and innocent compared to another conversation that also began with Iyal asking, "Mom, can we talk about something private?" I had been putting away clean laundry in my son's dresser drawers, fully aware that the chaos within them would grab my neat stack of underwear, socks, and T-shirts and torture them until they joined the no-man's-land of wrinkles, twists, and unidentifiable inside-out sportswear. Feeling like any sense of cooperation between his wardrobe and me would always remain lost in the dryer of life, I wondered why I even bothered.

Iyal was sitting cross-legged on his bed with Chancer protectively curled around him, a favorite position for each, when he hesitantly repeated his question. I turned away from the drawer where I was fighting a losing battle and said, "Yes, sweetie?"

His eyes searched mine, and I wondered if the way I put his laundry away had upset him. Later I would wish that it could have been something so benign. Iyal continued with a strained voice I didn't recognize: "Mom, I want to tell you something if you promise you won't get mad."

I gently put down the T-shirts in my hands, trying to preserve their dignity, and sat on the floor in front of Chancer and Iyal. "Honey, you can tell me anything you want to." I was already worried before the words came out of my mouth. "Do I usually get mad at you?"

Shaking his head, Iyal tiptoed out of his anxiety and said, "Something has been happening at school and I think it is . . ." He looked away, perplexed, as his eyes grazed the ceiling and his lips pressed together. *"Wrong."*

Uh-oh. This was territory I dreaded, an entire minefield of possibilities. I nodded for him to continue, never taking my eyes off him.

"Mom, this kid did something I think was"—he slowed down his speech to pronounce the upcoming word one syllable at a time with intention and an unusual accuracy—"*in-a-pro-pri-ate.*" I suspected he had practiced this over and over again to make sure he got it right. My heart sank, and I knew we were talking about a significant occurrence.

"What happened, honey?" I asked, bracing myself.

"Well, one time when I was in my first-period class," he continued with a severe gravity far beyond his developmental or even chronological years, "and there was no teacher, this boy took out his p-word and rubbed it on me."

Oh. God. Emotional shrapnel bombarded my rib cage as the bomb in my gut went off full force. I began to inwardly heave and retch inside but fought the impulse because I didn't want Iyal to think I was upset with *him*!

"This kid asked me a bad question, and I told him, 'No, I don't,' but he said it again and then touched me with it outside my pants . . . down here." Iyal pointed to his crotch and then looked up, scanning my face for some kind of reassurance that I wasn't mad at him for saying the *p-word.*

"Iyal, can you tell me more about it?" I informed my face muscles to soften. Reflexively, I reached out my hand toward him but held back, fearing he might shut down with my touch, the opposite of what most kids might crave at this moment.

I kept his eye contact as a moan escaped. "Oh. Sweetheart."

"I knew I shouldn't let him, Mom, but I couldn't tell him to stop! I think this was the second time or another time. Oh . . . and there wasn't any of that stuff that comes out. You know . . ." He used his hand in the air as if to wave off an annoying fly. That had been another conversation—one with Harvey—about ejaculation, wet dreams, guy stuff.

I felt dry sweat on my face that soon rippled down my entire body. I asked him how long ago this had happened, knowing this was a shot in the dark, and he told me right after we had seen snowflakes falling, an anomaly in Atlanta, so mid-January. A month ago. This happened a month ago, and I was just now finding out? Trying to act concerned but not scary-shameful concerned, I said, "Did you tell a teacher?"

"Well, there wasn't one around, so I went to the office. I told two people. But they didn't say much. So I decided it wasn't a big deal."

They didn't say much? Unbelievably, we had heard from *no one*! This was a month after Iyal's first experience of sexual battery, one he said he had immediately reported to the school, the one I had just *now* been told about. The tinder inside me was lit, smoking, kindling a firestorm that stole my oxygen and would not subside for the next five months.

Iyal shifted his position, now lying down next to Chancer, matching Chancer's length from head to paw. Iyal gently caressed him as Chancer's fur offered a sensory salve to Iyal's invisible wounds. Connected to his personal giant where he felt secure, Iyal described his sexual exploitation and sent me hurtling into space. I didn't have words yet to identify my emotions. My physical response was revulsion and fury.

And there was more.

Cautiously, I asked, "Iyal, is this the only thing that happened to you?"

He paused for a few seconds and said, "Well, there was another time when . . . that same kid rubbed his p-word against my arm, but he said if I told anyone, he wouldn't be my friend."

I knew now that I was numb, as if in shock when you must protect your body or soul from further systemic damage. I fought off my imagination, not wanting to picture what my son had endured. Tears weren't far behind, but I promised myself that I would hold it together for as long as he wanted to talk.

Iyal continued, his voice gaining confidence. "Mom? Remember in the beginning of the year, when it was still hot outside?"

Knowing Iyal wasn't always historically correct when connecting an event with when it happened, I was thinking mid-August, when he began the school year.

"The same kid told me he would 'bitch slap' me. What does that *mean*, Mom? Was that a bad word?" To be honest, I wasn't even sure I knew what that meant, but it couldn't have been decent.

Then, what I sorrowfully anticipated Iyal might say, "I'm sorry, Mom. Really, I'm sorry."

Along with the tears that could no longer be repressed, I felt bile rising in my throat. "Oh, honey." I soothed us both. "This was *not* your fault."

I couldn't grasp what Iyal was saying! I didn't want it to be true, but I knew he *couldn't have* made this story up. He had no prior experience in his life to which he could compare the meaning of this behavior. His IQ at the time was sixty; Iyal's memory likely rejected the experience, aware at some level of the violation, or else he simply couldn't bring himself to tell me before that moment. Harvey and I believed so deeply that most of his teachers cared about him and his education as much as we did. And letting it happen was one thing, but not responding to Iyal's attempt to get help? *Unconscionable.*

Thoughts were skyrocketing all over my brain, electrified by my own circuitry gone haywire. I was now in battle with my own primal flight-or-fight response; neither would help alleviate the angst my son was feeling.

Unfortunately, this wasn't the first time Iyal had been bullied both physically and emotionally. Two years earlier, in a session with his psychiatrist and me, Iyal spontaneously told us that in his last year of middle school, kids in his class had told him to "hump a chair." Because he had no idea what this meant, they had to demonstrate somewhat and then instructed him to do it. When they threatened, "If you don't, we will hang your dog!" Iyal, of course, complied. When Chancer was brought up in the equation, he knew there was no other choice. He had to save his best friend.

How did this happen to our son? I don't *want* to hear about the immature brain and how kids will say something without thinking . . . or act out because they themselves have been bullied. Of course, I know all this and am sympathetic to why it happens. I teach workshops about these behaviors! But God.

Chancer is Iyal's knight in shining armor. And their life is no fairy tale.

Tragically, Iyal's experience isn't that uncommon. Compared to those who are not disabled, individuals living with a disability are almost three times more likely to become victims of sexual assault. According to research by P. M. Sullivan and J. F. Knutson, experts in the field of disabilities and victimization, any type of disability contributes to higher risk of victimization, but those with multiple disabilities, like Iyal, are even more vulnerable.[4]

One staggering statistic circles above me like an albatross: 72% of adolescents and adults living with FASDs have been physically or sexually abused at least once in their life. Often the same perpetrators repeat the abuse because their victims don't register the abuse as "bad." Their limited cognitive understanding impedes an appropriate response.

Short-term memory may also be greatly impaired by their brain damage, so they may not remember when events actually happened.

So, the experienced trauma bypasses short-term recall and is stored in long-term memory before it returns to more recent memory. I imagine that's why people might not come forth when raped or assaulted until weeks, months, or years later. I just couldn't accept that Iyal had become part of this data.

As much as Harvey wanted to be involved and support this increasingly painful campaign for justice, he was immersed in his own sea of woes, the life of a synagogue riding the waves of human experience grasping for spirituality when it feels out of reach. Iyal's situation weighed heavily on him as he waited each day or night to hear news after a phone call or meeting I had insisted upon. I think he relied on my warrior-mom instincts and integrity to rise above the insidiousness of what had occurred.

I called the vice principal's office and arranged to come in. After I talked with his teachers and an administrator, I became livid. Not one of them came out and *said* Iyal made up the story of his abuse, but they might as well have. "You and I both know his memory's unreliable," one said, dismissing Iyal's perception of the incidents. I bit my tongue so I wouldn't scream.

In a period of ninety days that school year, Iyal said that he was sexually assaulted eight times, and he had reported the events *as they were happening* to five teachers, school administrators, or security officers. I calculated that fifteen members of the staff were informed of the abuse. But apparently no one did anything. They didn't notify the authorities or us.

Iyal even provided the names of the students who were responsible for the assaults, but because of laws protecting confidentiality, we didn't know what disciplines would be enforced. Between February and August of 2014, I was consumed with finding a justice for Iyal that seemed elusive. I felt my efforts were obstructed.

I didn't go directly to the police because I assumed my interaction with the school would resolve the issues of sexual battery against my son. Looking back, I'm dumbfounded that I continued to believe that the school would do the right thing by Iyal, not questioning their authority. I'm deeply saddened by the denial I was lost in, feeling that I should've known better.

The more Iyal shared with me, the more I cried in the privacy of our bedroom. Harvey held me, feeling helpless to make it better. My emotional barricade was shattered. Would a neurotypical teenaged boy talk to his mother so explicitly about being sexually teased, taunted, and coerced? Iyal recalled scenes with me that no mother would ever want to hear from her child, intellectually challenged or not.

On one particular afternoon, Iyal busted through the door into our foyer. Before I greeted him with my usual "Hi, honey!" I could see his demeanor was alarmingly agitated, as he would spill his guts yet again. He flung his backpack and then himself to the floor. Suddenly, he grew silent. Just when I thought there couldn't be anything else he could say to deepen my despair, Iyal stated flatly, "I want to kill myself. I'll never have any friends."

Not having any friends at school and always wanting them desperately, Iyal understood on some level he should say no when told to follow his abusers' instructions. But his impaired reasoning compromised his ability to actually say it. Seeming or feeling "normal" was most important in that moment.

Consequently, some kids had ordered Iyal to be a virtual marionette whose student puppeteer stood behind him and moved Iyal's arms and hands to touch a girl in the lunchroom, first her head and then her back. I recognized her name as another student who also lived with a developmental disability. After Iyal extricated himself, he met with his guidance counselor, but no one from the school reported the assault.

My mind raced around the rising complexity of the situation. I dreaded the nightmares that left me reeling and couldn't get the rest I so needed. Meanwhile, communication between me and school administrators was becoming increasingly disturbing, as I found their comments disingenuous and dismissive: "Oh, Mrs. Winokur, that's just terrible! I'm so sorry Iyal is having such a tough time right now."

I didn't give up, but I did get to a point where I didn't know where else to turn. Every direction looked like a dead end. The irony was that the more I sought help to end the abuse and bring the abusers to some kind of accountability, the worse it became. The promise to "look into Iyal's situation" seemed to carry an ominous veiled threat.

I knew an official administrative review of Iyal's accounts of these incidents could potentially harm him, because the credibility of his memory would inevitably come to attention. Because these bullying episodes also included another individual who struggled with cognitive impairment, Iyal's innocence would be challenged. I agonized with the recognition that the odds were stacking up against my son.

Harvey noticed that I dealt with the stress of this situation by reverting to my producer days: creating folders and binders and copies of the folders and binders containing every e-mail and notes from each phone call. They started in February with the awareness that all was not right in Iyal's world and continued to the end of August when the investigation came to a screeching halt. My compulsion for being a mistress of detail defined me, which usually made me nuts. But I couldn't come out from under the feeling that I might never do enough to fix the wrong done to my son. Not even my scrupulously organized notebook explaining the trajectory of this nightmare could steady me.

In my mind, the words to describe what was happening couldn't materialize fast enough. I wanted to scream my anger and spill out my grief before I slipped into hysteria. In these crimes, and they were crimes, Iyal had become the perpetrator as well as the victim. I no longer tried to hold back the tears when I was alone. I couldn't hide from my grief. I'm asking myself, How do I hold someone with a disability like

Iyal's accountable for his actions when he can't appreciate the impact of his actions?

Just when I thought this purgatory of abuse couldn't get any worse, Iyal returned home from school one Friday, telling Harvey and me that he told a teacher he wanted to see a guidance counselor because he heard in his head that people were telling him he wasn't good at basketball, and this made him very mad. Iyal dropped to the living room floor, scrunching his knees to his chest, not looking at us, not even looking at Chancer, who had ambled in to nuzzle beside his boy. He whispered that someone was telling him in his head to do bad things. With an alarming calmness, he added that someone was telling him to kill people in his home. To kill his family.

This was the first time Iyal had uttered these words. His psychiatrist had informed us a few years earlier that children who experience autism and fetal alcohol exposure may have intrusive thoughts and might not be able to differentiate whether they are their *own* thoughts or the words of *others* talking to them in their head. But I was deeply concerned that these distressing thoughts and images were now occurring in school to the extent that Iyal felt that he needed to leave a class or go speak to someone.

When Iyal was given the diagnosis of bipolar 1-with psychosis after his high school graduation, I was devastated all over again. I grieved with a new but familiar anguish. However, the diagnosis also provided a context through which we could frame the sensory hallucinations (although we didn't know how to identify them) that had plagued Iyal for years and the recent delusions that offered him unshakable beliefs of grandiosity. His raging was now understood as a characteristic of mania. I wanted desperately for Iyal to feel connected to others in *our* world. But I tried to take some comfort in accepting that he might live in coexisting worlds and feel a connection to others in both. How had my love for my son become large enough to contain all of these different Iyals? Many times throughout middle school and later in high school, the clinic would call Harvey or me to come pick up Iyal. He had been throwing up. He had a headache. He was crying. He couldn't concentrate and wanted to come home. His heart rate had soared. His blood pressure dropped dramatically. He was listless. He was hyperactive. His speech was pressured. He was agitated. It really didn't matter why. Iyal was miserable.

Those who had engaged in implicit and explicit coercive behavior to control, influence, or affect the health and well-being of a student (paraphrasing from the faculty handbook at my son's school) had threatened Iyal with reprisals. Over the course of these incidents, fifteen people, trained mandated reporters all, were aware of Iyal's assaults, and yet not one person called it in to the Department of Family and Children Services (DFACS), which is federal protocol.

Several years earlier, I was appointed to become a member of the Child Abuse Prevention and Treatment Act, a federally mandated agency, and, as an extension, served on the Children's Justice Advisory Task Force. My colleagues armed me with information as they supported and accompanied me through the grueling and unforgiving process of creating Iyal's case for maltreatment and abuse. Even though I had been an advocate and professional speaker on FASDs and the juvenile justice system for years, it was as though the reality of *my family* existed in another galaxy.

Besides the harm Iyal himself experienced, fetal-alcohol-affected individuals can become unwittingly involved in activities that escalate into sexual molestation and worse. I have always impressed upon other professionals that it is imperative that they understand the aftershocks that secondary disabilities can bring as a result of the primary brain injury.

A well-known statistic in the world of FASDs: 45% of individuals ages twelve and over living with FASDs have been reported to exhibit inappropriate sexual behaviors. Those who have experienced sexual assault are placed at even greater peril of committing these crimes. Sixty percent of people age twelve and over living with FASDs have trouble with the law. This deadly combination overwhelms the justice system, as kids living with FASDs enter and reenter the already crowded courts as if through a constantly revolving door. Futures that should have held promise for success are eclipsed by organic brain injury, creating a never-ending present or, worse, tossing them backward, where arrested development creates an even greater jeopardy for a perfect storm.

As Iyal continued remembering his abuses, it was evident that he clearly didn't know if what had occurred was teasing, bullying, or "just horsing around." Individuals who are intellectually impaired and plagued with a relentless need for approval will take on a subordinate persona. They attempt to make everyone around them happy, forsaking their own sense of self, which disappears because it's dependent on the happiness of others. What a burden.

And how do I even explain the layers of distorted thinking? Of course Iyal's capacity to respond appropriately in social situations included these heinous episodes of sexual harassment. But my God, he actually *apologized* to his perpetrators! Hoping that if he said he was sorry, his "friends" might forgive him for his own complicit behavior.

I believe that in Iyal's mind, no response he could offer would be the right one. But to my son's credit, he told me that he apologized because he also said to his perpetrators that he would go and report the assaults to some teachers. *That's* why he was apologizing to the kids! But then saying sorry made him feel guilty, and Iyal was obsessively worried about losing friends. It was an ironclad no-win situation.

As I would expect of someone with Iyal's brain differences, this period of time was like a mirage in suspended animation. He created a kind of still-life portrait for his reality, where things could remain safely static for prolonged periods. Change could crack his world, splitting him apart like Humpty Dumpty. He needed to feel in control. But not just like you or me. His every breath depended on it. So when Iyal told me and other adults at school that he didn't want to be a "snitch," my heart went out to him.

Nevertheless, he courageously agreed to describe to the school authorities a series of deplorable events that took place early one morning in an empty classroom. Iyal's arms became the canvas upon which some bullies wrote with markers; another morning in an unsupervised classroom, dry-erase-board erasers were torn up and stuffed into his mouth as a "joke"; and, in the cafeteria at lunchtime, other students pulled up porn sites on Iyal's cell phone and then shoved it in his face. Every time I heard Iyal recall these batteries, nausea overcame me. Lots of sympathetic nods, but no one believed us. Our cry for justice was dismissed.

When our case was reported to DFACS, it was "screened out" for investigation. DFACS would "not further investigate the charges of harassment" because they deemed the case "unsubstantiated"—"the allegation of maltreatment was not supported by the evidence and information provided."

Would this devastating wound ever completely heal for Iyal or for us? This face of FASDs is rarely reflected in the mirror of our culture. It's one that no one wants to see.

One thing was undeniable. Since Chancer had joined our family, Iyal had improved. He had shown remorse for his behaviors where he didn't before. Iyal now apologized for his tantrums and longingly asked me if he would ever change—ever control his emotions and prevent meltdowns before they reached the launching pad where they would sit waiting to be ignited. My son has grown and matured, despite the recent abuse and despite the fact that his IQ had dropped to fifty-six by the time he graduated high school. Iyal's initial score was ninety-eight at five years old, an average score compared to his peers'. Among individuals who experience FASDs, a decline in IQ can occur yet may level off by the mid to late twenties.

Over time, I learned the significance of Iyal's adaptive behavior score, which reflects the ability to be independent and get along with others. At five years old his score was seventy-one, in the moderately low range of functioning. While Iyal's score in this assessment has declined, too, he has mastered many day-to-day tasks needed to live interdependently. However, Iyal still misinterprets the motivation and behavior of others, showing his difficulty with social skills and causing us to constantly worry.

Iyal is compassionate and wants to help others. He would bend down to tie my dad's shoelaces for him without being asked. He tells Morasha "thank you" and makes it clear he loves her because she's his sister. My son has a good heart.

Which makes the following sentence I read after Iyal's abuse all the more heartbreaking: "To all my fellow FASD sufferers who have been through hell on earth before they die." This sentence posted on an FASDs blog knocked the breath out of me, and I just can't seem to get it back. The blogger went on to discuss the issue of suicide.

Comments like that one always exhumed my fear, as much as I tried to bury it. In truth, the idea that Iyal might choose death over life terrifies me. And maybe not even actively *choose* it. Choice implies an ability to weigh one concept against another, understanding the outcomes, and then realize the implications of making that choice. I wonder if an individual with cognitive impairment like Iyal can consider the real consequence of pulling a gun trigger aimed at himself or swallowing a pill bottle full of potent antipsychotic medication whose warning label can't be interpreted by him with any meaning.

Statistically, we have about a one-in-four chance that Iyal could lose *himself* and we could lose *Iyal.* The ongoing threat of suicide has only increased as Iyal grows older because the twelve-to-twenty age range is when suicide most often occurs for those living with FASDs. Current research shows that 43% of young adults affected by FASDs have threatened to complete suicide; 23% reported a history of suicide attempts throughout their lifetime. This is hell on earth for all of us.

Although individuals who live with FASDs are at a greater risk of attempting suicide as a result of damage to their central nervous system and their brain, I'm guardedly optimistic that Chancer (and any other service dog trained to support people like Iyal challenged by mental illness and the risk of suicide) hopefully will make a difference. However, no research has been done to show whether or not a service dog can help reduce these suicide numbers.

The truth is that the primary disabilities produced by FASDs include difficulties with the brain's executive function, sort of like a computer crashing because the CPU went on permanent vacation. Without strong executive function, the CPU is disabled, so a person can't hold more than one thought at a time. As a result, he can't judge these thoughts, one against the other, or set goals and make a plan. And if he does achieve the goals, he probably won't be able to measure the results and know if he hit a foul ball or a home run.

For people who are prenatally exposed to alcohol, however, their confusion is amplified by an inattention and impulsivity that barrels into the land of intellectual impairment. If a person can't squarely compare and contrast two thoughts, she can't appreciate the whole concept of choice, so decisions occur by default and sometimes without warning.

Primary disabilities can also challenge an affected individual's capacity to concentrate for any length of time; with Iyal, his maximum attention span was between four and six seconds when he was in fifth grade. In the past few years, though, we've seen him poring over the Internet, reading about a favorite movie and its actors. We know he can't read all the words or know what they mean, but he understands enough to create a scene in his head, imagining what the actors look like and how they might talk. He hangs on to every word he understands in a review, wanting to know why the director isn't rebooting the movie or why a particular actor wouldn't "surprise" (reprise) their role in the sequel! I love when he inserts his own version of words into his narratives. We never conceived that Iyal would match words to ideas that he hadn't actually seen.

These issues have not only impacted Iyal but also us, his family. For instance, sensory integration disorder was not only Iyal's disorder; it became ours. If Iyal didn't want to look at the colorful magnets on the refrigerator, it meant rearranging ourselves at the kitchen table so he wouldn't see the distressing images on the magnets. But with the help of his psychologist, we gradually increased his exposure to the offensive images, and he changed his seat! Since Iyal was about five, he could not look at particular photos, pictures, or objects without revulsion. From Barbies when he was little to telling me now to take off my nail polish or rings, he saw things we didn't. And if I asked him why it bothered him, he didn't know. In hindsight, Iyal's unique sensory challenges may have had more to do with hallucinations than with a sensory integration disorder.

His sensitivity to smell was off the charts. My body's odor, clean or otherwise, often spun Iyal into enormous tantrums, or even after Chancer, he flew into rages of rudeness and exaggerated responses to me. Sometimes I couldn't be anywhere he could see me, because he said he could smell me.

This issue with my smell only compounded our challenges, such as when helping with homework. I wanted to sit close enough to Iyal so I could see the words or the math problem with my reading glasses on but not physically come within a three-foot radius of his body, paper, or pencil. If I accidently breathed on his paper, we had to start all over, with me moving six inches farther away from him. Naturally, I couldn't get close enough to even pretend to read his assignments while reading upside down, remaining as still as possible, and holding my breath. It was pretty much a sensory disaster, with homework taking a direct hit.

I'm not sure I could tell you when Iyal's aversion to my smell or touch eclipsed my ability to be physically close to him. Most of the time, I have to monitor my own responses to Iyal or my needs to touch or hold him close. If Iyal is particularly bereft, however, he'll allow me to hug him or rub his back or shoulder. I may not always read the signals right—but after all these years, I have become a fairly accurate interpreter of his boundaries. Still, I wish his emotional force field didn't exist.

To return to the *primary* effects of prenatal alcohol exposure on the brain in order to provide insight on the high risk of suicide: Iyal has a diminished ability to read facial expressions or body postures. Sadly, he interprets our faces negatively or critically much of the time, especially if he's in a "bad place." If he doesn't see us smiling, he thinks we are angry with him. If I'm distracted by something, he imagines he has done something wrong. "Why are you mad at me, Daddy?" he frequently asks Harvey. "What did I do wrong, Mom?" "Morasha, do you love me?" Trying to smile pleasantly all the time for Iyal only works if you're Miss America, which I'm not.

Over these last few years, Iyal urgently and repeatedly asked if we were "happy." The intensity and frequency with which he inquired made it feel like his life was on the line. If we're not okay, then he can't be okay. He has assumed an inhuman responsibility to please his family and the others for whom he cares all the time. This burden drives him frantic as he runs interference for his own sake, trying to second-guess our thoughts and words. And if this sounds utterly exhausting for us, just imagine what it does to him. My heart hurts.

If *we* depend on the anticipated reactions of others to bolster us or to reassure us that we have the right to exist, imagine the constant panic and hypervigilant universe in which Iyal lives. He might think he doesn't deserve to live if he doesn't believe that his daddy isn't mad at him. If he can't understand that we're just thinking without a smile and it doesn't mean that we're mad at him or don't want him to be our son . . . how could he ever find any peace?

When impulsivity hasn't been filtered with the "what ifs" or "who might this affect," the results can be disastrous. Impulsivity linked with intellectual impairment, sensory disorder, and poor executive functioning create a potentially deadly combination. And I haven't even talked about the impact of mental illness on those already fighting the immediacy of their brain damage.

Depression, anxiety, and mood instability intrude on the already challenged central nervous system. FASD experts assert that up to 97% of fetal-alcohol-exposed people are challenged by mental illness. That's ninety-seven fucking percent! I am outraged by this number and what it implies. Outraged because I see it wreaking hell and havoc on my son's life. His mental illness underscores every action and brands his every thought. It is the undertow in Iyal's life, and out of fear, it drags us down with him.

Late in the day, Chancer must have sensed that, like my son, I was experiencing my own internal storm as I reflected on all the impossible challenges Iyal faced. He found me on the sofa and sat on the floor in front of me, which put us both at eye level. As I looked at him, he rested his massive golden head in my lap, setting it there and looking up at me with his intelligent dark-brown eyes. Chancer seemed to be willing me to feel better by sheer concentration. This thought made me smile, and after that happened, he knew he had me. Chancer licked my face and then resettled on the floor, his way of letting me know that despite the odds, everything would be okay.

Why? Because love never gives up.

Chapter Eleven

The drive from our home in Roswell, Georgia, to Birmingham, Alabama, was smooth and surprisingly without holiday traffic as we time traveled from eastern into central time on the penultimate day of the year. Our entire family, four humans and one large golden retriever, had already been counting down the hours toward our special New Year's Eve plans. And believe me, Chancer had an uncanny canine and otherworldly sense of human time.

Instead of midnight, 8:00 p.m. is the witching hour in Chancer's life because it's what we've come to call "chew time." Our initial discovery of a particular veterinarian-approved "chew" morphed into a highly anticipated nondiscretionary gastronomic event! In fact, witnessing Chancer's ecstasy brought on by even the mere sound of any word beginning with the "ch" sound, we invested in thirty-count bags of "Chancer's chews" months in advance.

We quickly learned Chancer would bark precisely at 8:00 p.m. for his chew no matter where he was in the house or where we were—somehow he just knew. It was astonishing. Even crazier, every year when daylight savings occurred, Chancer's internal clock changed as well. I am dead serious! How the hell could Chancer understand and respond to an external phenomenon when even *humans* fail to reset their clocks, watches, and other measurements of time?

That morning at the end of December, we loaded into the van with overnight bags, our evening ware on hangers. Harvey's rented tux hung next to Iyal's new suit, and Harvey and I, out of respect for each other's new-and-improved middle-aged bodies, didn't comment on the size. Shirts were pressed and black shoes were polished in size nine for Harvey and twelve wide for Iyal, with appropriate dress socks duly noted.

Morasha and I had purchased cocktail dresses for the event, although technically she was too young to even consider a dress associated with alcohol. We splurged on new high heels, my feet already howling with anticipatory torture, and chose sort-of-matching purses. Morasha and I were pretty sure we would be partying until early New Year's Day, so we studied her go-to websites for instructions on how to maintain your look for twelve hours. This exercise brought me to my knees with laughter. Were they kidding?

Chancer didn't need new clothes, but we made sure we had his kibble rationed out in baggies for the three days and two nights we would be away from home. Water bowls, poop bags, and special treats were stowed out of Chancer's reach for the drive to and from Birmingham. We had to be one step ahead of his nose.

More than a year before, a young couple from Alabama had contacted Harvey about conducting their marriage ceremony on New Year's Eve. Mutual friends had referred them, and the couple wanted to make sure they had Rabbi Winokur on the books for their wedding weekend. The bride's father was a well-respected plastic surgeon in the Birmingham area and had offered to put up our whole family for two nights in the hotel for the wedding. We'd informed him that the whole family included Chancer, our son's service dog. "No problem!" the father enthusiastically responded. "He's welcome to come! We'd love it!"

When the invitation arrived for Harvey at the temple, it indicated a concurrent celebration for both the wedding and for New Year's Eve. The couple told Harvey that they expected more than three hundred guests, so we were praying that Iyal would be in good-behavior mode for the festivities. Harvey and I agreed in advance that the kids wouldn't attend either the rehearsal dinner the evening we arrived at the hotel or the wedding ceremony the following day, but they would join us for the New Year's Eve party.

Upon arrival, we checked in to the hotel and made our way up to the two connecting rooms that would be home base for our short stay. Even though the rooms weren't particularly large, they were modern in style, each containing a king-sized bed and an adequately sized bathroom, and most important, they were *clean*. I was a clean freak when I stayed anywhere other than my own home. An immaculate bathroom, bed, and kitchen were nonnegotiables when I traveled. If I had to think twice about taking off my shoes and walking barefoot, it did not bode well for management of my OCD.

In fact, our hotel room was so modern that it didn't have a closet, per se. Our clothes would either be folded on shelves in the sleeping area or hung openly outside the commode room across from the sink and vanity area, which really wasn't a big deal. However, lack of "containment" might be an issue with Morasha's wardrobe, shoes, and other overnight essentials. For better or worse, this whole organization-and-boundary deal was an area for my personal best. And in this particular area, Morasha's lack of my DNA guaranteed I could keep my position intact. Morasha's overnight bags would explode with toiletries, curling irons, books, the required water bottle or two, and perhaps an additional set of headphones just in case. However, sharing a room with her often led to a cold sweat followed by dizziness, which might remain until we were no longer roommates. I once let my guard down and spied granola bar wrappers hidden under a pile of discarded dirty clothes.

When I scanned the bathroom as we unpacked our toothbrushes and makeup to lay claim to our territory on the vanity, I noticed that the bathroom also had no cabinets or drawers. All items were stored on shelves, some high and some at shin level. I noted the extra toilet paper rolls, wrapped soaps, and tissues boxes were also exposed. Okay, so I moved on.

A door that could be locked connected our rooms so that both parties could have access to each other. We could unlock our door but would still have to request permission, by knocking or shouting, to be allowed into the other room. I've seen this before and always thought it a bit idiotic.

A Rorschach inkblot would best describe how our rooms compared to each other. Equally designed in space with the same arrangement of shelves and supplies, they were mirror images.

With essentially more than a thousand weddings under Harvey's belt, or clergy robe, he had participated in events involving all manner of taste, food, ambience, and accompanying music, establishing a finely tuned wedding-calibration protocol. Yes, we both could become hosts of a reality series on *Weddings Gone Wild!* or *Honeymoon Truth or Dare?* or *Standing Alone at the Altar, What the Fuck Happened?*

On the first evening, the kids stayed in with Chancer to watch a movie on TV. Chancer kept an eye on things, especially with Iyal and his mood swings, always ready to prance in to rescue Iyal from his behavior if things went a bit haywire. We trusted that Chancer could manage Iyal if we left them alone.

Harvey and I drove to the location of the rehearsal dinner. An old railroad station had been converted into a combined bar and restaurant, creating a rusty ambience with clever sconce lighting. The room was crowded with people we didn't know, but we were used to being anonymous. Inevitably, it would be loud, so talking was useless anyway, which was often a bonus when we weren't in the mood to carry on conversation with other guests or each other.

Appetizers like puffs filled with warm filet mignon dressed with horseradish sauce and crunchy spring rolls with duck sauce were passed around. We had learned to pace ourselves so we could indulge on the food yet to be served. Dinner that night was a sit-down meal with choices from a carefully crafted menu, served in courses throughout the evening. Toasts to the bride and groom interspersed each course, and we suspected if we only knew the couple better we would be laughing just as hysterically as everyone else.

I've come to believe that the rehearsal dinner foreshadows the kind of reception that will follow the wedding ceremony. On a ten-point scale, you either suffered through a one ("Oh my God, when do we get to leave and go to Burger King around the corner?") or reveled in a ten ("Shit. Do we *have* to go already? Aren't there thirds?" followed by "How late is the bar open? Are you sure we already had dessert? I don't remember. I need another drink.").

This was definitely looking like a ten.

The next evening around nine o'clock, New Year's Eve, a little bit before the ceremony, Harvey, dressed in his conservative and respected traditional black robe of clergy, slipped out of the hotel room, leaving Iyal and Chancer to hang out, one on top of the other. I followed Harvey down to the ceremony a half hour later while Morasha had agreed to help Iyal get ready for the big night. Brave sister.

After a brief ceremony, it was finally time for our family to party! Three knocks on the door, a brief pause, and then one more knock was the signal for the kids to then ask, "Who is it?" Otherwise, they weren't to open the door to anyone.

Harvey and I reached the doors to our rooms; we knocked "the signal" and immediately heard Iyal yelling, "*I* wanna say it!" Which was apparently the password for all hell to break loose. Yes, we should've just used our key to get in, but there we were, trying to train our children to be spy kids.

"No, Iyal! It's *my* turn, be quiet!" Morasha yelled.

"Mom . . . *I* wanna ask. Where *are* you, Mom?" Iyal wondered aloud, still struggling with the concept of object permanence.

"Iyal, she's out there! Why are you asking that?" *Ah, Morasha,* I thought. *Don't you remember the rule—don't ask why?*

"Iyal, Morasha, please unlock the door so we can come in," Harvey pleaded.

Scrambling sounds, groans, and thuds accompanied the opening of the door. Much to our surprise, they were actually dressed and ready to go. Iyal looked rather like *GQ* junior in his new suit, even though one shirttail wandered around looking to be tucked back in and, upon closer inspection, buttons were protesting against their unmatched holes and remained askew, victims of the curse of Iyal's unusually large fingers and minimal fine motor control.

Morasha glowed with anticipation in her new dress and shoes. Makeup was subtle and jewelry minimal. Good girl! They were ready to party!

Harvey retired his black robe to the open closet and checked his face and hair in the mirror. No, he's not that vain; he's just aware that even without the robe, he's still Rabbi Winokur for the entire evening, subject to various greetings and introductions. Despite wanting to leave that role behind at times, it somehow always seemed to follow him/us around.

Case in point: a few summers ago, Harvey and I vacationed alone, just the two of us, for the first time in God knows how long. When our cruise ship docked near the Parthenon in Greece, we cautiously climbed up the uneven steps in our sandals, following our tour guide to the top, where we stood in awe before one of the great monuments of history.

Waiting on the rest of our group to catch up, I was drawn into my own trilogy of Greek mythology: chatting it up with Odysseus and Homer and looking (but not directly) at Medusa while recommending the latest hard-to-control-curly-hair gel. Oh. And that Trojan horse? I always suspected that a cascade of Greek-style condoms would come spilling out rather than soldiers. However, a shrill siren's song disrupted my inner travelogue before I could engage with Zeus about the new weather app on my iPhone.

By now the rest of our group had caught up to us, and the tour guide was waving his stupid flag held high for those who were travel challenged. But before he could even open his mouth, I heard from a good distance a woman's voice yelling above the rumble of dozens of tourists:

"Rabbi! Rabbi! Hey, Donnie, it's Kathy! Rabbi?"

I wanted to vaporize. I even *liked* Kathy! She was one of my favorite congregants. But shit, we were on vacation. In fucking *Greece*, for God's sake!

Harvey and I quickly exchanged glances that said, "Oh well, it was good while it lasted."

"Oh! Hi, Kathy! I can't believe it's you!" Harvey hollered across history.

I joined in the Greek chorus. "Oh my God, I can't believe you guys are here!"

It got better; their tour group joined ours for the rest of the tour. For the *rest of the tour*. And now Hebrew history was warring with Greek history in my head, leaving me totally confused. Did BC mean before condoms?

The four of us walked into the ballroom that had been transformed into another place and time, perfect for the coming new year. The ceiling had blinking light constellations against a midnight-blue tissue-like backdrop. Tabletops were dressed with sky-high flower arrangements, and tea lights twinkled and winked everywhere we looked.

The kids' eyes widened in disbelief, their beautiful faces reflecting that they had never seen a party like this before! Where were the Cheez Doodles and M&M'S? The chicken fingers and fries? Where were those obnoxious little plastic horns and Day-Glo necklaces searching for the eternal black light you could take home to annoy your parents? Nowhere to be seen. *This* was a classy party: black top hats and glittery Mardi Gras masks, high-end noisemakers that hit the top and bottom of two different octaves, and, yes, plenty of champagne.

This reception was one of the rare occasions where, instead of a deejay, a live eighteen-piece band with three main singers backed by a four-woman dance team played all night. They were outstanding! Harvey and I lost all control and danced with each other, with the kids, with strangers, and sometimes with ourselves for hours.

We gorged on a delicious dinner, survived toasts to the bride's and groom's families, which left the kids dazed and glazed, and finally had our desserts, which woke them up again. Celebratory hugs, kisses, and ear-shattering noisemakers at midnight were apparently the signal for more champagne and soda, and even more desserts. By the strike of 2:00 a.m. in any time zone, it was our Cinderella time, without the glass slipper that would have been welcome considering my wicked-stepmother high heels.

We were admittedly exhausted but happy, laughing together as we headed for the elevator back up to our floor. Then Harvey looked at me and said, "We left a *dog* in our hotel rooms!"

Yes, that's right—plural, *rooms*. The adjoining doors were left open so if Chancer got bored with one room, he could trot over to the other room and back again for some light entertainment. The four of us excused ourselves, and Harvey and I each dragged a kid through the lobby into the elevator, where we propped each other up against the walls, then flopped out and managed to navigate the hallway to our rooms.

We opened the door where Morasha and I were staying and fell inside, with all our souvenirs crashing onto the floor. We had barely stepped into the room when we looked up and saw Chancer staring back at us, standing just a few feet away. Harvey and Iyal had turned to open their door, but I whispered to Harvey, "Harve, I think you should look in here." He stopped in his tracks and leaned around the doorway to gaze inside our room.

Chancer had celebrated New Year's Eve without us! Shredded toilet paper confetti was playfully strewn about, and unwrapped soap bits littered the floor. Not to be forgotten, tissue boxes were decimated, their contents puffed up in cloud clusters adorning the bed, chair, and opened suitcases. We gaped, and Chancer stood there with pride, offering up his decorations. Not a guilty whisker on his face.

I realized Chancer had taken full advantage of the open layout of the room and supplies and knew where to find them and what to do with them. Smart doggie.

Oy. We remembered that we had left the doors open to the other room. We scurried through with Chancer following to assess his rearrangement of paper goods in our absence. I swear, he had seen the Rorschach inkblot too! He literally had swept the other bathroom of its paper contents and managed to duplicate his decorations in there as well! In addition, balled-up socks in black and white, a favorite impromptu toy, complemented the festivities, lying at the foot of the bed.

We recorded the decor of each room on iPhones along with Chancer, whose expression never changed. Smiling up at us, he knew he would never need to remind us that leaving him, a service dog, alone again wasn't okay, even if we left him with origami papers.

While he still behaved like a puppy at times, Chancer was getting older. And we knew that as Chancer aged, we would eventually have to consider getting another service dog for Iyal. Thank God that 4 Paws was based on a model where the dog placed with the family always remained with the family. We knew that Chancer would always be a part of our family, even when he could no longer provide the service work for Iyal. Some service-dog agency models require the dog to be returned to the agency when the dog is no longer able to work. I just can't even imagine how devastating that would be!

From the recesses of my mind, I recalled ten was the number that would signify the changing of the guard in our home. I'm not sure where this number came from, but it seemed about right. Had I heard it in our initial class when we got Chancer? That seemed like a lot of chews ago! I realized after Chancer began approaching the age of eight (roughly six years after he was matched with Iyal) that we would need to submit another application to 4 Paws.

Probably all our family members had been thinking about it for some time, but no one was ready to address the need or what it might mean for Chancer's future, so nobody was talking. I can't even remember what started the second-dog process; it might have actually been Iyal. After all, he had started worrying about Chancer getting old since we had brought him home! Some of this had to do with Iyal's distorted sense of time.

Iyal was aware that when Chancer became older, he would find it more difficult to work as his service dog, but Iyal understood that Chancer would always be in our home as part of our family and their friendship would never change. Many friends asked us how the transition between Chancer and our second dog would occur; would Chancer just know that he was retired and didn't need to be on call as much? As I anticipated when and how Chancer would take a backseat in the care of Iyal, I prayed the change itself would be seamless.

I knew that over the years of Chancer's life with us, I would have to be the anchor in an uneasy sea whenever Iyal started to wonder about the length of Chancer's life. When it came to emotional intelligence, both Harvey and I would step in to support his ability to grasp more complex thoughts and feelings. I treasured the job, even though it moved me into not only my own experience of deep sadness, but also took me into Iyal's world of sorrow. And illness and death wouldn't be easy areas of navigation for either of us.

Iyal definitely needed reassurance about Chancer through the first eight years of his friend's life with us. Often, something he saw on TV would unlatch the door to Iyal's cabinet of worries. Seeing any animal character, cartoon or otherwise, with any signs of sickness or injury prompted Iyal to ask how long Chancer would live. The good news, however, was the way these moments illustrated Iyal "catching" an implication, which was a significant step in his understanding of the abstract.

I suspect as Chancer opened up windows in Iyal's brain for better understanding, it also made a link about his Pop-Pop, who was much older than anyone else he knew. So as his brain began to catch up on development, with Chancer by his side, his world unfolded to a far greater expanse than we could have envisioned.

Even before my dad passed away in 2013, conversations between Iyal and me would consist of Iyal asking the same questions. "Mom, how long will Chancer live? Ten years? Fifteen years?"

"Gee, honey. I don't know. I hope so."

"Mom, will Chancer get old enough to be a grandpa like Pop-Pop?"

"Sweetheart, Chancer was never able to father puppies." We had covered these dog sex-ed questions many times. "So he couldn't really become a grandpa."

Iyal thought for a moment. "But, Mom, Chancer *could* live to be one hundred, couldn't he?"

Eeeh—now what should I say? "Well, Iyal, most dogs don't live that long. Smaller dogs tend to live longer, because they are, well, smaller. But even *they* don't live to be one hundred."

Iyal would tilt his head, sort of like how Chancer does with that quizzical look. "So, Mom, how long will Chancer live to *be*?" Early on, Harvey and I talked with Iyal about what we would do when Chancer died and how we hoped to get Iyal another service dog. The seeds of this conversation were planted and often revisited. And I'd try to close out the conversation with "Honey, nobody really knows for sure. Many golden retrievers live a good long life until they are twelve years old, or maybe even longer." I had to be *so* careful about picking a number, because it could linger in Iyal's thinking for a long time and come back to haunt me every day for years, whether it was the right age or the wrong one.

A concern that became more pronounced with time was the level of pain and decreased ability Chancer would experience as he aged due to his hip dysplasia and arthritis. Because we knew that he was living with this condition, we chose to follow our veterinarian's recommendation for a stem-cell transplant to strengthen his mobility. I had established what began as a client relationship with Dr. JoAnne Roesner almost forty years earlier and treasured the friendship it also grew into. I trusted her with my animals, knowing that their health was in her expert care and my heart was in her keeping.

Immediately after the procedure, we began a rigorous schedule of rehabilitation for Chancer, which was when I learned through one of my friends on my canine advisory council about a new facility opening. Georgia Veterinary Rehabilitation, Fitness and Pain Management is a state-of-the-art treatment center housing a pool, an underwater treadmill, and land rehabilitation, with exam rooms for laser therapy, acupuncture, chiropractic adjustment, and other supportive services. Dr. Evelyn Orenbuch, who opened and directed the facility, was a highly qualified vet who made all her clients, human and otherwise, feel safe and confident in her hands.

Chancer soon became a regular client and always received star treatment there. Our relationship with Dr. Evelyn and her colleagues helped considerably to keep Chancer "on his feet." Nevertheless, the whole process of treating and rehabilitating Chancer reminded us all of the inevitable.

So when I started to talk about Chancer's aging and the philosophy of 4 Paws during this time, I had everyone's attention in my family, including Chancer's. The process was still a ways off, but we needed to put it on our radar.

Chancer wasn't the only one getting older. My son and daughter were entering adolescence, which, being Jewish, meant preparing for their religious and cultural transition into adulthood. In true Winokur fashion, planning for Morasha and Iyal's B'Nai Mitzvah (the plural for children of the commandments) began years before their thirteenth birthdays, the traditional age for this sacred rite of passage. But now it was no longer so far away.

Preparation had started earlier for them as well and included seven years of basic Hebrew, Judaic studies, and further cultural education, leading up to the actual ceremony. The kids would also complete a mitzvah project, demonstrating their willingness to serve. Becoming a Bat, for Morasha, and Bar, for Iyal, Mitzvah meant that they were ready to take on the responsibilities that came with being seen as an adult in the eyes of their Jewish community.

During the school year leading up to their special event, Morasha became a cheerleader, earning a position as a "fly," a highly respected team member used in stunts and those Olympic-looking formations that left me wringing my hands. Morasha loved the ensemble feeling and enjoyed the practices and games immensely. Admittedly, she must have received these daredevil athletic genes from her side of the family. Neither Harvey nor I could even run and jump over a water hose lying on the ground without twisting an ankle.

When she turned thirteen and reached Facebook-page age, I knew she would master social networking in ways that I would never grasp. Already, whenever I asked for tech assistance in setting up a new computer account or removing a setting, she would roll her eyes and sigh simultaneously, which usually intensified my already low technological self-esteem.

But she made up for my distress when, to our delight but not surprise, Morasha mastered American Sign Language. And it was *her* idea! Her fingers usually danced by her side as she spoke, listened, sang, and probably even dreamed. She had captured the gestalt of this skilled language, and I was in awe. Well, actually I was jealous. This happened a lot as she matured. Don't judge me!

Iyal was also growing up. Although he struggled daily to navigate his middle-school landscape, he managed to improve his reading up to a third-grade level. That year he became increasingly aware that he was differently abled from his peers. Feeling the ever-widening gap of understanding and skills between himself and his classmates left him easily frustrated. And me worried. What would happen if he couldn't handle his frustration and his self-esteem plummeted further? Little did

I know then just how much we would all be tested by the harassment and sexual abuse in the years to come.

But at the time, Iyal continued to amaze us with unexpected improvements as he explored the Internet. He loved making PowerPoint presentations and began producing videos and short movies with the assistance and supervision of his helper friends. Soon thereafter he was writing scripts, directing others, and acting in his own movies. He seemed to have found a niche to develop his creative aptitude.

—

The rest of the school year flew by, and soon it was time for the actual B'Nai Mitzvah ceremony and accompanying celebration. We had chosen Memorial Day weekend for the event to allow more loved ones to travel to Atlanta. Over the holiday weekend, dinners, brunches, and lunches—not including the actual B'Nai Mitzvah itself—would connect our festivities.

—

Harvey and I had moved my dad down from New Jersey to Atlanta in the summer of 2010, around seven years after my mom died and the year before the B'Nai Mitzvah.

That June, Iyal, Chancer, and I drove up to New Jersey from Atlanta so Iyal could attend his sleepaway camp for the summer. Two days after we arrived, my dad took Iyal to a nearby zoo. My mom and dad loved the tradition of taking the kids to see animals, no matter where we were! On the way home, my dad briefly fell asleep while driving, and the car drifted across the two-lane road and into an oncoming car at the crest of a small hill. The road was literally two minutes away from the house.

After the impact, the airbags in Dad's car inflated. Someone from the other car called the ambulance, which arrived quickly and took Dad and Iyal to the nearest emergency room.

That's when I got *the call.* That's when I knew it *was time*. Although no one in either car was badly injured, thank God, the head-on crash changed the course of our family's future.

My dad had been on the fence about moving out of the house that I grew up in and that he had shared with my mom for forty-seven years. After her death, he'd been visiting retirement communities in the area for three years but couldn't make a commitment because making that decision was so complex. After the accident, he and I knew what he had to do.

Iyal, who had been sitting in the front passenger seat, didn't sustain any physical injury. Of course, at the scene of the accident, the EMTs discovered that Iyal couldn't answer their questions in a way that made any sense to them. He was unable to put the sequence of events together chronologically. And of course Iyal would say he was fine even if he wasn't. I believe he knew that if something was wrong with him, he might not be able to leave for camp the next day! Underneath the confusion in some instances, Iyal could put together the consequence of what might happen, which was actually a huge stride for him!

By the time I arrived at the ER twenty minutes after my dad called me, the ER staff was about to take an X-ray of Iyal's neck to make sure he hadn't hurt his spine. As I rushed into the curtained-off area, trying to compartmentalize my anxiety over Dad and my worry about Iyal, the technician asked Iyal to lie still. Given all that had occurred between the accident, the ambulance ride, and the ER, Iyal's adrenaline was racing around his body and pouring out of his mouth in a constant stream of words. He wouldn't be able to stay still even if he wanted to! I explained Iyal's disabilities to the tech.

"Okay, young man, I need for you to put down your legs on this table so your feet can lay flat," the tech said.

Iyal saw me come in and sat up. "Mommy! Where's Pop-Pop? Is he okay?" He began to cry. "Where's Pop-Pop? I don't want him to die!"

I hugged Iyal, more for me than for him. "Oh, sweetheart, he's okay, Iyal."

Iyal looked around and swung his feet off the table, trying to get up in search of my dad. The technician and I both grabbed him so she could resume the X-ray. I'm sure we looked ridiculous.

I pushed Iyal back onto the table while he wriggled to get free. The technician gently wrestled with him until finally his spine was lying flat so she could position him so the X-ray would cover the exact area that may have been injured.

"Iyal, can you show me how straight you can make your body?"

Iyal didn't respond as she placed a huge white plastic contraption around his head. She was determined to steady his neck.

This huge neck brace looked like a space helmet to me. "Wow, honey, you look like a spaceman!"

However, he couldn't hear me, because his hearing had involuntarily shut down, a physiological response to a traumatic incident. Iyal's flight response took over because the thought that something had happened to my dad was agonizing him.

"Mommy," he cried, "I need to see Pop-Pop! Where is he?"

Around the same time, my dad's dearest friend in the world, Harold, arrived at the ER after getting a call from Dad. Harold was with Dad while I tried to wrangle Iyal to stay still. Given my dad's history of cardiac disease and compromised renal function and the removal of an aortic aneurysm, I was panicking about what was going on. The hospital doctors and nurses performed an EKG after he had complained of chest pain. After I knew that Iyal was okay and would be released, I asked a nurse to stay with Iyal. I needed to focus my attention on Dad. I found his room; he was lying on a gurney in a hospital gown. I had no control over the scene. The ER doctor told me that he wanted to keep him overnight for observation. He believed Dad had fractured his sternum, which explained the cause of the chest pain. Thankfully, Dad was released after two days.

Meanwhile, Iyal went to camp the next day, and I wept with the realization that I could have lost my son and my father at the same time. The accident left my dad and me anxious, although a few days later, Dad stated he was fine. I knew he wasn't, and I knew that discussing with him how he really felt wouldn't be easy. He was deeply saddened that this accident had occurred with Iyal in the front seat of the car, and I'm sure he ran through the "what ifs" over and over again. I don't think he could ever have forgiven himself for causing an accident that could've harmed his darling grandson.

I had called Harvey as soon as I received the call from my dad after the accident, and he was waiting in Atlanta to find out what was going on. We said the same thing to each other almost simultaneously: we needed to move my dad to Atlanta. Even though we'd had this conversation in the past, this time would be real.

Dad reluctantly agreed to move to Atlanta, knowing that we had the stronger case in the argument. He also understood that this decision was the best thing for him and for all of us. Somehow I managed to pack up his house within two weeks, put it on the market to sell, and move him to Atlanta. Shit. Taking care of all of these details was critical while Iyal was away at camp. We didn't want to raise Iyal's anxiety level any further with questions that might come up while watching the move. We wanted to make sure that Dad was situated in his new home close to us before Iyal returned from camp.

The memory of the accident left us all shaken.

"Mommy?" asked Iyal while we drove over to my dad's in Atlanta. "I don't want to be in another accident."

"I know, Iyal, that was a really scary thing, wasn't it?"

"Sometimes I think it's going to happen again while we are driving."

"Hmm, I know what that feels like. When I was in an accident a long time ago, I felt the same way."

"Mom, that's why I'm sitting in the backseat of the van now."

I nodded. "Oh, that's right. That makes sense, Iyal." I smiled through my grimace.

I was so glad to have Dad six minutes from where we lived so he could attend nearly all the events that involved the kids or Harvey or me. His sheer joy to be with us gave me a unique happiness that poured over me every day.

My dad and I would go to the cemetery near where we lived in Roswell and visit my mom, who was buried there. We usually brought Chancer, whose liquid dark eyes saw our grief and whose love helped to absorb it. Even though my mom hadn't been alive to witness the dramatic difference in our lives since Chancer came to our family, I believe she was a pivotal player in this plan. Before my mom died, she was seeing the growing anguish Harvey and I had begun to experience over Iyal's behavior. We were in the early stages of his diagnosis but had yet to comprehend what any of the terms meant. I wanted to shield her from my distress, but she knew me better. She was my mom.

And my mom always knew what I needed. And so did Chancer.

That first year in Atlanta, Dad had settled comfortably into his independent-living residence and was quite the social networker. He didn't need Facebook. In person, my dad knew how to work a room, reminiscent of his own father's legendary charm. The Kanter men were always "chick magnets" wherever they went. He had an innate ability to draw women to him in a gentle, humorous manner. No matter where he went, he became the person that people wanted to be with.

At his new digs in Atlanta, Dad was the only male in his line-dancing class and served on the food committee, unable to escape his New York delicatessen memories. Now that Dad was living down here, he actively participated at the Lunch and Learn at our synagogue, to which he brought doughnuts every Wednesday. Because Chancer wasn't usually at the temple, Dad knew his jelly doughnuts would be hallowed until he was ready to unhallow them.

—

After we moved Dad to Atlanta, his body started to catch up to the calendar. He had earned a degree in physical education from Springfield College in Massachusetts and followed it with a master's degree from Columbia University in New York City. He loved athletics and coached swimming for more than fifty years. And after his heart attack forty-two years earlier, he had been vigilant in watching his diet and exercising.

Since Iyal was around ten, Dad had urged us to enroll Iyal in Special Olympics in Georgia. He saw the potential for Iyal to succeed, and for Harvey and me to become a part of a unique community. We're so glad we followed his advice, because it was one of the best things we have done for Iyal. He joined a team that practiced near where we lived, and as my dad thought, the Special Olympics community embraced us with open arms. We met some of our closest friends and best supporters of Iyal through being a part of this organization. During the state track-and-field events, Iyal's ability to run shone like a lightning bolt. Since 2012, he has participated in basketball as well as track, earning gold, silver, and bronze medals as well as ribbons. Iyal has since become a bodybuilder, proud of the muscles he has developed and unbelievably obsessed with getting a six-pack!

Recently, Iyal was telling Harvey and me that he had done 150 sit-ups in three sets. It didn't occur to me that he had figured out how to count to 150.

"Did you use a calculator to help you count?" I asked him.

"No, I wrote it down after every set of ten until I got to one hundred and fifty!" Iyal exclaimed.

My dad loved to come with me and watch Iyal run, play basketball, and do anything, actually. That's what a Pop-Pop should do.

And Dad faithfully attended basketball games at the middle school that year to watch Morasha cheerlead. And yes, he was still driving at age eighty-five, which weighed on me heavily. Every time my dad left our house to traverse the three miles back to his place, the kids lovingly called after him, "Drive safe, Pop-Pop. We love you!"

The "driving conversation" was inevitable. I rehearsed that conversation over and over in my head until I finally knew I had to have it. We began by cutting down his night driving until we phased it out completely. Dad realized that soon he would not be driving during the day.

As we watched changes in my dad's lifestyle due to aging, Harvey and I agonized over what to do. My dad loved to explore where he was and where he wasn't almost more than anything else. "Taking away his keys" left us all aware that the end of certain abilities meant the beginning of a chapter that no one wanted to write. The anticipated loss of independence was already a shattering blow no matter how I softened the impact with as much love as I could offer.

When that shift began, everything else in my world became unstable. I'm sure that the conversations about replacing Chancer as Iyal's service dog didn't help either. They formed the first imminent layer of a grief that I knew would become mine.

Iyal began to understand that Dad's health was failing, because he noticed Dad's walking pace had slowed. Lovingly, Iyal adjusted his own pace to match my dad's. At fourteen, Iyal would hold Dad's hand as they walked in the neighborhood or from his car to a movie or the playground. On Wednesdays, Iyal and sometimes Morasha would join Dad as his dinner guests at the dining room where he lived. Dad loved to show them off; you know how seniors can be about their grandchildren.

They might tell the same stories about their grandkids over and over again, but because many of their friends had failing memory, it was as though their friends were hearing these tales for the first time.

Conversations between Iyal and Dad around this time would inevitably contain a question-and-answer period that went something like this:

"Pop-Pop? When are you going to die?"

"Honey, I don't really know."

"Will you be with Giggy, Pop-Pop?"

"I know I will, and she'll be happy to see me."

"Do you think you'll die tomorrow, Pop-Pop?"

"I hope not."

"Me, too. I want you to take me to a movie."

Dad had developed a close friendship with a couple, Marian and Don Mohr. During one particular conversation, Marian was explaining that she had had four heart attacks. Iyal, standing beside us, listened attentively and abruptly turned to Marian and asked, "Did you survive?" We all laughed while Iyal looked at us, wondering how we could be laughing at such a serious thing.

Sometimes I would hear Iyal and my dad talking together during lunch, and Dad's health would come up again in the conversation.

"Iyal, would you like to come with me to the store?"

"Sure. But how is your kidney today? Is it still alive?"

"I think so, sweetheart."

"Okay. Let's go."

Iyal could head straight to the bottom line of any topic.

Morasha was deeply distressed as Dad aged, but she had difficulty talking about it. I sensed her sadness and would hug her when I caught her face registering the changes she saw. Dad found it harder and harder to walk up stairs as his arthritis became more difficult to address with medications and physical therapy. But Morasha and I had an unspoken pact that helped us share without words our worry and our pain knowing that he was ailing.

My dad and I often talked about his dying during his last year with us. He was deeply concerned about how the kids would handle his death. And it wasn't just about Iyal. Dad knew the impact Mom's death had had on little Morasha, and it grieved him. I would reassure him that the kids would be okay, without diminishing his own fear. There was only so much I could say. He and I held hands everywhere we went just like we always did.

—

My dad's last three years of life in Atlanta gave him the emotional and physical support he needed as his health became increasingly challenged. His involvement with the kids was everything he and I could want, the brimming presence of his grandchildren creating a daily carnival.

Chancer and I would often visit Dad at his independent-living place, the three of us walking the hallways and greeting other residents. Chancer also came with Dad and me to almost all of Dad's doctor appointments over the last year and a half he was with us.

When we needed to admit Dad to hospice, I raced the clock, keeping him as comfortable as possible. He and I had discussed what would happen when there were no longer any other choices or chances for improvement. When my dad had been discharged following his last hospitalization, at first he knew what was happening around and to him. In his case, as we were told by the hospice social worker, the physical transition of moving him from his assisted-living apartment where he resided for only three months into the hospice location would be psychologically and physiologically traumatic, and we would see a vast decrease in his cognition and ability to communicate. And sadly, it happened just that way. Dad began to slip away from us within the first day.

My closest friends and congregants and Dad's friends from Atlanta came to visit and say good-bye. Judy, a dearest friend I'd made when I first came to Atlanta in 1979, stopped by each day to be with me. Her mother had stayed in the same hospice before she had passed away, and Judy knew where I was in my grief. We would sit quietly in the garden outside Dad's room or take a walk and just share the same space together. It made a difference.

I thought I had prepared myself for Dad's leaving, but the ache was deeper than I would ever reach.

For fourteen days, Dad hadn't eaten, and he was no longer communicating in a way we understood. Iyal asked me what language my dad was speaking.

"Mom? What is Pop-Pop saying?" asked Iyal.

"Honey, I'm not sure. What do you think he's saying?"

Iyal paused. "I think he is telling us he loves us."

My voice trembled. "I think so, too."

Morasha and I stayed overnight with Dad while he was in hospice. She wanted to stay, and I wanted her with me. We cried through the night as we took turns holding his hand and holding each other. Witnessing my dad dying was so terribly difficult to grasp in our hearts and in our minds. Morasha was brave to let the heartache touch her while she touched my dad and murmured her feelings to him. I worried how Morasha would be able to weave this great sorrow into her life. I needed to trust us both in this choice. Because it seemed that this was the only one.

I told dear friends and my cousins that there was nothing holier in my life than being with Mom and Dad as they died. That was a truth. And being with death, in life, as I was with my parents, is being with God. Although I felt so broken when each of them died, I also knew that healing would come, even when the grief was unbearable. Harvey, Morasha, Iyal, and Chancer would move through the grief with me and I with them. That's what families do.

As I watched the relationship deepen exponentially between my dad and Harvey, I realized how Harvey had ultimately become the husband, father, and friend I wanted and needed more than anything. On and off through my marriage, I became silently embittered when I wanted Harvey to be less of a rabbi and more of a husband. He seemed to be more comfortable in the rabbinic role, and I didn't know how to address this disparity. Harvey's relationship with Dad offered an intimate, regularly hilarious, and mutually loving opportunity. Perhaps it was the role of son-in-law that shortened the distance between the rabbi and the husband. I truly wouldn't have survived the illnesses and deaths of my parents without Harvey's love and caring for them and for me.

As a result of coping with my dad's aging, I tried my best to engage with even more vigor all the other wonderful things going on in my family and in those who made my world alive.

Harvey pursued his spiritual direction program, which gave him another opportunity for both personal and rabbinic growth. He hoped to encourage more folks to explore this form of spiritual enrichment and enjoyed the diversity of faiths these relationships would bring. I have to brag that Harvey had fine-tuned his "menschness" (all the attributes that shape a person to be kind and good, without ever being asked), as he would spend so much time with Dad watching sports; frequenting their favorite breakfast sanctuary, Waffle House; and running errands together.

We were also so fortunate that Harvey's mom, Miriam, was healthy. After Harvey's father died, my mother-in-law's grief—after sixty years of marriage—was immense. We all mourned with her and offered as much comfort as we could. But ultimately, what sparked new life in her was ballroom dancing! She even started competing on the dance floor! We were grateful she would be flying in from Buffalo to share in the kids' B'Nai Mitzvah celebration.

Between worrying about our guest list, restaurant reservations, and the imminent mortality of people and dogs I loved, I had something else weighing on me. At this point, even after fifteen years of being married to a rabbi, I still hadn't memorized the entire Hebrew alphabet, nor did I have a significant number of prayers in my repertoire. Yes, I know you're shocked, but *please*, be kind.

When we first married, I realized I could solve the problem by joining the High Holiday choir—what better way to learn than by *singing* Hebrew! By singing Hebrew, I could master, in theory, how to pronounce the words, maybe even get a sense of what they mean within the context of High Holiday prayers, make new friends, and score big points with the congregation.

After we adopted Morasha and Iyal, I no longer had the luxury of Tuesday-night choir rehearsals, so I would have to learn the many Hebrew prayers, readings, and passages some other way. Unfortunately, with life being life, I just never found time to do it! So I secretly began squirreling away prayer books after Friday-night services so I could study on my own when Harvey wasn't watching.

I also kept a prayer book with me at all times, even hidden in the glove compartment, so when the kids were napping, or later when I was driving car pool, I could whip it out and memorize a letter, maybe two if it was a good day. Sometimes, and this was risky, I even hid one in my nightstand, as inevitably Harvey would fall asleep before me and he'd be snoring so loudly that if he woke up and thought he heard me chanting Hebrew out loud, I could just say, "What, really? That was just your own snoring! I can't believe you didn't recognize it. Go back to sleep."

Still, it wasn't enough. So I learned to compensate and became amazingly adept at lip-synching Hebrew prayers while sitting among the congregants. With our entire family under the stained-glass microscope at the B'Nai Mitzvah, I worried my cover would be blown, so I took matters into my own hands and decided to tackle the situation from a different angle.

Even though most of the weekend formed a collage of special memories, I have a sparkling-clear recollection of the waves of pride both Harvey and I felt during the ceremony. I'm confident both women and men wept in awe at the combined performance of both our children as they were called to the Torah. Or maybe it was the record-setting two-and-a-half-hour length of the service that inspired their tears! Either way, the kids evidently surpassed any expectation people had prior to this momentous and poignant occasion.

Morasha, bright and poised as ever, carried herself through the service with dignity and grace. Iyal, having been tutored by our beloved friend Kelly for four years, blew people away as he chanted his Torah portion directly from Hebrew. Chancer was a part of Iyal's tutoring for his Bar Mitzvah, sort of like a study buddy. At home and then in the sanctuary, as the date of the B'Nai Mitzvah loomed closer, Chancer joined Kelly and Iyal, offering his physical and spiritual presence. The day of the B'Nai Mitzvah, Chancer had a reserved spot just in front of the first row. He lay on the floor between my dad and me so that he and Iyal could maintain eye contact throughout the service. I imagine that most of the guests in the sanctuary wondered how Chancer would participate in the B'Nai Mitzvah. We didn't let them down.

Then it was my turn. During the Saturday morning of the actual B'Nai Mitzvah, the parents of the young honoree customarily present a speech. For most families, it offers a moment for the parents to relive memories of their child, talk about their kid's goals, and describe the path taken to achieve said goals. Usually, one of the parents was more inclined than the other to deliver the speech.

Often one parent wrote it and the other delivered it. Harvey and I had agreed that I would be the one to deliver the parents' speech at the kids' B'Nai Mitzvah. We assumed that the congregants, family, and friends would have had enough of Harvey talking on and on and on . . . a marathon to beat all marathons. So being in my element, I wrote about seven drafts, just to perfect my participation. Here is an excerpt of what I said after I thanked family and friends for being there:

"God gifted us with the blessing and responsibility of raising a son and daughter to become our forever family. Today is a celebration of learning, Judaism, spirituality, and community. Today I have the chance to tell you what an honor it is for Harvey and me to acknowledge how, in many ways, *we* are the students in our family. Both of our kids have taught us, without even trying . . . how to be better parents. They *each* have shown us that there are no disabilities when it comes to spirituality.

"It seems sometimes the bad news about adoption and the sad news about disabilities is all you read or hear about. And it is terribly important to reveal what is often hidden or considered shameful by some individuals. Because *without* information, things cannot change for the better. Voices will not be heard and needs may remain invisible and unmet.

"Yet we are all here today to celebrate a significant milestone in the life of our family. One that includes adoption, disability, and challenge as well as spirituality, family, commitment, and community. Morasha, while initially an *involuntary* ambassador, has become an amazing advocate for her brother and others with disabilities. She has remarkable sensitivity and a great capacity to sense what is going on with people around her.

"And Iyal makes me think about ideas I might *never* have considered. A few weeks ago, he asked me, 'When do we find out if we are a human, a dog, or a dinosaur? How *old* are we when we know that?' These are philosophical questions. I consider that rabbinic thinking . . . pretty impressive for an almost-thirteen-year-old!

"So this is a day about faith and fate. Harvey and I believe it was *b'shert,* fate that he and I met and married when we did in 1997. It's obvious that God put our family together very strategically when we were given the chance to adopt. We could not imagine our lives without Iyal and Morasha. And we are very grateful for God's trust. Yet it is not enough to talk the talk. So in our family, we walk the walk. Four of us with our heads held high in focused tenacity. The other lumbering diligently by our sides on four paws, giving a quiet dignity to a devastating disability. You see, it was when a golden opportunity romped into our lives in an enormously soft, furry body with outrageous affection and patience, happily wagging its tail . . . that we received another gift."

A good thing I'd memorized most of my speech, because at that moment, I couldn't see everyone else's tears for my own.

"We *all* navigate through darkness in our lives. And like the *N'er Tamid*, the eternal light that never goes out, I hope the brightness of today stays alive in all of us."

Harvey walked over to the podium while I "freed" Chancer from his "down" in front of my dad and led him up the steps of the bimah. I put Chancer in a "sit" next to me, and both kids joined us. And that's when the sniffles began as Harvey and I shared with Morasha and Iyal our final words of the service, as Chancer gazed lovingly at his whole family. I'm sure I saw a tear or two of pride in Chancer's eyes.

Chapter Twelve

"Mom! I can't get Chancer to come up the stairs! What's wrong with him?" asked Iyal.

"Just be patient," I said with encouragement. "He's probably just tired today."

The problem, however, was that he seemed tired most days. But I knew he was doing his best.

As difficult as it might be, we had to get serious about a second service dog, a replacement for Chancer. Almost eight years earlier, our golden wonder dog had joined our family and began assisting Iyal.

Doing the math, I knew that Chancer was coming up on his tenth birthday, which, in dog years, means it's time for retirement. The hip dysplasia continued to be an issue, and it was just clear that Chancer was slower, more easily fatigued, more content to lie on the cool tile of our foyer or beside Iyal, wherever he might be. Chancer still did his job, but we could all tell the cost for him was greater than ever before.

So I took the necessary steps to get the process in motion with 4 Paws. Overall, the procedure to get another dog would be relatively the same as when we first got Chancer. We still needed to obtain a prescription for Iyal, stating that his medical condition was such that the physician believed he would benefit from having a service dog. We then needed to submit the formal application with a video of Iyal demonstrating his need for a service dog and his current level of functionality.

Since Chancer had become a part of our family, the change in Iyal was monumental. We had seen and experienced such significant improvements in so many aspects of his life. Iyal was no longer an eight-year-old boy; now he was a young man. I accepted this reality one day recently when I told Iyal he needed to wash his face—he had something (Oreo crumbs?) all along his upper lip and jawline. When he told me his face was clean, that he'd just taken a shower, I put on my glasses and walked over for a closer inspection. Oh my God, my son needed to shave! When did this happen?

Despite the physical changes adolescence had brought to his body, and despite the progress he had made, his need was still great. Iyal's meltdowns had morphed into a vertical version instead of the historical horizontal position. His frustrations still triggered his arousal dysregulation, but with his maturity came new triggers. And we knew they would come. A few years ago, if his electronic games froze and changing the batteries didn't provide the luck he needed, Iyal would first freeze like his Nintendo before melting down into a pool of anger and agitation. And more recently, the storm brewed when a slow computer tested his endurance or his cellphone died or he decided he was just too tired to do any kind of anything. Over the years, Chancer performed the nuzzle command, consistently a calming intervention, from a lying-down position for both Iyal and Chancer. But Iyal was no longer that boy playing on the floor or rolling around after the collapse of a fatigued brain done for the day.

On our video for the second dog, we needed to show how Iyal's rages took place while he was either sitting in a chair, say, at the computer, or lounging on the sofa playing an Xbox game, with a controller trembling in his hand, waiting to be launched against the wall behind the TV if his score started going in the wrong direction. And then we had to show Iyal careening around a room, pacing with his hands over his ears, his muttering quickly escalating into screaming.

However, catching the older Iyal in these situations proved more difficult than before. He was more self-aware now, more self-conscious, reluctant to let others, even our friends at 4 Paws, witness him in full Hulk-transformation mode. So it was an exercise in cajoling Iyal just to get his cooperation to make the video.

When I tried to interview Iyal on camera, asking him how he wanted his new service dog to help him, I practically had to be a ventriloquist.

"Iyal, can you tell me how another service dog like Chancer could help you?" I asked in my best radio voice.

He shook his head and grinned bashfully. "You know . . . helping me."

"How does a service dog help you?" I tried to stay in anchorwoman mode.

"Helping me . . . do stuff." He looked outside. He looked underneath his bed. Everywhere but at the camera. *Barbara Walters never had to put up with this,* I thought.

The way he clammed up during the video really floored me, as he talked about how Chancer was his best friend on a daily basis! But try to capture it on camera? Oh noooo. That wasn't happening. As a result, this second video was probably only half as long as the first one.

Ironically, Iyal had become quite the film director, with his childhood passion for playing video games transformed into making videos with him in starring roles. Interestingly, Iyal didn't cast Chancer as a supporting actor in his films. Maybe he, too, had heard the old adage that dogs could upstage even the most talented actor! Using his favorite music and various special-effects apps, he would create "mini movies," usually focused around his superpowers and fighting prowess. After launching his own YouTube channel, he quickly had more than a hundred subscribers! In fact, he loves to give updates, sometimes hourly, on how many likes, new subscribers, comments, and fans he has. We're thrilled, of course, because this reflects incredible creative accomplishment, showing us and everyone else how far he has come.

Despite these amazing advances, Harvey and I continued to worry about Iyal more than ever. We know that sometimes Iyal can be an accurate historian about certain episodes he has experienced, but other times he is so confused about what time something has occurred that none of us can make heads or tails about it. Iyal's lack of patience pummeled us when *we* couldn't follow him!

As he has grown older and been exposed to more of the world, his inability to recognize what is real or not has been deeply disturbing. This part of his brain development had become arrested like that of a young child, a child who believes in fantasy and fairy tales.

For instance, after watching the latest superhero sequel, Iyal asked, "Mom, that part where the bad guy dies and the good guy comes back to save Earth . . ."

"Yes, honey?" I said, knowing what was coming next.

"Is that bad guy still dead? Or did he come back to life after the movie ended?"

"The bad guy is still dead, sweetheart," I said. "It's a made-up story. The *actor* who played the bad guy is still alive, but the bad guy he *pretended to be*, he's still dead." See how complicated this becomes? And I'm getting no help from the producers of these superhero action films who often kill off a character only to bring him or her back in a sequel or two down the line. What seems crystal clear to you and me becomes neurological quicksand for Iyal, pulling him into a chasm of uncertainty and confusion.

Harvey, Morasha, and I take turns running interference for Iyal. We are acutely aware that his brain damage presents an ongoing setup for misunderstanding, more sexual and physical abuse, other mental illness, and aggression that leads to violence and the possibility of self-harm. We are enlisted in an involuntary battle to keep an individual experiencing FASDs safe. Even from himself.

Raging in a recent storm of anger and frustration, Iyal screamed, "I'm going to blow something up! It's not fair that Morasha can write and I can't. I'm going to make it so she can never write again. I don't care!" I remind Iyal that his language is a threat and that as soon as he says these words out loud, he can't take them back. If I'm lucky, he'll pause to consider what I've said. And then, "I can change, Mom. I'll show you I can change." But the words are empty if he can't remember that this refrain was sung earlier this morning, yesterday, and probably the day before.

Or consider a less urgent but nonetheless dangerous assumption: sometimes Iyal talked about creating a time machine or some invention that would allow him to become immortal and live forever. Because he read on the Internet that such things were possible, he believes it must be true.

Iyal's most recent IQ is fifty-six. The most commonly used criteria stipulate that an IQ of seventy or below renders a person with mild cognitive impairment. Although the brain dysfunction may not seem apparent on the outside, Iyal's emotional world is tumultuous as he stumbles around trying to find even ground. And then he does. When he finds Chancer. Iyal looks to his side where Chancer has ambled over, leaning against his leg. Iyal smiles and drops to the floor, finding the medicine made especially for him. He curls up around Chancer, letting the healing in.

I hadn't thought that much about how getting Chancer impacted Morasha until she cornered me one day in the kitchen.

"Mom?"

"What, babe?" I asked, putting away the groceries.

"I don't know if I really want Iyal to have a service dog."

I stopped and closed the refrigerator door. "What do you mean, Morasha?" I was honestly startled by her comment, remembering all the months she and I had scanned the 4 Paws for Ability website, wondering which gorgeous puppy face might belong to our dog.

Morasha looked at me briefly and then turned away. "Well, how do I know my friends won't want to play with Chancer instead of me?"

I thought, *Crap. How could I have not considered the real possibility that Morasha could be jealous?* I came over to where she was sitting at the table. "Oh, Morash, I'm sorry I didn't think about this. This is what I think," I said. "I bet the first time your friends meet Chancer, they may make a fuss over him. But then I bet the next time and after that, they may say hi to Chancer and pet him, but they won't be distracted by him." Morasha looked at me, considering the truth of what I was saying. I said, "Do you know what I mean?" She nodded her head, and I came over to her with a big hug. She reminded me that I needed to be more sensitive to hear her part in adding this new member to our family.

Even though my daughter was now older and more mature, I was determined not to make the same mistake when we got this second service dog. I wanted her input throughout the process. I needn't have worried, though. My beautiful Morasha was becoming more mature, beyond her years. As a single sibling of a brother or sister who lives with a disability, from the moment the sibling recognizes the problem for what it is, playing a supportive part in the family becomes their starring role.

There were a few years during middle school when I believed that Morasha felt pressured to stay positive all the time, denying her true feelings. However, I'm sure resentment was percolating, especially since a preteen can be vulnerable. I worried that the media and society reinforced messages that told siblings like Morasha that they were "blessed to have a special family member." This was not our definition of "blessed."

Those who did not know our situation well might tell Morasha how lucky she was to be "normal"! But *I* heard myself asking Morasha, "How can you feel lucky all the time when you are living with anger and embarrassment and guilt and no one seems to really understand just how horrible your life feels!" I would think this made Morasha feel even worse.

I continually worried that we made too much of a fuss over Iyal's accomplishments compared to Morasha's. For every "Wow, that's great, honey!" I exclaimed to Iyal, I felt that I needed to do a somersault and a roundoff while shaking my pom-poms for Morasha. The flip side was then wondering if Morasha would doubt her own self-worth, thinking that she wasn't quite good enough—otherwise, why would her mom need to do cartwheels over just signing her name and date on a homework paper?

On one occasion, when the kids were probably seven or eight, Iyal had become so obsessed with an art assignment that he literally couldn't be separated from his picture. He was at school, drawing a portrait of Harvey's mom, unable to fill in her face with a crayon to his satisfaction. Nothing the teachers told him stemmed his mounting panic. Iyal was rubbing the paper so fiercely with crayons that his artwork ripped, sending him into even greater spasms of despair. He refused to take a walk outside the school with his teacher and would not let go of his paper, which was shredding further with each spike of his torment.

That day, nobody from the school contacted me, which was unusual because I practically had my phone number engraved under the school's emblem in the front foyer. In fact, I wouldn't have known about this mother of all tantrums if not for my daughter. The teachers had summoned Morasha to Iyal's classroom to see if *she* was able to contain her brother's raging storm.

What the hell were they thinking? Bringing her in like some ambassador from the Winokur embassy was so unfair! I was outraged that they had put her in a position to either succeed or fail at an attempt to rescue her brother from his behavior and restore peace in the third-grade special-needs classroom. None of us expected her to be her brother's keeper. I was left reeling from their response to Iyal and the pressure they had put on his sister.

Part of the difficulty with trying to prevent my daughter from being a default caretaker was her natural temperament. You'll recall her regal elegance as Zipporah at an early age. From the beginning, she just possessed a poise and quiet confidence. It seemed like Morasha could hold her own as she grew up. But that didn't keep me from obsessing. The three of us understood without it ever being said that our lives would always be circumscribed by Iyal's needs. I worried that Morasha felt smothered by Iyal and then by our intentional need to bring her into our fold if we felt she was drifting.

Kate Strohm writes in her insightful book *Being the Other One: Growing Up with a Brother or Sister Who Has Special Needs*, "We want to believe that our normal children have grown wiser and more compassionate through the family's trials."[5] I knew that I had wanted to see Morasha act like a character in a movie, one who lovingly and willingly puts her sibling's needs before her own, taking on the role of hero, but only as a tireless saint, rarely ever as the protagonist in the movie.

After the kids graduated high school, I had a distressing conversation with Morasha about Iyal having been abused. I didn't know what she understood about this episode in her brother's life but wanted to be respectful of her silence in the matter. I felt torn about having this conversation with her while they were both in school. I suspected that Morasha had a sense that something very big was taking place in Iyal's life, but navigating this devastating topic left me anxious about its impact on her.

When I finally broached the subject that Iyal had been abused by other students at their high school, she became thoughtful and remained silent.

"Honey?" I asked. "Did you know that something was going on with Iyal?"

She said, "Yeah, I knew something bad was happening, but I didn't know what." Morasha spoke softly. "Mom, I wish you had *told* me." She was clearly and understandably upset. "If you had *told* me, maybe I could've stopped it."

We looked sadly at each other. I wanted to cry. What else did she feel responsible for?

Strohm adds, "Single sibs often experience the strange combination of feeling like an only child but missing out on the attention that an only child receives. At the same time they often feel compelled to take on the second mother role to their sibling."[6] Morasha had ridden this ride way too much as far as I was concerned. I worried about her just as much as Iyal, even if he consumed more of my time and actions. I agonized about Morasha receiving the leftovers of my day. Where would I ever find the energy to listen and see her life as she drew it so beautifully? Where did Harvey and I fit into *her* picture? I wanted so badly to provide a balanced way of parenting, but I knew doing so was impossible. Iyal sapped our energy and patience and usually left me empty and unable to attend to her experience the way I would want.

Morasha, like so many other siblings, felt she had to compensate for Iyal's behavior. She witnessed our struggles and didn't want to create any more headache or heartache for us. Eager to please, she longed to make things right. And in order to do so, she often had to force herself to be okay, not wanting to add additional needs we'd have to address. But how unfair to feel so much pressure, wanting to be an emotional superhero who didn't need more from her parents than she thought they could give.

When Morasha told me that she mourned the loss of having a "normal," healthy relationship with a brother, I wanted to wrap her up inside my heart. This suffocating grief held no way out, no matter how old they were. More understanding and empathy would find their way in, but this distinctly different kind of sibling relationship would remain the same.

But as much as she could *not* imagine Iyal living with any other family, fearing no other mother and father could rear a child with his disturbing behaviors, at times she certainly didn't want him living in ours!

For at least the whole year before the B'Nai Mitzvah, Morasha began to feel like an afterthought to this special milestone. Later she told me she felt that she had done all the work but Iyal had received all the praise, diminishing her participation in this rite of passage. At other times, she said she'd wanted to say to Harvey and me, "I have it hard, too!"

She absorbed message after message that told her we had no choice in this chaos of a household. With no apparent choice, she had no chance to redefine her role in our family. And as hard as I tried, I couldn't hear her silence.

And how I wish she knew the laughter she brought me without even trying. One time, Morasha, who was probably around eight, and I were once again standing outside Newark Airport, waiting on my dad to swing by in the car, performing his infamous airport pickup routine. Our arrival plopped us into what I refer to as "Jersey jungle weather," stifling hot with a humidity that instantly plastered one's clothes to one's body.

Here was what my dad's side of the phone conversation typically sounded like as he poked along the miles-long pickup area: "Donnie, what door did you say you were near? Are you sure? Honey, I don't see you! Where is Morasha? Look again. What number does it say? Can you see me yet? I'm in the Toyota. The white one." We had only one Toyota. "What are you wearing, honey?" You get the drift.

With the unforgiving heat, not many people were waiting outside. Or even inside, from what I could tell. However, I noticed an unusual number of Hasidic Orthodox men pushing their carts with luggage toward the curb. They had *payes*, the uncut curling sideburns held down on both sides of their heads by a yarmulke underneath broad-brimmed black hats. Each had on the traditional black robe, which, considering the weather, made me sweat just thinking about it.

I turned to say something to Morasha, but then I stepped back for a minute, quizzically watching her. She was looking from right to left, bobbing her head as she murmured something to herself. I watched some more. There she went again. This time from left to right. Nodding her head one nod at a time, while saying something very softly.

"Morasha!" I said, suddenly worried about things like dehydration and heatstroke.

"What, Mom?" She stopped nodding for a moment and looked up at me.

"Sweetie, what are you doing?" I asked. "Are you okay?"

She smiled and said, "I'm just counting Jews."

Many siblings of brothers and sisters living with disabilities may express their unmet needs by acting out or by turning inward, fueling depression with their unchanneled anger. I thank God that our daughter seemed to have risen above the white water, neither drowning in her own pain nor hurling it against a dam only to have it recycled and roar at her again.

Of course, Morasha was frustrated that we let Iyal "get away with stuff" when she would be held accountable for her actions. Iyal was allowed to tease her incessantly, but she couldn't tease him back or let off steam with her own outbursts. The one-sided story left her confused when I was really just trying to spare her more angst as Iyal exploded over and over again. But that's not how she interpreted it. *She needed to express her anger just like everyone else, and I just didn't get it!*

If I saw her frustrated about "living in this family ruled by Iyal," then I would failingly try to give her some perspective: "Honey, do you know how bad it can get for other families?" Then I would roll call the list of "what ifs." What if Iyal had cerebral palsy? What if Iyal had a life-threatening seizure disorder?

It didn't matter how much or how often I made this comparison; she would ultimately become exasperated with me, raising her voice and saying, "But, Mom! We are *not* that family, and our situation is just as bad! We are *not* that different! No one knows what goes on in our house!" And to Morasha, that part was very true.

We generally kept the really bad episodes close to our vests. I know, certainly, that Harvey did. He might share the frustrations and challenges we experienced with his fellow clergy and some temple board members or office staff. And they genuinely were concerned and would express their support to me if I stopped by the office or bumped into someone at Shabbat services. But they certainly didn't hear what my closest cousins and dearest friends heard. I don't know if I could've survived this life without the help from my therapist.

At ten, thirteen, or seventeen, I didn't know how many friends Morasha could turn to. I didn't think I could ask, which made me feel inadequate as her mother. When the turbulent life at home drained her of the compassion and patience she believed she was supposed to have, she didn't turn to her friends. She didn't think they would understand.

At times when I thought Morasha might be receptive, I would suggest that she speak to a counselor or therapist. But inevitably her response was always "How would they know how *I* felt? They don't know what it's like to live with Iyal!" I knew I'd have to wait until her maturity gave her an opening for this intervention. Not until she soared through her AP psych class did she put the pieces together and see the value of cognitive therapy. This was one breath for help I no longer had to hold.

—

During her senior year of high school, Morasha told me, "Mom, I'm sure you've already thought of this, but sometimes I feel so bad that Iyal won't have the kind of life I'll have."

I said, "What do you mean, honey?" with sadness growing inside me.

She said, "I just hate that he won't ever have a driver's license or his own car, or probably his own house."

I murmured, "Hmmm."

"Mom, I know that Iyal must be jealous of me, going to college, you know."

I nodded. She was right. Iyal certainly understood enough that he wanted to be like his sister, who, according to him, "got to go away to college and would probably get married and do everything she ever wanted." I told Iyal that there was no reason he might not be able to do these things in his own life. And Morasha did, too.

But we all knew there would always be certain limitations.

When Iyal was in a "bad place," he was unable to hear how terrific *his* life was, how much *he* had grown, and all the wonderful things he had achieved. Morasha was torn about her feelings that she was abandoning us, leaving us with two fewer hands to juggle our complicated lives. I didn't know how to relieve her of her presumed responsibility. Yet she was ready to spread her wings, and I was determined not to let another cocoon spin into place around her. All we could do was reassure her that it was her time. We were all ready. It truly was okay.

—

A photo of my mom and Morasha hangs on Morasha's bedroom wall. Occasionally, I go into her room when she isn't there (Oh Jesus—she'd kill me if she found out!) just to look at this photo. My mom, before she became ill and when Morasha wasn't even three, is sitting on the floor of the babies' room with her. Morasha, in a little animal-print flannel nightgown, is curled in front of my mom, sucking her thumb. My mom has her legs up in a crisscross-applesauce cradle and her arms circled around Morasha protectively, holding a book in front of them both.

This photo is how I remember my beloved mom—sharing one of her most favorite things to do in the world, reading, with one of her two most favorite little people in the world, her granddaughter. Whenever I look at the photo, I can hear my mom reading to her. I look at the photo and see her holding my daughter in the safety of her arms. She holds both Morasha and me to her heart.

Falling in love with your challenged child is the easy part. Staying in love with them may be the hardest thing you'll ever do. As they grow older, the love changes, evolves, becomes more of whatever they need at their new stage of growth. And this was happening with the love between Harvey and me. We were fortunate that we could stabilize through the tectonic shifts in our marriage, recognizing and even celebrating our own positive growth.

My intention had always been to create a healthy and affirming relationship with my children. I never thought that digging in and navigating from the trenches would give me cause for surrender. But I found myself flailing against the demons in my son, which brought my own to the surface. I was then forced to ask myself, Am I more afraid of being unable to reach *Iyal* or of him not returning a loving and meaningful relationship with me, his mother?

Many years ago, Iyal's psychiatrist at the time flatly warned me, "Iyal will never really be your *son*, Donnie. I mean, come on—does he *look* like the children you see with their mothers at this age?"

I was dizzy with grief, slayed by this monster of a woman. How dare she presume whether or not Iyal could really love me the way a son is "supposed to love a parent"? She thought she was helping me by explaining that emotional reciprocity couldn't be achieved with some-one as "damaged" as Iyal. I was stunned that a professional would so casually define my maternal future and dismiss Iyal's ability to be a significant part of it.

I never returned for another session.

She's not the only one with this mindset. Over the years, after hearing about our son's eruptions and nosedives, several well-meaning people have whispered, "Did you *know* that Iyal had special needs when you adopted him?" These words translated to "If you knew he had these challenges and that your life would be a living hell, would you still have brought him into your family?"

Along the way, as we parented Morasha and Iyal, friends and family tried to reassure me that at least I have Morasha to love and guarantee me that she could love me back. *She* was the good one. *She* could make up the difference and fill the hole that only grew bigger the more Iyal's disability kept his love unreachable.

But what a burden for Morasha to inherit just because she didn't cause trouble or send us reeling into madness like her brother often did! Others scripted her life as a stabilizing force. And sometimes I did it, too.

Giving them the benefit of the doubt, I embraced their question as a backhanded compliment, a way of saying, "Wow, you and Harvey are the most astounding parents we know. Just look at all you've done for Morasha and Iyal! No one else would've done as well!" But most days, I fell off their perceived pedestal at least once if not more, simply overwhelmed by all the problems orbiting my son.

All along, I've known we would continue to expand our umbrella over Iyal's future, but lately, I fear getting buried in the fallout. With the constant managing of our son's behaviors, accurately seeing him or seeing ourselves, for that matter, has been difficult. Are we really helping him or just validating the choices we impose on Iyal because we have run out of options?

In the past, friends and family cheered me on from the sidelines with words of support: "Oh, Donnie, you can do this! Look how much you and Harvey have accomplished with Iyal." Their encouragement explained away my fatigue and sustained me for another day. But lately, with Iyal looming over six feet tall, well above both his parents, everyone in our supportive network has sensed a change. When cheering no longer seemed to fit, friends and family began gently instructing me, "Donnie, you need to let go."

The first time I heard this, it stopped me in my tracks. *Let go?* Let go of *what*? Let go of Iyal? The physical being or the spiritual one? The one who sleeps safely in his bed in our home or the one who's in college in my dreams? Amid this jungle of tired and tangled expectations, others' and my own, I'm afraid to comprehend the incomprehensible. Am I supposed to "let go" of the already relinquished child or the young man who heroically fights every day for his independence?

Don't they understand I can't leave Iyal behind, even if I *am* losing my mind? Even if the bough has been breaking for over a decade? Iyal has already been abandoned once by his birth mother. I simply cannot allow this to happen again. Ever.

If I give up on Iyal, I am giving up on God.

I cannot *let go*! A parent doesn't let go of loving someone like it was something that *happened*, an event that came and went. This is your child. It is not a finite experience. It continues.

Iyal is a part of me, like my own flesh and blood. His life courses through me, just like Morasha's. It does not have to be reciprocated by anyone else's standard. Adoption was merely a legal means through which we attached ourselves to each other, Iyal to me and me to Iyal. Morasha to me and me to Morasha. I am their mother. Morasha tells me this is so. Is it really any different when two adults bind to each other as a married couple? We aren't related to our spouse by blood, yet it feels that way. Severing the emotional umbilical cord that Harvey and I created when Iyal became our son and Morasha became our daughter would be impossible. There's no difference.

If I let go of mothering Iyal, I have given up *the fight*. If I let go of lifting up Iyal to become the best Iyal he can be, I won't know who *I* am. I have no compass to live by without Iyal and Morasha. My children are my world. *This* world didn't exist before them.

And I can't rely on anyone else to do my job as painstakingly and lovingly as I do. For many years, my days ached from morning until dark, when I staggered at last to bed, aware that I just couldn't take it anymore, couldn't catch my breath as the intensity of Iyal's needs suffocated me. In the middle of these nights, when my faith all but collapsed, praying no one was listening, I would whisper, *"I give up."* And I would cry until I couldn't.

Then the next morning, I'd get up and somehow find a way to keep going, to keep giving. I have worked hard. I have given my all and then some to my husband, to my daughter, and to my son, scraping the bottom of my soul in search of just a little bit more. I grieved too much in that unrelenting twilight, tempted to believe I had nothing left to offer my family or myself.

And then hope arrived on four paws, wagging and slobbering, chewing up cell phones and nuzzling away the demons inside my son. Chancer's intelligence, innate desire to please, and enthusiasm to be loved created a safety net that no human could knit together.

He saved us.

Not just Iyal, but our entire family.
All of us.

Commencement. It was finally happening. I appreciate how the word captured the bittersweet taste of one chapter ending and another one beginning. As Iyal and Morasha finished their senior year, ready to graduate, nothing conveyed this spirit of transition to me better than getting our new service dog. His name is Quinn, and he's every bit as lovable, playful, and well trained as his big brother, Chancer. Quinn has picked up the bone and immediately earned Iyal's love and devotion—something I worried about, considering how much Iyal adores Chancer. So now we have both dogs, and of course Autumn the cat, taking care of the Winokurs.

We even considered bringing all three of them to the kids' graduation. But when the time came one late spring evening, only the human members of our family attended. Harvey and I sat on hard cement bleachers, bursting with pride as Iyal and Morasha walked together across the school's football field to receive their high school diplomas. Both being Winokurs, they were alphabetically tortured and had to wait at least nine hours and forty minutes. Well, maybe it just felt that way to them. To me, it had all flown by way too fast.

Sitting there under the twilight stars, a gentle breeze cooling us down, I reflected on the bumpy road our family had traversed to get to this point. Nestled against his shoulder, I smiled up at Harvey, more aware than ever of how much I need him to ground me. He remains my anchor, and without him I would continually dive headfirst into every experience, disregarding the "no diving" signs posted on life's beach. He rescues me from myself when my tenacity gets in the way. And I let him. Harvey has grown wiser in this untidy life of ours. I treasure our life together as I watch the dogs and Autumn edge him into a softer world when our life feels hard. He has needed this animal intervention as much as any of us. For Harvey and for me, letting the animals in gives way to a greater space for us to grow our love.

Watching tearfully as the kids moved their tassels and tossed their mortarboards up into the night sky, I was no different from any other parent there sending their young adults off to write the next chapter in their lives. It was a sweet ache inside, a good thing.

Harvey and I could not be more proud of Morasha's academic prowess, and she did this by herself. Earning the highest scholarship possible from her university only confirmed her competence and drive. To her credit, despite being drafted into an almost daily battle, she has become a gentle warrior protecting her brother. She now has to leave. She can soar without a parachute, always landing on her feet. Morasha grounds us in her own unique love. And we hope she feels grounded in ours.

Iyal is ready, too. He just doesn't know it. Graduating high school is a triumph none of us could've imagined nine, five, or even three years ago. He proved us wrong over and over. It was one step forward, eight steps backward much of the time, but he never gave up. And neither did we. Sometimes we had to drag him and ourselves to the next finish line.

As exhausting as it was for us all, Iyal remains the real hero in this lifelong battle. We know it and so does Chancer. And as the torch has passed from Chancer's paws to Quinn's, I know Quinn will discover it for himself, serving this beautiful, brave man who is my son.

So who hasn't heard "just add water and stir"? Well, our "instant" family was made from a different recipe. It wasn't water that was added. It was alcohol. And while the alcohol happened *to Iyal*—Iyal happened *to us*. So alcohol became part of our family's story. But it's only one of the ingredients that make our family, well, our family.

I could say that Iyal's disability doesn't define us, or that Harvey's being a rabbi doesn't define our family. I think they do. Does Morasha believe she is the glue that keeps our family together? She has told me as much. I wish she didn't. Do *I* feel responsible for weaving together and repairing our family's safety net over and over again so no one slips through beyond our reach? Of course I do.

What binds us together as a family is not the *bad* ingredient—although at times we all feel it is *just too much*! Especially for Iyal.

You see, the good ingredients bind us together. Even if the recipe keeps coming out upside down or inside out, we can always try again.

The ingredient that matters most can come from many sources; you'd be surprised. It doesn't take a lot, but it must be true, and it must be forgiving. It might even come from a different species. Don't underestimate this possibility.

When I look back at our story so far, I see this. Moving a marriage or a relationship forward is a two-party deal: it requires mutual respect, especially when the dream of one partner leaves the other dumbfounded. Remember, you chose each other. For a reason. Even if sometimes you forget. Figure it out. It matters.

Raising kids is always hardest on the parent. Just ask any parent. Raising parents is always hardest on the kid. Just ask any kid. Now ask a service dog the hardest part of *his* job? I'm confident he would answer, "Not working." The love of a service dog for their person or their human pack is undeniably true and forgiving.

They have it figured out.

They know it matters.

EPILOGUE

My son's voice echoed toward me from our driveway, where he had been shooting basketball. "I suck at basketball, I'll never be a pro! They'll never take me because I'm no good." Iyal roared, "Fuck it!"

I sighed, waiting a beat while Iyal continued to rant, "God damn it! It's *their* fault. They made me suck!"

The swearing continued to escalate until the episode culminated in Iyal crying and screaming at the same time. I was thinking, Whose *fault?* Who *made you do it?*

Iyal then started throwing the basketball at the house just above the open garage door. Without wasting another moment, I flew downstairs from our top floor, through the house, with Chancer and Quinn at my heels, the three of us bringing a triage team to Iyal.

Out in the glare of the afternoon sun, I squinted at Iyal as Quinn immediately started doing his special greeting: "Don't be upset, Iyal—you're my favorite person!" Starting out with a play bow, he then jumped up, purposefully placing his front paws on Iyal's chest, as he'd been trained to do in order to de-escalate Iyal's rage. In fact, Quinn's "touch" command included a specific bark to alert us or another adult that Iyal was losing it. Frankly, we rarely heard Quinn bark, since other than when necessary with Iyal, he is a behavioral-disruption-assistance dog trained not to cause any further disruptions in *anyone's* behaviors.

Chancer moved behind Iyal, attempting to "hump" him with an "I got your back, buddy! Please don't cry!" I know, this may sound ridiculous, sort of like an Iyal sandwich between two goldens, but for Chancer, almost eleven years old, this was how he tried to get Iyal under his control. Iyal, uncertain how he felt about this intervention, continued crying, but stopped swearing.

I would call this a success.

Observing our changing of the guard proved to be fascinating. If Iyal fell apart when the stresses of the day were too much to handle, both dogs stepped up for service at the same time! In fact, 4 Paws supported the idea that the first service dog would become a role model for the second.

Initially, Iyal was overwhelmed by all the attention. He wasn't quite sure which dog he should pet first! His default was to lay down with Chancer on top of him, embraced by his paws, as Chancer covered him with kisses. The full length of Chancer offered comforting deep pressure from Iyal's head to his toes. For the first six months, Harvey, Morasha, and I needed to remind Iyal that he had *another* service dog that also wanted to help, and wasn't he fortunate to have two wonderful best friends who cared very much for him? Ultimately, both dogs would lie on either side of Iyal, and he could pet them both at the same time. Chancer and Quinn quickly became our dynamic doggy duo. Not only did they serve Iyal, but they also continually cavorted together, keeping us highly entertained.

Consider this scene, for instance: the dogs ceremoniously crouch low and circle each other with lips curled, gleaming gums exposed, and teeth bared as the requisite rope-toy tug-of-war between them commences. Their canine tango remains an ancient, timeless, archetypal moving chess match we never tire of watching. Only the age and size indicates they are not identical golden twins.

Whenever the dogs enthusiastically roughhouse, one variation requires Quinn to try herding Chancer, although goldens aren't known for this canine characteristic the same way a border collie or Australian shepherd might be. But Quinn somehow uses his head to guide Chancer in circles by putting it underneath Chancer's chest and moving him around. In fact, figuring out where one golden ends and the other begins is hard to do! As they romp, Quinn is usually on the inside running while Chancer tries to keep up the pace, like a motorcycle sidecar, except the front wheel is missing, so he bumps along.

In another version, Quinn emits cartoon-like gruffs, his play bark, interspersed with his now famous chuffing. I had absolutely no idea what this chuffing noise meant at first. During our training at 4 Paws, Quinn would occasionally cry out with this ridiculous sneezing sound! Jodee Kulp, our dear friend, renowned FASD expert, and dog trainer, grinned and said to me, "Oh, Quinn's chuffing. It's sort of his laugh. It's like he's chortling and telling you, 'Oh, my life is so good, and I want you to know, and let's share a bone!'" I thought, *Well, don't we all wish we could chuff!* Sometimes chuffing is accompanied by a head twist, especially if the cause involves a tennis ball or other toy in Quinn's mouth.

The noise inevitably makes us giggle and exclaim, "Oh, Quinn. You are soooo silly!" or "Quinn, we love you and your laugh!" and his favorite, "Ohhhh, Quinn . . . whaddagoodboy you are!" Our exclamations typically make him even giddier, thereby increasing the snort chuffing exponentially as he parades around, enjoying the attention.

Chuffing often elevates the dogs' play into a furry free-for-all, one jumping on top of the other, a front leg flung over the other's shoulder, as *that* one dips down to throw off his partner's balance. Quinn loves play bowing and scooting underneath Chancer so he can throw him to the ground, a winning wrestling move. Even though Chancer is at least a third larger in size than Quinn, Chancer's arthritic hips tend to give way, causing him to momentarily sit on his hind legs until he regains his balance and scrambles up for the next round. Their shared panting carries the action from one scene to the next.

One of our favorite turns is watching Quinn clamp onto a leg, gently gnawing up and down (like corn on the cob) before moving on to Chancer's ear, all this without ever stopping the rumble. Head butting might follow intermittently before Chancer tries to hump Quinn (much to our chagrin, and Quinn's) and then swing back to look at Quinn to assess the outcome, which is always nothing.

We usually double over laughing when the dogs begin "attacking" each other! Chancer would literally put Quinn's snout in his mouth, and then Quinn would rear back, his mouth open, his kohl-black-outlined eyes squinting like those of an angered wolf. The "wolf look," as we affectionately named this pretend predatory play, would appear and disappear as they dove into each other, reared back, and then dove again, nosing shoulders, faces, and any other body part within the vicinity.

And then there was the "lying-down version," also ridiculous because this tousle usually meant they were too exhausted to really play but couldn't pass up an opportunity to mess with each other. So here, they are prone, sometimes at forty-five-degree angles, other times at a ninety-degree intersection. They are nosing back and forth, the pace slower than the standing-up version. A paw comes over to hug a shoulder, a mouth chomps down on an ankle, and Quinn is falling all over Chancer in slow motion, landing on his back with a thud.

This maneuver enables Quinn to assume the "belly-up bicycle," where he rapidly pedals his hind legs back and forth in an upside-down tadpole position. Quinn's scrawny front legs bend at the elbow, his wispy fringes hanging, so he looks like a pony resting on its side. All this activity happens while Quinn is lying on top of Chancer's head, theoretically suffocating him! Chancer doesn't move a whisker. You simply hear him panting beneath the blanket of his brother's fur. Chancer is such a mellow fellow.

Sometimes when Quinn is playing with a tennis ball and Chancer is resting nearby on the floor, the ball will "accidently" smash Chancer in the face. Without flinching, Chancer watches the ball roll slowly off his massive snout, and Quinn dives in for the kill. It's as though Chancer's body is a graceful mountain range that slopes down near one end, silently anchoring the terrain of the land, with mayhem swirling all around.

Among Chancer's repertoire of communication is the "Can Quinn come out and play?" bark. Even *I* know what *that* bark means! Chancer will stand at the bottom of the stairs, looking up, or at the top of the stairs, looking down, waiting to see if his buddy has heard him. Quinn, on the other hand, doesn't announce his intention to play; he merely comes over to Chancer and pushes his entire body against him so Chancer cannot remain still. They each offer a unique invitation to frolic.

Chancer and Quinn freeze in free-form ice sculptures when we've interrupted their play with the "rest" command. Yes! We made up that command all by ourselves, and it works! Harvey and I can recognize when they are "done" even if *they* can't. Like toddlers. Quinn, as the new kid on the block, still behaving nicely, is always the first to go into a "down," huffing and puffing and chuffing as a footnote to their mischief. Chancer looks at us indifferently before circling around several times to find a spot and recover. He plops down very close to Quinn, with paws touching, so as to not lose connection.

At the end of the day, literally, the house looks like the aftermath of the US Open; every level is strewn with tennis balls. A rope toy is splayed in a corner, more frayed than before, and Nylabones or other chew toys lie in an upheaval, piled high, branded by an army of chomping teeth. But I grin deliriously with love as I bend over to gather up the remnants of the afternoon's duel, pull apart the remains of a staged "battle of the bone," all evidence of a day well lived by our precious dogs.

I couldn't have been happier.

I awoke earlier than usual on a Tuesday morning in February. Before I was even out of bed, an immediate panic soared up inside me as an anchor of anxiety pulled me down. Somewhere in the house I heard Chancer's yodeling, a distinct way of talking to us, which we usually found hysterical. Chancer's yodeling was an invitation for us to join him. He was informing us that he was feeling lonely and wanted us nearby.

Dread stalled me, though, as I made my way toward the kitchen, where I found Chancer lying next to his water bowl, his nose resting on the rim. Something was wrong. In all the years of living with Chancer, I'd never seen him in this position.

The night before, around ten o'clock, Chancer had seemed listless, unlike himself. Harvey and I agreed that if he appeared the same way the next morning, we would take him to JoAnne, our veterinarian. My gut felt heavy and bottomless. I followed Chancer into our bedroom, where he'd been sleeping at night since Quinn joined our family. Quinn now used the gargantuan kennel next to Iyal's bed, which seemed to suit all three guys.

Once Chancer was resting on the bedroom carpet, I lay down next to him. He wasn't on his side, so I couldn't spoon with him, but I curled against him nonetheless. Lying down, my length perfectly matching his, I whispered, "Oh, Chancer . . . you know how much I love you, don't you?" I buried my face into the fur on his back, smelling the familiar musty wool-rug scent that I adored. "Chancer, my love . . . I knew you before I met you." I wrapped myself closer, wishing he and I could somehow become one being. One soul. I held his paw in my hand and drifted into a twilight sleep next to him, afraid to be too far away.

So on Tuesday morning, as soon as I saw Chancer by the water bowl, I crouched down to pet him while looking at his face. His nose and ruff were wet as he looked up at me, almost apologetically. I assured him with my eyes that he was a good boy, no matter what. I ran to get Harvey, and we both looked at Chancer, mutually understanding the impending crisis that was unfolding before our eyes. I was on the phone as soon as the clinic opened. Iyal had made his way upstairs from his bedroom to get ready for his internship.

Chancer was unable to get up by himself. As the three of us stood looking down at Chancer, Iyal told me, "Mom, Chancer didn't really seem like himself last night."

I asked, "Why, honey? What did you notice?"

Iyal answered, "When I lay down to get my kisses, he didn't give me them. He didn't lick me or put his paw on my arm."

I said, "Oh, Iyal, that must've made you feel sad." *I* was sad just thinking about it.

Iyal asked hesitantly, "Mom, is Chancer . . . okay?" Iyal was taking in the unspoken tension, the fear, in the room.

Harvey tentatively said, "We don't know, Iyal, but we'll find out what's going on as soon as we can."

Gently, Harvey and I walked Chancer down the stairs, instructing Iyal how to carefully transport and lift Chancer into the van. I didn't want to look at Iyal's face, worried that I'd have to reassure him. But he didn't seem to register any emotion. Harvey and Iyal stayed behind to begin their usual day. Although nothing about this day felt usual. As I left the house with Chancer, I knew Harvey was deeply concerned. Our love for Chancer was entwined with our stronger love for each other. We were both frightened.

During the thirty-minute drive to Loving Hands Animal Clinic, I began to cry. I didn't *want* to cry, because crying meant that something terrible was happening to our Chancer. Crying was an emotional statement that defined this experience as serious and perhaps life threatening. When I arrived, JoAnne, our vet, quietly entered the exam room and said softly, "Oh, Donnie, I'm sorry this is happening. You know you did the best thing by bringing him here right away. So now let me take a look at our boy." She hugged me tightly as tears began to stream down my face. JoAnne hadn't even examined Chancer yet, and she was, without words, already communicating her worry that Chancer could be seriously ill.

This couldn't be happening. Chancer was fine yesterday afternoon. He and Quinn had even been groomed! Nothing seemed out of the ordinary. Yesterday. Chancer ate, went potty, and spent the evening in the living room with Harvey and me, our predictable but comfortable routine. I heard Iyal come upstairs to find Chancer, with Quinn following. Quinn didn't like being left behind. Next to the sofa where I was sitting, Iyal lay on the floor, his six-foot body circling around Chancer, connecting them together with their own canine-human language. Quinn was nearby, as backup.

Now in this exam room, I began asking myself questions. How could something be threatening Chancer's life so suddenly? What had we missed in the last twelve hours? JoAnne told me that she'd take X-rays and do blood work and have the results in an hour. I went out to our van and called Harvey. "Harve, JoAnne said it could either be pancreatitis, which could be treatable"—I was stumbling over words as my emotions disabled my speech—"or something much more serious." I couldn't think as I tried not to cry. "Harve, I'll call you back in an hour with the results."

"Okay, Don. I'll wait for your call. Let me know as soon as you do." I could hear the worry in his voice.

There were no signs. No way to prepare. I couldn't imagine how I'd ever navigate this great grief that began to descend around me. An hour later, I was called into the same exam room and was told that

Dr. Roesner would be in shortly with the X-ray results. Again JoAnne murmured as she came into the room, "Oh, Donnie, I'm so very sorry . . ." She reached me with her arms raised for a hug—all of the oxygen escaped from the room and I couldn't breathe. Everything that grounded me in this world was fractured—including me, and I didn't think I would ever be whole again. I wanted to rewind the morning, rewind this day, and erase this horrible suffocating experience. Holding me tight, she said the words I'd only heard in movies and on television. I didn't want to hear them in my world.

JoAnne spoke slowly and carefully: "We found a tumor on his spleen, Donnie, and we cannot operate. Chancer wouldn't survive a surgery."

I shut down. I don't know where I went, but I wasn't here. I didn't want to concede to this nightmare. I wasn't ready. Nightmares like this would require me to recruit every emotion I didn't want to feel. I gasped, "Oh my God. No!" JoAnne held me up in our hug. I was stunned. "Oh no . . ." I shook my head back and forth. Even though I was preparing for the worst over this last hour, every cell in my body was screaming, "This doesn't happen in *my* world. Not now!" It wasn't time, even though Chancer had turned eleven only twenty-three days before. The world was disappearing—and so was I along with it.

JoAnne explained that this cancerous tumor was the most often diagnosed tumor in older golden retrievers. It could appear suddenly and quickly grow large enough to threaten the health of the organ it was near.

Somehow I found the words between my tears. "Why was Chancer okay yesterday and now he's so ill?" I couldn't fathom how fast Chancer's health had declined.

Holding both of my hands, she answered, "It's possible that he hemorrhaged overnight, Donnie, which is why he couldn't move this morning." In my mind, I'm seeing Chancer lying by his water bowl, lifting his head, trying to be attentive to his family, trying to do his job.

I had to look away from inside my mind. I was too afraid to consider the image from this morning. But the present was no better.

JoAnne said, I suppose out of a veterinarian responsibility, "Donnie, you could take him home for the night, but it may take a lot out of Chancer."

I cried, "Oh, I don't think I can." I visualized the ride home with Chancer, me sobbing uncontrollably. Having to take him into our house, when he couldn't even stand up or eat. "JoAnne, I can't do that to Chancer." I saw us keeping vigil all night, next to his prone, exhausted body. I imagined pieces of my heart giving way to grief as the hours passed until morning, and we'd need to return him to the clinic. Struggling to talk, I whispered, "Will he still be alive when . . . when we come back later?" Oh my God, how was I even asking these questions? I hadn't thought I was strong enough to string these words together. A part of me was determined to stay grounded, pretending I could handle this devastation.

I heard from a distance, "Donnie, I think we can keep him alive until you all come back. If we give him fluids and keep him hydrated, he'll be comfortable. What if we meet back here around six thirty? Can you do that? It'll be quiet, and you could have as much time as you want to say good-bye." I nodded my appreciation. She asked, "Now, would you like to stay here with Chancer? You can if you want."

What should I say? Of course I wanted extra time with Chancer. But I also felt guilty that I'd have more time with him than the rest of my family would. Would that be fair? I told JoAnne that I wanted to stay for a while, but I had to call Harvey to tell him what was happening.

Holding on, feeling like I was sinking into quicksand, I dragged myself out of the clinic and back into the van, then called Harvey. I sobbed and told him there was nothing we could do for Chancer, except be with him to say good-bye. I heard Harvey trying not to cry. "Oh, Don . . . there's nothing they can do?" With an urgency, a desperation,

Harvey asked, "Why can't they do surgery?" I explained that it would be too dangerous a surgery and Chancer might not even survive. I heard Harvey's silence as he tried to comprehend all that was crashing down. I heard the ache.

Then Harvey switched to rescue mode: "We have to call Morasha and get her home. She has to be here! I need to call her right now."

My words ran into his: "But how can she get here so quickly? She's in Charlotte; it's four hours away!" I continued, "Harve, it's one thirty now, and we need to be back at Loving Hands by six thirty so JoAnne can be with us."

Harvey said, "Well, can't Morasha be there with us tomorrow morning?"

The tears wouldn't stop. "No, Harve," I had to force myself to say. "JoAnne said Chancer might not be alive that long." I listened to myself saying these words out loud. Who was *speaking* these words? It couldn't be me . . . I could never do this. "Harvey, we have to come back at six thirty. Tonight." Thoughts swirled around in my head. "How could Morasha be here five hours from now? It's Tuesday. She has classes."

Harvey said, "I'm getting her on a flight from Charlotte. She'll be here. I'll call you back."

I interrupted him. "She doesn't even *know* yet! You'll . . . you'll have to *tell* her." I moaned, "Oh my God, she's going to fall apart."

Harvey said, "I'll tell her. It'll be okay." I knew if he wanted to make this happen, he would. He can get these things done.

I went inside the clinic again, straight to the exam room. I didn't want to make eye contact with anyone. I didn't want to have to explain my growing anguish. It seemed vital to concentrate my entire being on every moment now. Two veterinarian technicians brought Chancer to me, on a gurney that was as high as my chest. He was strapped in. The sight of Chancer looking so helpless . . . so vulnerable, made my heart crumble even further.

One of them asked, "Would you like us to lift him so he could be on the floor with you?" She nodded at Chancer. "Or would you rather he stay here, on the gurney?"

I couldn't believe it was taking so much energy for me to form a sentence. Making a decision, *any* decision, in that moment, seemed impossible. "Oh, please, can you . . . would you let him be with me on the floor? Would it be okay to move Chancer?"

One of the techs answered, "Of course."

I watched as they gently lifted Chancer off the gurney and onto the floor.

As a tech slipped out of the room, I collapsed on the floor next to Chancer, weeping. The other tech silently slid down the wall across from me, respecting my sadness. Chancer lay between us. "Oh, Chancer . . . I'm sorry. I'm so sorry you have to leave us." I was petting his head and stroking his large muzzle with both hands. I felt his whiskers tickle my palms. I never could've imagined that a dog, *this* dog, with a heart big enough to hold so much hurt, could've found *us*, when we were lost in our family and lost in ourselves. What had we done to deserve so much love? And how would we be able to give him back to God? I truly didn't know.

I stayed that way, murmuring my love into his ears, his eyes, wanting to share his breath. Sometime during that hour, Harvey called back. Morasha would be flying into Atlanta and would arrive at four twenty this afternoon. I could only nod on my end of the phone. I didn't want to leave Iyal's boy now. Not ever.

But I had to. Iyal would be arriving home from his internship, and Harvey would be going to the airport to get Morasha. I drove home, wondering how Morasha would manage to keep herself together. I wondered how I was going to tell Iyal. How *was* I going to tell Iyal that his boy would be leaving our family? Our world. *This* world, as Iyal would say when he couldn't discern what was real and what wasn't. He would have to work out in his brain what was happening now, not in the past or the future. And *I* had to figure out what words I would say and how I'd say them. Iyal would be getting home just a few minutes after I did.

Iyal walked through the garage door into our foyer, dropped his backpack on the floor, and loped around, looking for Quinn and Chancer. "Hey, hon," I said, trying to sound normal as I walked down the stairs. "How was your day?"

Iyal mumbled, "Okay." Then, "I'm hungry." He passed by me and up the stairs to the kitchen. I had to tell him. I couldn't wait.

"Iyal?" I asked.

"What?" he said.

"I need to tell you something. Something about Chancer."

Iyal turned toward me as he opened the refrigerator door. He asked, "Is he all right?"

I anchored myself. "Well, remember how we had to help him get into the van this morning, because he was weak and couldn't stand up?"

"Yeah?" he said as he closed the refrigerator door.

"He is very sick. And we can't fix it, sweetie."

Iyal said, "Oh." I saw a shift in his body. Perhaps he was already steeling himself for the worst thing I could say.

"Iyal, I'm so sorry, but we'll have to say good-bye to Chancer tonight."

He looked at me, his face softening. "Why tonight? I don't want it to be tonight," he insisted.

"Oh, Iyal, Chancer's really sick. I know it happened so fast, but he can't live that much longer. We have to do it tonight."

Oh God, how I wanted to hug him, to rub his back . . . to spare his heart from a hurt I couldn't prevent. But that couldn't happen. "Are you okay, honey?" I asked.

"Yeah. So when will we do this?"

I soothed with my voice, since that was all I could do: "In a little while." I told him that Daddy would be here soon after he picked up Morasha from the airport. Earlier I had called Morasha when I knew she was at her gate in the Charlotte airport. Our words became tears over the phone. But I knew she'd make it here okay.

Harvey and Morasha picked us up from the house, and the four of us, and Quinn, went to say our good-byes to our Chancer. To Iyal's boy. And to ours.

In our room at the clinic, the four of us protectively encircled Chancer as he lay quietly on the rug. He lifted his head slightly, acknowledging our presence. We pet him and kissed him. His fur was damp where our tears fell. Each of us told him in our own way that he was such a good boy. In the end, it was Chancer's love that gave us the strength to say good-bye.

—

Two days after Chancer passed away, we buried him at Oak Rest Pet Gardens north of Atlanta. Chancer would be among other service dogs in the Garden of Honor. His deceased companions were guide dogs, K-9 dogs, therapy dogs, and others.

Harvey lovingly placed Chancer's collar with his tags and his working vest on top of the casket for our small service. Iyal was negotiating his way through these difficult moments. He'd walk away from us, not looking at the open grave where Chancer would be buried. I couldn't stop my tears as I looked from Iyal to the grave and back. I worried that he would be lost without Chancer. Had Chancer given Iyal the balance he would need to live his chaotic life? Would he soar into his future without Chancer there to offer him a safe place to land? I believed that Chancer would always be a part of him and hoped the memory of him would sustain Iyal when his life felt broken. Chancer offered a simple, profound holiness. All we had to do was let it in.

When Iyal drifted back to where Harvey and Morasha were standing, they recited English and Hebrew prayers while I knelt next to Quinn, my hands on Chancer's casket. Favorite memories were shared among us—there were many. I'm so glad Morasha flew home from college and was with us; we couldn't have said good-bye to Chancer without her. I needed her here with me. We all did. Morasha said through her tears, "Chancer would be so happy that he's in a dog park forever. And if someone in heaven said 'Sit'—*all* the dogs would sit!"

Perhaps the most poignant moment of that morning took place during a conversation between Iyal and Harvey. We had chosen the words for Chancer's plaque, which would say:

CHANCER
JANUARY 16, 2006–FEBRUARY 7, 2017
THE FIRST FASD SERVICE DOG

While they were walking around the cemetery, Iyal asked Harvey, "Can we also say on the plaque, 'Iyal's Helper'?" Iyal and Chancer had come full circle. And so had we.

Did Chancer's assistance for Iyal also help restore the very essence of our family? Without question. Chancer reunited us with each other and with ourselves. His enduring patience, playful spirit, and canine understanding pulled our family back together when we were falling apart. Though Chancer was specifically trained to be Iyal's assistance dog, his bright countenance brought us all out of a threatening darkness.

Quinn has been well taught by his big brother, and we're grateful for the year that Quinn was mentored by Chancer. And we're particularly thrilled that Quinn has *not* demonstrated Chancer's talent for stretching up almost four feet to reach our kitchen counter—to decimate muffins, wedges of Gouda, and cooked or uncooked hamburgers, with or without the buns. And if he did, it would be okay.

He would still be a good boy, too.

If someone had asked me many, many years ago if a dog can sense when a human lives with a disability, I would have said, "Gosh. I don't know. But wouldn't that be astounding if it could?" If someone then asked me, "Well, how did your son's service dog Chancer know?" I would share my ideas on the brilliant intuition Chancer was born with and honed through his training and his exquisite ability to alert to an impending chemical storm that could drown our son in his own neuronal vortex.

And if someone asked me, "When is a dog not just a dog?" I'd say, "When it's an anchor for a little boy or a young man whose life swirls around him like tidal waves of confusion and fear threatening to pull him under; when a dog's very presence releases the boy from the grip of unforgiving nightmares that flood his brain, numbing his ability to feel safe; when a dog's canine calm opens a gateway to words locked away in a neuronal safe, yearning to be freed; when a furry paw reaches around the boy's sleeping body, embracing his charge; and when a dog's love penetrates the barriers of others' unrealistic expectations and misinterpretations."

That's when a dog is so much more than a dog.

That's when a dog can find what's been lost.

That's when love is found.

—

NOTES

1 FASD: What the Foster Care System Should Know," National Organization on Fetal Alcohol Syndrome, accessed February 7, 2017, https://www.nofas.org/wp-content/uploads/2013/10/FASD-What-the-Foster-Care-System-Should-Know_2013.pdf.

2 Susan Doctor, "Susan Doctor on Intervention for FAS," (keynote at FEN Conference, Madison, WI, April 1, 2000), http://www.come-over.to/FAS/SusanDoctorIntervention.htm.

3 Bruce Ritchie, "If It Quacks Like a Duck," FASlink Fetal Alcohol Disorders Society, accessed February 7, 2017, http://www.faslink.org/If_it_quacks.htm.

4 "Sexual Abuse," Disability Justice, accessed February 7, 2017, http://disabilityjustice.org/sexual-abuse.

5 Helen Featherstone, as quoted in Kate Strohm, *Being the Other One: Growing Up with a Brother or Sister Who Has Special Needs* (Boston: Shambhala, 2005), 124.

6 Strohm, *Being the Other One: Growing Up with a Brother or Sister Who Has Special Needs*, 36.

ACKNOWLEDGMENTS

This book might never have been published without the patience, sense of humor, and brilliance of Dudley Delffs. Thank you for taking such good care of my work and of me.

Thank you to the whole team at Grand Harbor Press. To my editor, Erin Calligan Mooney, thank you for your confidence in me and my work and for creating an expert crew whose members include production manager Dan Byrne, marketing folks Marlene Kelly and Eric Duggan, author relations manager Gabby Trull, copyeditor Laura Petrella, proofreader Monique Vescia, and my dedicated publicist, Kristin Lunghamer. You are my SWAT team behind the scenes. Thank you!

Chad Sievers, you pushed me hard and let me push back, and we created an editing language that was new to us both. Thank you.

I owe much gratitude to Susan Brower and especially to Natasha Kern of the Natasha Kern Literary Agency, who helped launch this memoir and offered her friendship along with her expertise and experience.

I extend my deepest love and respect to Jodee Kulp, whose generosity of talent and knowledge of FASDs supports me always. You helped raise my children, and you are my sister for life.

Marian Mohr, your unconditional love embraces us as a surrogate grandmother and mother. You keep my dad and my mom alive in each of us. We love you.

Huge hugs to my dearest cousin, Jody Kanter-Doud, for her unending love during this process and beyond.

And to her sister, Adair Kanter, for weathering many storms with us while at 4 Paws for Ability when we first obtained Chancer.

To my cousin Evan Skinner, whose reality checks all through this process kept me focused.

To Karen Schwartz, thank you for helping me find myself and always celebrating my creativity.

Much gratefulness to Bill and Joanne Simmons, for your gifts of photography and friendship.

To Melissa Fay Greene, you captured my heart and our story and then set them free.

A huge thanks to everyone at 4 Paws for Ability, especially for the gifts of Chancer and Quinn.

Love to my many friends, who sustain me in ways you may not know and do so graciously and gently.

Great appreciation to Elizabeth Parra Dang and team. Your work is critical, and we are honored to help bring awareness to the public health crisis of FASDs. Our story is yours.

Morasha and Iyal, I thank you with all of me for the privilege of being your mom. My love for you grows in ways I never thought possible.

Finally, I thank my husband, Harvey, for your humility and trust in sharing our story.

ABOUT THE AUTHOR

Photo courtesy of Bill Simmons, 2016

Donnie Kanter Winokur is a writer, speaker, and human rights advocate. A native of New Jersey, she studied theater at Catholic University and earned a degree in psychology from Emory University in Atlanta. After honing her skills writing and producing advertising campaigns for clients throughout the Southeast, she created award-winning projects for Discovery Communications, the Smithsonian Institute, and Broderbund/Random House.

Donnie has authored two award-winning children's books and contributed to national and international magazines and journals, including *Guideposts* and *Adoption Today*; her journey was captured in India's *Reader's Digest* and Australia's *Marie Claire*. In 2012, Donnie's story was featured in "Wonder Dog" for the *New York Times Magazine*.

Donnie and her husband, Harvey, the founding rabbi of a Reform synagogue, live north of Atlanta with their son, Iyal, and daughter, Morasha. The family now includes Chancer's successor, Quinn, also trained as an FASD assistance dog; and Autumn, their cat, who tolerates her canine brother and enjoys the occasional swat.